D1217396

What I Didn't Know

True Stories of Becoming a Teacher

What I Didn't Know

True Stories of Becoming a Teacher

Introduction by
JAHANA HAYES
2016 NATIONAL TEACHER OF THE YEAR

Introduction by
IRVIN SCOTT
DEPUTY DIRECTOR OF EDUCATION
BILL AND MELINDA GATES FOUNDATION

Edited by
LEE GUTKIND

Copyright © 2016 Creative Nonfiction Foundation.
All rights reserved.

Kristin Leclaire's "Inside the Labyrinth" was originally published in
Biting the Bullet: Essays on the Courage of Women (Chatter House
Press 2015) and appears here by permission of the author.

Portions of Anne Raeff's "Mayans in East Oakland" were published in
"Reimagining California," a partnership of the California Endowment
and Zócalo Public Square.

Requests for permission to reproduce material from this work should
be sent to:

Rights and Permissions
In Fact Books
c/o Creative Nonfiction Foundation
5119 Coral Street
Pittsburgh, PA 15224

Cover design by Seth Clark
Interior design/layout by The Printed Page

ISBN# 978-1-937163-27-3

Table of Contents

Foreword from the Editor: Making a Difference

Lee Gutkind

When my brother Richard was nearing the end of his college career back in the 1970s, he didn't quite know what he was going to do. He was a math major but had no interest in accounting, he didn't want to become a CPA or tax attorney, and in truth, he wasn't crazy about the idea of playing with numbers for the rest of his life. So, in his senior year he took a couple of education courses in a program that was a shortcut to teacher certification, and upon graduation he was offered a job in a newly opened middle school. He pondered for a while, then decided to try it out. It was a way of starting adult life with a steady paycheck, decent hours, long summer vacations. For my brother, becoming a teacher was a beginning, not a passion or a mission—just a job for a young man seeking a direction.

Many of the contributors in this collection became teachers under similar circumstances, as an interim thing, a first job out of college. And for most of them it was the first stop in a long journey leading to a real career and fulfillment, professional accomplishment, and personal satisfaction. That's not to say that all of these writers have remained in the K–12 sphere—many have moved on to universities, community colleges, and administrative positions—but in one way or another, all have stayed connected to the teaching profession.

Some of the other writers in this collection were not teachers first; among them are an attorney, a research scientist, and a network TV producer. Dissatisfaction with what they were doing led them to teaching, despite all of the obvious and well-known challenges. Like low pay. Or the political agendas of outsiders, who measure progress by often irrelevant standardized testing. Or conflicts with parents—or with the students themselves. But these writers remained teachers despite the frustrations because, they discovered, teaching makes a difference—not only to students, but to teachers, too.

For an example of the difference teachers can make, we can look to the story of Jahana Hayes, who contributed one of the introductions to this book. Jahana grew up (as too many American children do) surrounded by drugs, violence, and poverty. She became pregnant at age seventeen. But twelve years later, after working her way through a community college and a local university, she returned to her hometown and got her first teaching job. In 2016, she was named National Teacher of the Year by the Council of Chief State School Officers. In Hayes's first appearance as Teacher of the Year, with President Obama at the White House, she discussed the passion and commitment required of teachers. She also talked about the great responsibilities with which we entrust our teachers, including the responsibility, as well as opportunity, to share their "empowering stories with students and communities and elevate this profession."

This is exactly what *What I Didn't Know* is all about: teachers sharing their experiences in the trenches of the school system and exploring what those experiences meant—and still mean—to them. Some of these stories may be difficult to read or believe because of how hard these teachers work, how much they care about their students, and how frustrating and sometimes downright devastating their days—and their semesters—can be. In *Order*, for example, Michael Copperman labors to understand his most troubled student until, suddenly, the boy storms into the classroom, knocks over desks and chairs, and spits in Copperman's face. In *Ancient Beef Made Me a Teacher*, Lori D. Ungemah observes a fight between two high school boys in her classroom. She is horrified at the sound of cartilage popping and the explosion of blood, and she breaks down sobbing. But she is even more horrified when, after the fight is broken up by security guards, her streetwise students file out of the classroom, silent and seemingly unfazed.

And yet these teachers stayed in the classroom—not forever, but for several more years. And they are not alone. Education is the fourth largest major at universities and colleges in the United States. The annual overall attrition rate for teachers is barely 8 percent (though it's higher for early career teachers and for teachers in lower-income schools). In a recent study conducted by researchers at Arizona State University, nearly 60 percent of respondents (they were all K–12 teachers in Arizona) reported that they were "very satisfied" or "satisfied" with their jobs.

One thing that makes teaching special and fulfilling is the amount of independence teachers have and the influence a teacher can wield. While it is true that teachers must follow a curriculum, they are pretty much on their own behind classroom doors, with anywhere from twenty to fifty individual, unformed personalities, kids seeking answers to questions that they might not even understand. Teachers must advise, communicate information, solicit and encourage ideas, and maintain discipline and an atmosphere conducive for learning. And they must be flexible, able to roll with the punches (literal or figurative) and fill voids, sensing and responding to their students' needs.

It's a tall order, to be sure. And not every teacher can reach every student, every day. But the best teachers can reach most of the students, most of the days—and that can make a tremendous difference.

In a statement to the White House, Jahana Hayes recalled the importance of teachers in her life. Teachers recognized her potential. They did not give up on her. They gave her books to read at home. They "encouraged me to do more, be more, expect more." Her teachers made a lifelong impact; ultimately, she says, "They inspired me to become a teacher so I could make the same kind of impact in my own students' lives."

Sometimes, it's impossible to guess at the impact a teacher can make; sometimes it takes years, and sometimes the impact is quite unlikely.

My brother Richard stayed in the classroom for many years, and then he became a principal, and then an executive director of the school system in which his teaching journey began. He is now the director of a graduate program in education, but his students from his middle school teaching days still remember and appreciate him. No matter where I go with him in his hometown, Richard is recognized. Former students, who now look almost as old as he does, come up to thank him for his guidance and wisdom. Not long ago, we attended a production of the Tony Award–winning musical *Kinky Boots* together. After the show, he was welcomed at the stage door and embraced by one of the cast members.

"What was that all about?" I asked him later.

Richard explained that during his first few years in that middle school where he first taught, the teacher coordinating the annual play—that year, it was *Babes in Arms*—could not follow through with the production and had to drop out. Even though he was a math teacher and knew nothing about musical theater, Richard volunteered to fill in, and he learned how to produce and direct a play. The actor who hugged him—then in the sixth grade, and now in his forties— never forgot how Richard jumped in to save the play and, in a way, launched the actor's career. That actor—Billy Porter—went on to win the 2013 Drama Desk Award for Outstanding Actor in a Musical and the 2013 Tony Award for Best Actor in a Musical.

All these stories in *What I Didn't Know* do not end so triumphantly. But even those with more complicated endings convey the importance of the work teachers do. The hard work is worth the effort.

Whether you are a teacher, a prospective teacher, a parent, or just someone who cares about kids and the future of our country, *What I Didn't Know* will open your eyes and your heart. The true stories collected here vividly capture that moment of truth when a teacher first comes to grips with the fundamental challenge and awesome responsibility of shaping minds that will someday shape our country and our future. Although they may have hoped, or even expected, to influence their students' lives, it's only after living, breathing, suffering, and celebrating in the classroom day after day that they could fully appreciate the profound and lasting impact they could make. These teachers—all teachers—make a difference every day.

Introduction:
The Importance of Connection

Jahana Hayes

My first day in a contracted teaching position should have been easy. I had graduated in the top of my class with a 3.97 GPA, passed all of the certification exams in my state, and had been hired to teach in the building where I had just completed fifteen weeks of student teaching under a wonderful teacher. He was comfortable in his role, which he had occupied for more than twenty-five years. He knew everything and never had to refer to any notes. He did not follow a traditional lesson plan format, but somehow it worked. It always worked. I could never tell the line of demarcation between active learning and closure, but somehow it always worked; students always learned. The discussions were robust and the student responses were evidence that they "got it."

I watched in awe as he moved the conversations forward. He was a very distinguished gentleman with a PhD, working in a large urban public school with a very diverse population. Somehow he had commanded the respect and admiration of all the students. I watched as he allowed students to express their opinions and take risks without fear. I watched as he fostered a culture that was inclusive and democratic. What seemed like casual discussions always ended with a history lesson. I took lots of notes, but I still couldn't really put my finger on the chemistry that existed between the students and the teacher.

I had started my student teaching experience in September, and then a series of amazing opportunities and doors opened up for my cooperation teacher. Suddenly, he was out of the class, and there was a job waiting for me. I knew the routine, was working with a collaborative staff, and I was taking over as the teacher with a group of students I had worked with all year. Changing my title from "student teacher" to "teacher" should have been easy.

But it was not easy. In fact, I was unexpectedly panic-stricken, paralyzed in fear at the beginning of a new journey. No longer an apprentice under the tutelage of a master teacher, I was totally responsible for the teaching and learning. If things went wrong, it would be all my fault.

Secretly, I knew I was not up to the challenge. I was a history teacher: what if I forgot something as simple as the date of the attack at Pearl Harbor? December 7, 1941, December 7, 1941...I rehearsed this date and many others, repeatedly going over them in my head, but still I wasn't ready. I wasn't ready. Mentally I replayed a variety of scenarios in which a student asked me a question and I didn't know the answer. Even worse, what if a student was smarter than me? After all, this was high school, and I was not much older than the students in my class. I was not up to it; I could not do it; I was not prepared.

With the benefit of more experience and some hindsight, I can see that maybe no one is ever fully prepared for that first day alone in the classroom. Certainly, that's the case for many if not all of the teachers whose stories are included in this collection.

On that first day, I made so many mistakes. We had a fire drill, and the bell schedule was altered. I had planned for a forty-two minute lesson, but all the times were shifted. I was nervous and afraid. I was not sure what to do and could not find my center, I fumbled in front of classes for the entire day and had more questions than answers. A part of me wanted to pretend I was sick and just go home but I stayed. And I survived. I was honest with my students and shared some of my concerns and—believe it or not—they helped me. I maintained control, but I asked them questions, and we helped each other. On that day I realized that no teacher preparation program can ever fully prepare you for what is to come. It is an ongoing process.

I read history books and committed to memory the lesson plan format. I anticipated questions that I would be asked so that I could always have an answer. In order to be a good teacher, I had to be a great student. I continued to read and learn and became more comfortable in my role as a teacher, and over the years it got easier.

But finding that delicate balance between teaching academics and addressing all of the intangibles took many years. For the first few years of my career I was never fully satisfied or fulfilled. I loved teaching, but I didn't feel like teaching loved me back. Something was missing, I needed more. I started to think about my experiences as a student and all the things I remembered, and I realized that although I could not remember many specific lessons, I remembered dozens of personal interactions and how they made me feel. It was then that I realized in order to teach my students, I had to know my students. It did not matter how much I knew; if I could not connect with them, I could not teach them. They might not remember what I said, but they would always remember how I made them feel.

Things started to make sense in my fifth year of teaching, when I had a group of students who seemed unusually distracted and unmotivated. I could not figure out why, but after a series of conversations I realized that seven students in this one class had lost a parent to cancer, and their families were still dealing with the effects. We decided, as a group, to get involved with the American Cancer Society. These students became more active and engaged in class, and I realized that there was a direct relationship to the work we were doing in the community. The lightbulb came on. Students will not learn from someone they have no connection to.

It was around this time that I began to further develop my personal philosophy of education. As part of my graduate work I became increasingly interested in the writings of Dr. Martin Luther King Jr. My philosophy is rooted in the ideas of Dr. King, who, in 1947, wrote an essay for the Morehouse College student paper, in which he described the purpose of education. He writes that most students are confused about the role education should play in their lives and society. Dr. King eloquently sums up the essay with this conclusion: the purpose of education is twofold, to build knowledge and character. I realized that by focusing on only the academic side, I was not providing students with a complete education and therefore not experiencing the chemistry I had longed for so many years ago. The connections we make with students are as important as the content we teach.

Thirteen years later, as I write the introduction for this critical collection of stories in teacher voice, I am reminded of how important it is to connect with students by learning about their stories and including them as participants in their education. In May 2016, I was named the National Teacher of the Year, and I believe that what separates me from more than 3.5 million other amazing teachers in America is the fact that I have fostered strong relationships with my students and their community, which I have used to build capacity and give them a heightened sense of worth. I have learned that my job is to teach much more than academic content.

Most of us have vivid memories of a teacher or educator who was a major influence. I too have those memories. At every stage in my life, I can remember a teacher who had a significant impact on me. There was Mrs. McKinney, my 3rd grade teacher, who baked me a chocolate chip cake for my birthday. And Mrs. Turner, a high school guidance counselor who came to my house to inquire why I had been absent so many days from school. There was Dr. Burt Saxon, my amazing mentor and college professor, who taught me the value of making personal connections with my students before any real learning could occur. I can think of a dozen other teachers just like them, and my memory always includes the way I felt during and after the interaction.

I also remember vividly—down to the blue floral dress and the earrings she was wearing—the teacher who said no one in my family cared about me because they hadn't attended parents' night. You see, we used to put all of our work in a folder for our parents to see on parent's night. The folders were left on the desk and our parents were supposed to take them home. My grandmother didn't drive and there were no late busses in my neighborhood, and my folder was always left on my desk the next morning. I always tried to be the first one in the class so I could remove the folder before anyone noticed. I remember overhearing my teacher tell another teacher in the hallway that "their parents don't care and no one ever comes to inquire about those students." I knew exactly what she meant. In spite of everything that has happened in my life and all of the amazing interactions I have had with teachers, I still remember the razor sharpness of that comment and how it made me feel.

While my role as an educator includes ensuring that students learn the required academic content, I also want them to feel valued, respected, and free to take risks in my class. Fostering a collaborative culture and building relationships is one of the often overlooked lessons in schools. I want every one of my students to have felt included and represented in the conversation and to remember how they felt in my class. As educators, we must work together to find ways to empower our students intellectually, socially, and emotionally. We should use our students' cultural experiences as a way to impart knowledge and skills and begin to change attitudes, and not as reminders of the obstacles that monopolize their daily lives. Our country has so many different communities—urban, suburban, rural, regional, and even Native American reservations. Our schools have to address the needs of all these communities. We must explore creative and inclusive ways of reaching students. Every child is entitled to an educational experience that is rich and robust and reflective of their personal journey.

The collection of personal stories in this book illustrates the many ways that teachers show students they care about their academic success and their personal growth. These teachers have engaged families and communities to work together to ensure that students succeed. They have taken the time to learn the stories of their students and understand their journeys and are now sharing those stories here today.

Jahana Hayes is the 2016 National Teacher of the Year. She is a history teacher and the chairperson of the School of Academic Renown (SOAR) Program at Kennedy High School in the Waterbury Public School district.

Introduction: Teaching Moments

Irvin Scott

I will never forget my first day in the classroom, nearly twenty-six years ago. All had gone relatively well: I'd taught five classes, supervised a study hall, and caught a quick meal during my thirty-minute lunch period. I had made it to the end of my final period—the last minutes before my thirty-or-so students would be set free to attack the waning days of summer. The bell rang, signifying the end of class and the day, and something happened that I will never forget: the students jumped up while I was still speaking. Not only did they completely ignore the fact that I was in the middle of a sentence, but they actually seemed oblivious to the fact that I even existed. And then it happened...

"Whoa, whoa, whoa!" I exclaimed, raising my voice just slightly above the rumbling of books and feet. It was almost instinctual. And incredibly, all thirty-or-so adolescents froze, almost in mid-air, and slowly turned their eyes to me as if to ask, *now what?* I was stunned. I honestly hadn't expected such obedience. "The bell is not your teacher," I said. "I am, and I am not done giving the assignment for tomorrow."

All teachers experience "teaching moments" like this throughout their careers. Those moments are usually an opportunity for teachers to impart some vital, timely knowledge or wisdom to their students. Yet, I have found that these opportunities are often as much about the teacher as they are about the learner. With my end-of-the-first-day power play, for example, both my students and I learned valuable lessons. The students' lesson? The bell doesn't save you in Mr. Scott's class. The lessons for me? If you expect it, they will meet it. Also, begin class with the end in mind; post and bring attention to the assignment at the beginning of class.

The funny thing is, I don't remember ever having been taught—during my methods classes in college or anywhere else—how to stop students from running out of the class when the bell rings. (Of course, there is the possibility that I missed that class.) Some of the most powerful teaching lessons happen in real time, in the classroom. Of course, there's a need for teacher preparation experiences that truly ready teachers for actual classrooms, and I am happy to see the field moving in that direction.

But there is another way to impart readiness: read actual stories from the field. This is what's in store for you in *What I Didn't Know*. These practitioners speak from the heart and the intellect, bringing the reader into close contact with both the *sage on the stage* and the *guides on the side*. Whether in elementary schools or high schools, these teachers chronicle real stories about real students in urban, suburban, and rural communities across the United States (and, in a couple of cases, internationally). If you're an educator, reading about some of these students may prompt memories of similar students from your own experience. If you're a parent, you will begin to gain a new appreciation for the joys and challenges of building America's future by teaching its children. As a former teacher and, now, an educational leader who works to elevate and celebrate great teaching and teachers, reading these stories made me think of my own unforgettable classroom experiences.

For example, the day one of my senior students, Tracey, asked to talk to me after class. I could tell that something was wrong; Tracey was usually full of life and energy, with a smile that you couldn't help but respond to in kind. After class we found a quiet room where we could talk. There, she shared with me that she was pregnant and wasn't sure what to do. She talked about the internal and external struggles she was experiencing. As you might imagine, these difficulties centered on her family, her boyfriend, her peers, and—most of all—herself. This was a first for me, and I was at a loss for what to do. She begged me not to tell anyone, and I felt compelled not to betray her trust. So, I just listened to her. I really don't remember saying much at all. I just remember her sitting, talking, crying, and talking some more—all the time pleading for me not to share this information with others, which I promised I would not. So, I just listened and then went home and prayed for her.

Soon after our talk, Tracey's smile returned and she seemed to be herself again. Because this was happening close to the end of the year, I had no way of knowing what decision Tracey had made. While I continued to wonder, I learned another powerful lesson. I learned how important it is to be there for students. I learned that, most of the time, the best approach is not to tell them what to do or to speak from your own belief system, but rather just to be there, listening, reminding them that they matter enough to be heard.

This story highlights another key theme that runs through the stories in this collection—teachers are often called upon to occupy roles that go well beyond teaching content. Make no mistake: the role of teaching content is critical and, in my opinion, our number-one responsibility. However, as the saying goes, *students don't care how much you know until they know how much you care.* In Mary Ann Hutcheson's "An Honor and a Privilege," for example, a teacher guides an entire classroom toward embracing, rather than shunning, a fellow classmate who has done everything imaginable to rebuff the teacher and his fellow students. The teacher's wise guidance and show of love leads to a poignant moment, which then opens up the floodgates for reciprocal kindness from the student who has caused the most hurt.

Such displays of love, care, and respect must accompany rigorous and challenging teaching and learning. In my experience, one of the pitfalls that some teachers fall into is the erroneous assumption that it is wrong to push vulnerable students too hard. The logic goes that these students face unbearable challenges and conditions outside of the classroom. Consequently, for these students, school should be a safe, caring, and nurturing environment. It should be a place where students have agency, a way to counter the uncontrollable nature of their environments outside of school. And while I agree with some of that, I am happy to say that this collection also includes stories where teachers take issue with the notion that vulnerable students need to be protected and coddled, not "pushed." Sure, that pressure and push should be personalized from student to student. Sure, the pressure and push should be accompanied by an authentic relationship with and personal interest in the student—but *pressure and academic push* must be there.

After fifteen years in the classroom, I became a principal, and students would occasionally come to my office to complain about a teacher. I would provide a listening ear for a few minutes, but if I saw the conversation shifting toward concern about how hard the teacher was on the student, I would abruptly interrupt the student and say something to the effect of, *the next time you see this teacher, I want you to thank him or her for caring enough to hold you to high standards.* Like children who can't fully appreciate the methods of their caring but strict parents, these students would leave my office somewhat unconvinced. But I can't tell you the number of times that those same students—years later, sometimes—would come back to visit those teachers who had relentlessly applied that gentle pressure, in the same way (as one of my mentors used to describe it) that diamonds are made. Henry Brooks Adams has written that "A teacher affects eternity; he can never tell where his influence stops." The stories collected here show how these influences begin.

Regarding Tracey, the student who just needed me to listen as she dealt with an unexpected pregnancy: when the year came to a close, I lost track of her. However, one day during the following year, I was teaching and a knock came at the door. I went to open the door, and there stood Tracey—but not alone. She was holding her newborn son in her arms. She had made the decision that was best for her and her circumstances. She would go on to ask me to do the honor of marrying her to her boyfriend, which, of course, I agreed to do.

I'm reminded of a short, powerful poem by American poet and state legislator John James Ingalls on the importance of seizing the day. In "Opportunity," Ingalls uses personification to implore us, through Opportunity's voice: "I knock unbidden once at every gate! //

If sleeping, wake—if feasting, rise before / I turn away." For teachers, every day you walk into the classroom is an opportunity to impact lives. The following enriching stories will show readers how teachers all across America are maximizing these opportunities.

Welcome to their classrooms.

Irvin Scott began teaching high school English in 1989 at J. P. McCaskey High School in Lancaster, Pennsylvania. After eleven years in the classroom, Scott became a principal and continued to teach at McCaskey East High School from 2002 to 2006. From 2006 to 2011, Scott was a doctoral student at Harvard University while he worked in a district leadership position (assistant superintendent for high schools and chief academic officer) in the Boston Public Schools. Scott was the deputy director of education at the Bill & Melinda Gates Foundation from 2011 to 2016, where he was engaged in supporting and connecting teachers nationally. Scott is currently a faculty member at the Harvard Graduate School of Education in Cambridge, Massachusetts.

Teacher Edit

Lynn DeFilippo

I am sitting with Stephen waiting for him to tell me a sentence. Before we write the sentence, I want him to speak it. If he can say it, he can write it, or so conventional educational wisdom goes. Outside my classroom in Nome, Alaska, snowdrifts and blue sky beckon Stephen and this class of seventh graders like a siren singing to a sailor. *Come speed across the tundra on your snow machine. Slide down my hills, reckless. Why write sentences, or paragraphs, or anything, really?*

I teach writing to Stephen and his classmates, mostly Inupiaq and Siberian Yupik boys, during the last class of the day when the allure of the outside world competes against me for their attention. Squirrely boys, they concentrate on how many minutes before the bell rings and what they have to do to stop me from bugging them. Being allowed to line up at the door even three minutes before the bell rings qualifies as a reward. Some boys can't stop talking while others, like Stephen, hardly talk at all. They all hate to write, or so they proclaim.

It's 2010, and I've been teaching for eight years, five in Nome. Perched on the shores of Norton Sound in the Bering Strait, Nome— population 3,500—is a regional hub for the handful of surrounding Native villages that dot the coastline of the Seward Peninsula. You can't drive to Nome from anywhere, but you can fly there on a jet from Anchorage. With a hospital, two grocery stores, a movie theater, several restaurants, a lively bar scene along Front Street, and road access to beautiful, remote countryside, Nome offers the bush Alaska resident a quality of life not found in smaller villages.

There are thirty-eight seventh graders this year, an especially small number that we've divided into three groups. Most of them, thirty-one according to the school enrollment packet, identify themselves as Alaska Native. The remaining seven students include four whites, one Latino, and two who checked off two or more races, though it can safely be said that most people in Nome are two or more races, mainly Alaska Natives and the white settlers from the Gold Rush days.

Stephen's class is typical of the "low" tracked language arts/English classes offered at Nome Beltz Junior/Senior High School: they speak the least standard English, are more likely to be raised by a grandparent, and have the darkest skin on average. It's a good bet they all qualify for free or reduced lunch. Indeed, food is a powerful motivator for this group. At the start of class, I circulate with handfuls of pretzels, and they rush to their seats, pens and notebooks at the ready.

The boys and I are somewhat adrift on the ocean of English language literacy. Fluently reading—never mind writing a complete sentence without my assistance—proves daunting for many of them. I am the captain of our ragtag ship, forever heading off mutiny. They are considered "struggling learners," but in reality it's me who does most of the struggling while they laugh about farts and draw snow machines in their notebooks. Our current writing assignment, the "me essay," a standard for this age group, demands that they compose anywhere from one to five paragraphs detailing their favorite activities, what they want to be when they grow up, their favorite subjects in school, etc. Most of my students embrace it as an opportunity to do what they love at this age: talk about themselves.

But Stephen is not most of my students. He doesn't really talk about much of anything, never mind himself. Most of his communication with me is nonverbal: lifted eyebrows signaling *yes*, a shrug of his shoulders, a smile, a wrinkled nose, a slight head nod, a pointed finger.

The low January sun casts a golden light into my classroom's west-facing windows. Stephen and I confront his run-on list of words, probably four sentences' worth of writing. I attempt to charm one more sentence from him, to complete one fragment of his thought into standard, written English.

Say the word *essay* in the English classroom and students slump in their seats, roll their eyes, and groan NO! And I can hardly blame them. For me the essay is a personal and fluid form of literary prose exploring ideas and linking experiences. But the academic essay demanded by American schools and codified into state standards threatens students and teachers alike to a jail sentence of hyper-structured boredom loosely interpreted as introduction, body, and conclusion. Yeah, sure, such linear papers are easily graded with rubrics. But the truth is no matter how you dress them up in flowery adjective-adorned skirts that twirl and dance with active verbs, no one in real life ever wants to read, or write, these academic assignments, least of all middle schoolers.

Twelve- and thirteen-year-olds want most to fit in with their peers: *How do I look? What do my friends think? Do they like me?* As an English teacher I capitalize on my seventh graders' self-absorption by using the "me essay" as a doorway into the world of academic essay writing. I begin the unit with writings projected onto my digital whiteboard. Previewing student work from years past satisfies my students' need for peer comparisons. Essays with titles like "Me, Myself, and I" and "All about Me" illuminate our darkened classroom. Invariably they ask, *Is this real? Did you make this up?* Their interest piqued, we read, talk, and brainstorm. I model my own lists: *Hobbies: knitting, bird watching, dog training. Sports & outdoor activities: hiking, biking, berry picking. Reading: mystery novels, historical fiction, field guides. Favorite subjects in school: writing, art.*

I challenge students to find an inspirational quote to begin their essays, something that reflects who they are or what's important to them. Students in my other seventh-grade classes will excitedly peruse the Internet in their search. Quotations from athletes, pop culture stars, former presidents, and Helen Keller all inform their adolescent imaginings of themselves: *Life is nothing without friends. Everybody* dies, but not everybody lives. *Success is often the result of taking a misstep in the right direction.* A twelve-year-old will rise to lofty heights given the opportunity.

But Stephen and his classmates do not subscribe to the introductory "hook" concept. It's confusing, or it's boring, or something. After a class hour of distraction while they search Google images for basketball stars leaping into jump shots, not a single boy in this class has a quote, or wants one. They prefer the straightforward beginning: *My name is Sam. I am twelve years old. My favorite sport is basketball.* I hope for capitals at the beginnings and periods at the ends of sentences, but I'm happy with even the most rudimentary conglomeration of words on paper, sans punctuation. Eventually they, and I, will be judged by the school district, the state, and the federal government on standardized tests that will require their facility of complex language skills. But today we are still just wrangling single words into coherent sentences.

The State of Alaska English Language Arts standards for seventh grade loom over our word-by-word sentence construction:

Write informative/explanatory texts to examine a topic and convey ideas, concepts, and information through the selection, organization, and analysis of relevant content...

Write about yourself, I tell them, explain who you are.

Introduce a topic clearly, previewing what's to come...

Tell people what you're gonna say, say it, then tell them what you said. Hopefully you can do this before they, or you, fall asleep.

Develop the topic with relevant facts...

It's not enough to love basketball. What position do you like to play? What's your favorite team?

Use appropriate transitions...

For example, next, also, in addition, ad nauseam.

Establish and maintain a formal style...

Other ways to say awesome? Amazing, remarkable, awe inspiring, astounding. Give seventh graders a thesaurus, and *Call of Duty: Black Ops II* becomes "transcendent."

Provide a concluding statement…that follows from and supports the information presented…

For Stephen and his classmates, I make it painfully, achievably simple. Repeat one important thing from your beginning, preceded with *In conclusion.*

Administrators walk into my classroom weekly for a ten-minute "snapshot" to see how well I'm bludgeoning my students with the standards. They want to see a "learning goal" posted and a dutiful student regurgitating some edu-speak. I'll look up from a student's desk and see a stone-faced man poking his index finger onto an iPad, checking off the "Observe4Success" teacher evaluation form: *Student Engagement–Compliant 100%; Learning Goal Posted–Observed; Expectations Posted and Enforced–Limited.* One earnest administrator asked when was I going to post my classroom expectations, so he could check me off. Like a student who had failed to complete her homework assignment, I lied: *Oh yeah, okay. I'll get to that.* He wants me to care about my grade. He also wants what the English sentence wants: an explicit statement declaring something that is otherwise perfectly evident. Somehow writing down and posting on the wall that students should come to class prepared, do their work, and be respectful will legitimize my respectful, quietly hardworking classroom.

My first teaching job landed me—literally, in a twin-engine Piper Navajo—in the tiny Koyukon Athabascan village of Huslia. Population just under three hundred, Huslia sits on the banks of the Koyukuk River, deep in the interior of Alaska's boreal forest. I rented a comfortable two-room log cabin that was walking distance from the school where I was a generalist teacher for eight students grades six through eight. I'd spent the prior year in an intensive post-baccalaureate teacher-certification program at the University of Alaska Fairbanks. "You're in Indian Country now," a resident elder said to me on the runway when I stepped off the plane.

I had moved from the East Coast to Alaska with an ex-boyfriend in the late nineties, on somewhat of a whim. I liked it enough to stay and for several years pieced together seasonal work while living in a dry cabin far from the nearest town. The searing subzero cold and darkness of winter, the blizzards, the limited groceries, the lack of entertainment or a social life, that part of Alaska was familiar to me when I moved to Huslia to teach. Despite the coursework in cross-cultural communication, and the few days I'd spent in a village school for my rural practicum, and the district-sponsored culture camp where we listened to stories, it became clear soon after my arrival how utterly unprepared and foreign I was. How few decent curriculum materials there were. How many hours I'd have to work each day, each weekend, each month. How the loss of the Native language, silenced with an assimilationist educational policy enacted at the turn of the twentieth century when the first schools were established in the territory, had created an undercurrent of hostility in the current generation. How becoming "a part of the community," as we were told to do, was a daunting task given my job demands. How I'd be perceived, despite seeing myself as a progressive and an Alaskan of some years, as just another white lady from outside.

The sentence. The sentence embodies the English language's complete unit of thought. As an English teacher, I accept the fundamental rightness of the sentence as a given. Subject and predicate married into their world of action or concept or state of being. The subject *does*, *thinks*, *feels*, or *is*. But children learning to write carve their thoughts and ideas onto the paper with little concern for subjects and predicates. They repeat, ramble, and join endless streams of consciousness with conjunctions.

I can and do directly teach sentence construction to Stephen and his classmates. But if there's one thing I've learned, it's that direct grammar instruction does not usually translate into student competency in writing. Children need to talk and read and write and mess with language on their own. Identifying subjects and predicates on worksheets? Anyone can get kids to figure that out in a lesson or two. Making students compose sentences from the nebulous world of memory and experience, shaping thought into ideas and words, requires relationship, excitement, interest, and talk.

Stephen's English and my English hail from two different worlds. His English, also his first language, resonates with the rhythm, volume, and tone of his ancestral tongue, Inupiaq. Sometimes referred to as village English, it possesses an economy and straightforwardness I admire: *I go store. Why? Pop.* So much less explanation, so much less *blah, blah, blah.* In the classroom Stephen might simply say to me, *bathroom,* while holding the pass and standing at the door. Most likely his grandparents learned English as a second language, and I don't know about his parents. Given the history of public and Bureau of Indian Affairs schooling in Alaska, there's a good chance Stephen's parents were shipped off to a boarding school and punished for speaking Inupiaq. Is his reticence at talking a generational consequence of this linguistic violence? Or perhaps it's a natural, cultural trait of a people whose ways of living on the land embodied other methods of communicating that go beyond the Western dependence on verbal and written exchange.

In the treeless, white, monochrome world of the tundra in winter, I'm coldly aware of how different is my perspective of the world compared to the Alaska Native students I teach. The landscape of my New Jersey youth featured suburban streets, shopping malls, and racially mixed neighborhoods. Hot summers at the shore, three months of winter, April showers to bring May flowers, and crimson maple leaves in autumn.

Here, I sometimes feel disembodied, utterly powerless in this vast and rugged wild place, a nagging sense that I don't belong. Shushing wind. A croaking raven. I try to imagine a father and a son, an uncle and his nephew, in the hills or on the sea ice. Maybe they're hunting for a seal, searching the black water of an open lead—a fracture in the sea ice. The boy watches as the man performs some action: aiming his gun, hoisting a boat. Traditional Alaska Native teaching and learning emphasize close observation. I too watched and learned skills and crafts from my parents and grandparents: rolling out and cutting pasta dough, sewing a hem, crocheting a hat. But the majority of my formal education was in mainstream American schools. My students learn how to live on their land by watching adults, performing a task when confident of their ability to do so. This makes sense if you're using precious resources that mustn't be wasted, or if the hunter whose clothing you sew relies on your craft for his survival.

It took me years to realize that some of my students spent considerable time thoughtfully composing sentences prior to committing their words to paper. I'd watch students sit for a long time in class, paper blank, and think they were confused or simply refusing to write their rough drafts. In reality, they were taking their time, thinking, crafting sentences and not just scribbling their thoughts unheeded. Their process demanded more time than I usually gave. But consequently, their writing required less revision. In my educational world, freeform talking and quick verbosity are too often valued at the expense of depth and deliberation.

In Eskimo and Aleut linguistics class I learned that Inupiaq words can be lengthened with a variety of suffixes and prefixes to provide syntax, meaning, and tense, expanding a single word into sentence-like complexity. Prior to contact with white colonizers and the introduction of written language, what need had they for punctuated sentences? Oral language histories demanded an excellent memory and the ability to listen closely and pay attention. Information given in the form of stories and songs, as well as direct advice, were woven into the fabric of lives, I imagine, and not discretely chunked into separate parts, as currently modeled in our schools: science, math, history, reading, writing, art.

As a teacher, I've had to learn over the years to moderate my fast-talking, often sarcastic, sometimes ironic, and frequently argumentative verbal speech patterns so as not to offend people. Alaskans, both

Native and white, don't usually jump in on conversations and fight vigorously and loudly for their point of view. Instead, one must wait and say nothing while another person finishes their complete idea. Waiting for people to stop talking is an exercise of extreme endurance for me, coming as I do from the Land of Interrupters, otherwise known as New Jersey, where being loud and animated means people like you, or at the least are having a good time. Had I grown up here, the timbre of my voice would naturally be lower, the speed of my speech slower, and my verbal approach more polite. If I spoke in my natural, East Coast volume while working with Stephen, I'D BE YELLING at him.

After students write an introduction paragraph or sentences for their essays, we embark on the body. *Details*, I reinforce. *You like to hang out with your friends? What do you do? You like basketball? Are you on the team? How long have you played?* Most boys in Stephen's class have a paragraph devoted to video games, with random forays into sports, snow-machining, dirt bikes, and hunting. One student's favorite president is John F. Kennedy because "he looks nice and he's on *Black Ops Zombies*." That's right, President John F. Kennedy, zombie slayer.

After fleshing out the requisite video game and basketball paragraphs with compelling details, we embark on the Conclusion, a concept some seventh graders require almost a year to grasp. Many simply stop writing, and conclude with "The End." I've told you everything, and now I'm done. No need to tie it into a bow, or refer back to the beginning, or reach an epiphany. But school wants a conclusion, and tests require it. To that end, I've perfected a color-coded method of teaching conclusions. I project student work onto the whiteboard and mark with pink, blue, and orange highlighters sentences, ideas, and fragments from the intro and body paragraphs destined for repetition. *Finally. In conclusion. To sum up. All in all. Pick one,* I say. *Link back to your intro. Just a few sentences,* I plead. *What do you want the reader to remember about you,* I coax.

Conclusion or not, now comes the word processing. If the high school teachers only knew the pain involved in teaching these budding humans to type their writing in a Word document, double-spaced, with a centered title, name in the upper left corner (or any corner for that matter), and spell-checked. Despite their weekly practice on keyboarding programs, Stephen's class resists the wisdom of the home row. They want to look at their fingers picking out each letter. O n e. B y. O n e.

Typed rough drafts in hand, students begin to edit, or pretend to. They must read their writing out loud, twice. Once to themselves for the self-edit, then once again with a friend for the peer edit. Red pens and editing checklists in hand, they scan for spelling mistakes, check capitals, periods at the end of sentences, and any grammar skill we're practicing: commas placed correctly in their lists, the use of transition words, simple tense verbs. Lots of kids don't really use the checklist because either they don't understand it, or they think I don't check.

The miracle of Stephen's typed rough draft lies before us: a correctly formatted document in sixteen-point font. I feel a triumph, a sense of satisfaction at his accomplishment. He has been patiently waiting for me to work with him this class period. He even possesses an editing checklist. Instead of using periods, he's chosen the comma. And why not? The comma signals a pause, a breath in his story of himself. Now at least he identifies and separates complete, written thoughts. Earlier in the year his writing was one long stream of thought detailing in a repetitive stream of consciousness his detailed long stream of thinking. To hear him speak in his low, whispery voice I must sit right next to him: *My name is Stephen, I was born on November 24, 1996, in Nome, Alaska, I'm fourteen years old.* Who am I to bemoan his lack of artistry? I am happy with this exhibition of correct sentence structure because it is one crucial measure of his success or failure in this school: facility with standard, written English.

Among Stephen's classmates, many will not graduate with their peers in five years. In 2010–11, only 55 percent of the Alaska Native students in Nome graduated from the high school. When Stephen's cohorts were sophomores in 2013–14, the last year for which public data is available, that number had climbed to 62 percent. A class that had entered seventh grade with thirty-eight students was down to nineteen rising sophomores. A few had probably moved away, and a handful had enrolled in the state's boarding school, Mount Edgecumbe in Sitka, where rural students have greater opportunities for elective classes and advanced placement. Still, the hard truth remains: by tenth grade, when they turn sixteen, many Alaska Natives drop out.

Some fail their freshman English class and have to retake it. Sophomores bogged down with two English courses lose an elective space in their schedule. A student like Stephen, who longs to get his hands dirty in small engines, will instead be slogging through English twice a day. Tired of the boredom and the failure, many simply stop coming to school. I'm afraid Stephen will be one of these students. Or maybe he'll stay the course, taking an extra one or two years to graduate, his high school career marked by class repetitions, remedial reading, and computer-based tutorials all attempting, and often failing, to deliver on the promise of a public education.

Paul Ongtooguk, an Inupiaq from Northwest Alaska, attended Nome Beltz in the early 1970s, when it was a regional boarding school. Until 1976, if they wanted a high school education, Alaska Native students living in the villages had to leave their homes to attend boarding schools in other parts of the state or outside in the lower forty-eight, because schools only taught up to the eighth grade. In many larger communities, including Nome, the local high school taught only white students or those Natives of "mixed blood" who were considered "civilized" enough to be in the same classroom as their white counterparts. Tobeluk v. Lind, a class-action suit more commonly known as the Molly Hootch case, after an Eskimo girl whose name headed the original list of plaintiffs, forced the state to build high schools in any rural village that wanted one, and most did.

In his essay "Their Silence About Us: Why We Need an Alaskan Native Curriculum," Ongtooguk writes: "The curriculum at my high school in Nome was virtually silent about us, our society, and the many issues and challenges we faced as a people caught between two worlds. In fact, educational policy since the turn of the century had been to suppress Native culture and 'assimilate' us into the broader society. Everything that was required—everything that had status—in the curriculum was centered on white people and was remarkably like what might have been found anywhere in the US."

Yes, some things have changed. Local communities have more control over their schools, the State of Alaska has adopted cultural standards to guide districts, and Native language programs in the schools are springing up across the state. But a lot remains the same. Ninety percent of all teachers hired in Alaska are white, with the majority coming from outside the state. There is no formalized Alaska Native curriculum adopted at a statewide level, and with the current climate of testing regimes and newly adopted Common Core–like state standards, more and more districts are purchasing corporate curriculums designed to be taught anywhere in America. And what is that if not assimilation?

My classroom, like many in Alaska, exists in a kind of purgatory, a place where I must somehow bridge cultures: the daily lives of children who do not see themselves reflected in our school's culture, student needs versus state and district requirements, administrative demands versus classroom reality.

As a teacher, I'm lucky in some respects. Small classes allow me the frequent opportunity to work one-on-one with my charges. Together we read their work out loud and review every word, every period, every sentence. At first, many children are scared of me, of this "teacher edit" process. Their writing, however banal and repetitive and convoluted, or however brilliant and funny, is a tender thing to them, and I am not often a tender person. I am direct and my pen wields power.

Come sit here, I command. *Get me your checklist.* They sit and we correct misspellings, capitalize, de-capitalize, insert commas, answer questions. *What do you mean by this? This is a run-on sentence. Can you show me where the period goes? I'll read it and you tell me when to stop and put in a period. This is a fragment. Can you make a whole sentence for me? This paragraph only has two sentences. You need more. Should this sentence go somewhere else? Where?*

I also say, *Awesome intro! That really drew me in. Wow, your writing has really improved since September. You've got periods and capitals in all the right places. This is an excellent organized paragraph. Cool, you go hunting with your dad? What for? Tell me and I'll write the sentence for you.* If we can speak it, we can write it.

Much to their chagrin, I bust them on their checklists. *Here you checked off that you had four to six detail sentences in each paragraph, but you don't. Sorry, I can't give you credit for that. You haven't capitalized any names! Wow, a whole paragraph here and only one period at the very end? Hmmm, you checked off that you looked for periods. Can you redo this please?* They return to their desks with a sheepish look.

Written sentences necessitate a distance from the world. The English sentence individuates, separates, raises the tactile, the real, the sensual, into a thing apart. Does the experience of being a human living in this arctic place lend itself to the kind of written sentences, paragraphs, and essays that I demand in the classroom? How often, out in this country, dwarfed by the omniscient sky and horizon, mesmerized by darkened water clouds above an open section of otherwise frozen ocean, have I been at a loss for words? What sentences contain this world? The human words that first arose from this earth here—different from the ones I now possess—must be perfect for expressing this reality.

On seal hunting, Stephen writes: *I went boating with my dad when we got back, we had no gas for our boat. So my dad went to get gas for the boat, when we put the boat in the water, the water went in the boat.* I hear this spoken in his quiet voice, his soft words. When I sit with him waiting, sometimes for several minutes, waiting for his words, I see his mind in some faraway place where the action or the idea happens. But time ticks away and another child, another boy, is talking, wandering, asking for help.

Stephen is just one boy, a man's son. This man is one of many competent, smart, strong, and capable males out here for whom writing an essay, writing anything short of a job application or a materials list, is just plain silly. This sort of academic literacy may never be a part of their real lives. I suspect this concept of writing down thoughts and experiences must appear strange, foreign, and incomprehensible to them. These men are the backbone of the community. They build houses, deliver fuel, and keep the roads clear. They are hunters and fishermen, mechanics, tradesmen, working men of all sorts. You'll find them in the fire department, on maintenance and custodial crews. These guys will save your ass, fix your car, and put meat on your table. But they're not gonna write shit down.

Stephen isn't going to say another sentence, at least not in the little bit of time we have left before class ends. I'm pushing too hard. This sentence business, this essay business, it's urgent only to me. Reading the words and thoughts on his page, I discover he wants to be a hunter when he grows up, and work on search and rescue. I'm certain he will do well at both things and I'm glad for that. He will likely have a family to feed, and no doubt there will be people to rescue out in the wilderness, possibly even me. To be on search and rescue, Stephen will have to complete EMT training, so he'll have to write at least some things. As a hunter, he'll need to fill out forms for fish and game, but sentence and paragraph writing won't necessarily help him communicate knowledge to his son or nephew. I hope that my pushing for a sentence furthers his literacy and increases his odds at a successful life, but the conclusion to this story eludes me. And what can one do, really, in the last ten minutes of class, in the last class of the day on a Friday, but call it "good," get ready for bus duty, and start fresh on Monday.

You Can't Say That in Here

Anne P. Beatty

I was constantly shocked by what came out of my students' mouths. In the same way foreigners learning a new language can scoop only a few familiar words out of the conversation soup, during my first few months at a public high school in South Central Los Angeles, I could hear only the curse words, sometimes strung together five deep. *Jacked-up motherfucker. Fucking asshole. Crazy-ass bitch.* To their friends, they said, "Shut the fuck up," with as little venom as I might say, "Oh, come on." Then the insults—mostly misogynistic—filtered through: *skank, ho bag, hood rat, tramp.*

"Go to hell, you Cambodian muskrat," I heard Joseph tell Craig. Neither boy was Cambodian.

"That's not appropriate," I said, which seemed to me (as their twenty-four-year-old English teacher) the right thing to say, even if it sounded like a line I'd cribbed from a script about teaching. Secretly I marveled that Joseph knew the word *Cambodian.* Our student body was African American and Latino, with a smattering of Native Americans and Pacific Islanders. The day I was hired, before I'd even taught a class, I was walking in an otherwise empty hallway behind a teacher who was unaware I was there, when suddenly she yelled out, "I am so fucking sick of this place!" To say it seemed a bad omen would be an understatement.

Whenever I heard a curse word I would stop class, call the student out, and…what? My plan ended there. What did I want? An apology? To kick him out? To string her up by the toes and make an example of her? I was not sure what I wanted, so I usually ended up with a power struggle. The student would mutter, "Damn, why you gotta be such a bitch?" or regale me with the other forty-three raunchy words she knew.

Teachers in inner-city schools like these are often said to be "on the front lines" or "in the trenches." Some districts even offer "hazard pay" for positions at these schools. The obvious implication is that teachers are soldiers. The less obvious implication concerns the enemy. Is it ignorance? Poverty? We teachers would like to think so. But all too often, the enemy becomes the students. After all, it is their ignorance and poverty we are up against. The fact that teaching in a hostile classroom feels like fighting in a war zone will come as no surprise to any two-year-old's parent, who knows how the person you love and strive to help can be so maddening as to become your de facto enemy.

In this battle, language becomes a weapon. A teacher, like an out-numbered general, clamps down on her power, overreaches, makes threats she cannot deliver on and perhaps wishes she could retract. Students who are forced into submission, captives at the mercy of their overlord teacher, trudging en masse through filthy hallways when the bell tones—well, they revolt. Deprived of so many freedoms, uninhib-ited by the middle-class norms that would have made such profanity unthinkable in my own high school classrooms, my students call a spade a spade, saying, mildly even, "This is some *bull*shit!"

It took several years of teaching before I respected the sentiment, if not the colorful expression, of their outrage.

It doesn't work simply to tell a student he can't say *fuck*, because in fact he can. He can say, "Fuck, fuck, fuck, fuck, fuck…you!" to your face and then cross his arms to observe how you deal with him. Students like that must be disciplined, but how? There are logistical problems in bodily removing them from your classroom.

You cannot touch a student. This is one of the most important lessons taught in the five-day training the LA Unified School District provided in July 2003 for new teachers like me who did not have an education degree or any experience student-teaching. We reviewed this point each day. Can you hug a student? No. Can you touch a student on the shoulder to say good job? No. Can you tap a hand to remind a student to get on task? No. And you most definitely cannot grab a student by the ear, as a retired schoolteacher once confided to me was her favorite approach. The trainers, retired teachers themselves, spent the rest of the week teaching us how to take roll and do our grades on elaborate Scantron sheets. On the last day, they served us cake and ice cream, as if we were the second graders whose classroom we had inhabited for the week. But we still did not know what to do with a defiant, disrespectful student.

Students who will say *fuck you* to your face probably won't leave the room when you tell them to. They will leave only if it serves their purpose, if they are bored or perhaps can't read and are embarrassed to be in an English class lest they be called on. In that case they'll flounce out with a haughty "Fine!"—often before you can fill out the referral slip for the deans. If the students do wait long enough to take the referral slip, they will just tear it up in the hallway and hang out in the stairwell for the rest of the period. If they have the misfortune to be caught by a security guard, they will say, "My teacher kicked me out."

A security guard then has the choice of telling them to go back to class or escorting them to the deans, who yell at the security guards just like they yell at the teachers. "We can't have fifty kids in the deans' office! We're not babysitters! Take them back to class!" The security guards don't like being yelled at any more than I do. They also don't like taking a kid back to class when the teacher refuses to accept him; both guard and teacher lose face haggling as the student stands off to the side, smirking. So the guards merely tell the kids wandering the halls to go back to class and the kids say okay, and then they walk off in opposite directions. These kids find each other and travel in packs as large as eight or twelve. There is always a new stairwell if they are forced to move on.

Recall for a moment—and most people can—a classroom where the students made the teacher cry. Remember that dynamic of power, shame, resentment, and schadenfreude. Students torture teachers casually, pounding the saltshaker over the slug, and teachers do the same. The potential for such brutality lurking in every classroom makes people on both sides feel fear or anger—two emotions that nearly always surface in our words.

Every faculty meeting during my first semester of teaching included a segment devoted to the number of children roaming the halls. During fifth and sixth periods, especially on Fridays, the administration estimated that as many as three hundred kids were out of class.

"Teachers," the principal would exhort. "You cannot send a child out of your classroom without a referral slip."

This was the equivalent of a teacher saying to a student, "You can't say that in here." An empty statement that holds no power; it was a Band-Aid rule. Some teachers were going to keep sending kids out of class, because they'd outlasted seventeen principals in their thirty years of teaching and they'd be damned if they were going to put up with a mouthy kid in sixth period on a Friday. Then there were other teachers, like me, who meekly followed the rules but suffered an internal collapse of discipline in their classes because kids had to do terrible things before they got kicked out. No matter where a teacher fell on that spectrum, none of us liked hearing we couldn't send kids out of class. The subtext troubled us as well: the only reason kids flooded the campus was that teachers did not follow the rules.

A murmur of discontent would ripple through the teachers, slouched in our folding chairs with stacks of ungraded papers at our sides. Sometimes a veteran teacher would raise her hand and point out that a lot of these kids just walked out, or never came to class at all.

"Don't you realize," she would ask, "that some of these kids lie? They lie to the guards and they lie to the administrators and they lie to us. They are playing us all against each other, because there is no real system in place with real consequences for these roving students."

"That, uh..." The principal would clear his throat nervously. "That is a real problem." He would look for a minute as if he wanted to delve into it, wanted to hold a symposium where we could all contribute. You could almost see this look transform itself into mild panic as he grasped where such truth-telling might lead, staring out above our heads, a little sweaty, earnest and manic as a preacher. He would compose himself by looking at the agenda. Then he would announce, "Teachers, you have to send your attendance sheets for homeroom down by 10:30 a.m. No later. 10:30."

The wave of discontent would roll through us with an audible groan and then settle someplace deeper, someplace that is the root of apathy and revolt.

We teachers forgot our own apathy and revolt, though, when confronted with it in our students. So a student has just said *fuck you*, to you. You can't pick him up and hurl him out the window, much as you would like to, because the architects designed the windows to open only at an angle, a crack wide enough to drop an empty Capri Sun packet through and no larger. You have told the student to go to the deans' office and he has said, in one form or another, "Make me." You have no choice but to play your remaining card, if you are a skinny white woman with a maddening compulsion to follow rules. You move to the phone to call security, referral slip in your hand. For a few of them, this is enough. They will get up and leave when you put your hand on the receiver, as it's their last chance to roam the halls unescorted. You can check on them later and see that they never went to the deans' office at all, and you can call their house or write them up again, and very occasionally the deans will actually call the students in the following day.

The deans' feedback: "Call his house."

"I did," I say.

"Then he'll straighten up. Or call again." Case closed.

Okay, I'll dial that disconnected number again. Or I'll talk to his seven-year-old brother who promises to translate for their mother. Or I'll talk to a foster mother for twenty minutes and end up consoling her that *Craig's not such a bad kid, he'll get through it. He's actually smart when he bothers to do the work. Don't worry, I'm sure he'll come home sooner or later.*

———

January. Second semester at our year-round school. A new start. At least half of my students I had never seen before. In the intervening two-month vacation, students had moved, teachers had quit, classes had been collapsed. I stood at the door at the beginning of the period, greeting students and directing them to their assigned seats, just like the discipline books suggested. I had vowed to redefine my role to be a good-humored, exacting, encouraging teacher, which seemed a real possibility until fifth period. Just as the tardy bell rang, William slouched in, six feet of attitude, smacking his lips and looking down his nose at me.

"Okay, everybody, let's get out a sheet of paper!" I said after obligatory introductions. I tried not to acknowledge William's scowl. I was going to stay upbeat. Fast paced. Keep 'em busy.

"I hope we're not going to do something boring!" William announced, looking around for support. The class tittered.

"Sometimes people say something is boring because they just don't get the subtleties of it, or they haven't given it a chance," I said, a serrated edge to my voice. "So let's get out a sheet of paper." Even I, who unlike my students understood the word *subtleties*, wasn't sure what I meant by this. But William got the gist.

"Are you calling me stupid?" he demanded.

"Nobody said anything about stupid, William. Let's just try to—"

"Man, fuck this," William said, and put his head down.

We were three minutes into class, and I was as angry as ever. How dare he come in and mess with my new start?

"William, this is not a good way to begin your semester," I said, knowing it was true for me too.

"Don't talk to me," he said, his voice muffled.

"And there's no cursing in here. So you'll need to stay after class."

"Don't. Talk. To. Me."

I was losing ground fast. "Fine, get a zero on the first assignment— that's a great start to your year."

I turned back to the class, ready to sacrifice William for the rest of them. The students were still quiet, awaiting further direction, but the scent of my desperation must have been strong because the possibility of mutiny now hung in the air. It would be months before I realized that in our first few minutes together, I had lost William for good.

The day before, I had hung a hand-lettered poster in my classroom that read, "Language is power. Use it wisely." I thought it was a message for my students. In retrospect, the message was just as much for me.

One afternoon that February, from my classroom, I heard the beginnings of a commotion. Since I'd grown accustomed to a baseline level of noise (shouting, cursing, thumping sneakers, and the occasional backpack dropped down two flights of stairs), it took a while for the sounds to register as anything out of the ordinary. It was late enough that most of the regular students were gone, but those who attended the evening adult school held in our classrooms—many of whom had previously dropped out or were parents—were arriving. I heard the words echo again and again until their individual meanings formed a whole sentence that finally penetrated my brain: *I'm going to kill you, motherfucker.*

I stepped into the hall to see a huge guy pressing a girl against the wall, his massive hand clamped around her throat. It wasn't the strangler who was threatening to kill, but the girl, sobbing and shouting and delivering quick, hard jabs to the stomach of her assailant.

My strongest emotion, even stronger than my horror, was the seed of relief that two teachers, both males, were already running toward them. The guy and the girl were much bigger than me. They loomed like giants against the dirty light passing through the opaque window behind them. The girl's fist pumped in silhouette, as practiced as a boxer's.

One teacher—whom students unaffectionately called Super Mario—barked, "Break it up! Break it up immediately! I'm calling the police right now! Do you hear me, young man? I'm calling the police!"

The teacher wasn't actually calling the police. He was tugging at the boy's sleeve, and the boy was paying him no more attention than an elephant does a fly. The girl stopped forming words and began making choking sounds, though they sounded more angry and hostile than desperate.

The other teacher, Mr. P, always had kids in his room at lunch and after school. Kids had nicknames for him, affectionate ones, and pounded his fist in the halls. Mr. P stepped up to these two people and somehow put a hand on each of their writhing bodies. "You're gonna get in trouble," he pleaded in a soft, mournful voice. "Listen, you guys, this is not what you want to do. You're gonna get in trouble!" He sounded so sad, like he wasn't scared or mad about their actions, but had seen beyond and knew how it all turned out: the cops, the handcuffs, the sentencing. "You're gonna get in trouble," he repeated, not as a threat but as advice. "You don't want to do this."

The two of them, in a burst of arms and torsos, hurled themselves apart. The guy must have stepped back and released the girl's throat. She immediately lunged for him, red braids swinging, but now there was time for the teachers to throw themselves in between them. Super Mario pushed the guy toward the stairs. Just before he disappeared, the guy turned to survey the hallway, a young man coursing with adrenaline, so hot he couldn't see anything in front of him. The light caught the ridges of three small scars on his cheek, and then he was gone.

The girl, whimpering and cursing, huddled against the wall. Mr. P still had his hand on her arm, murmuring to her.

"Now I'm calling the police!" Super Mario announced and stomped into his classroom.

The girl glared after him and then heaved herself off the wall to run the length of the hall, past me in my demure suede skirt and sensible shoes, and shoot down the opposite staircase.

Security came ten minutes later and left, shrugging. Only we three teachers remained.

"Those kids are not our kids," Super Mario declared. "They are from the adult school, and they are crazy. Some of them have been to prison. That's why we always have to lock up the TV and VCR every afternoon, so no one from the adult school steals them." He looked pointedly at Mr. P, whom he repeatedly accused of not sufficiently securing their department's audiovisual materials.

"They *were* our kids, though," Mr. P said, still with a hint of accent from his childhood in Mexico. "They were our kids until they got in trouble and got kicked out, for something exactly like what just happened." The way he bent the word *trouble* made my heart heave, it was so heavy with feeling and suggestion.

Super Mario gave him a haughty look and said, "Of course our kids are crazy, too. Our kids steal. Some will never learn…But they'll learn one day. They'll learn when they're locked up for thirty years."

"And what good will that do any of us?" Mr. P asked.

The two men looked at each other. Super Mario stalked into his room. Maybe they'd had this argument so many times over the years there was no need to continue. But it was new to me. Were these kids ours or not? This question framed everything I'd been grappling with in my classroom. When the students were foulmouthed, violent, disrespectful, or lazy, the easiest thing to do was write them off, get hostile, deliver a reprimand, and feel self-righteous. I saw some of myself in Super Mario.

Mr. P and I talked in the hall a minute longer. I apologized for not doing more to help. My new friend shrugged and said it all happened so fast, we just got lucky it wasn't worse. I remembered the English department chair telling me that she'd once solicited Mr. P to come speak to her class about how he'd crossed the border illegally as a child. During a unit on the book *The Crossing* by Gary Paulsen, she had observed prejudice in her African American students toward illegal immigrants and she wanted them to be more compassionate. "He talked for an hour, giving details like how his jacket got caught on the fence as his family ran ahead of him. By the end of his story," she said, "kids were crying."

Super Mario, on the other hand, back in the fall had told me gruffly, "Don't smile until Christmas." The kids toed his line, because he did not hesitate to kick them out. He'd been known to kick kids out for the rest of the semester or go to their counselor and demand to have their classes switched without even telling the students. They may have feared him, but they didn't respect him. Super Mario's students were my students and were Mr. P.'s students, yet they behaved differently for each of us. They respected Mr. P. They feared Super Mario. They didn't seem to respect or fear me, perhaps because I did not know myself which side of the battle line I was on.

Are you scared of your students? people asked me. Not really. Yes, it's true that Destiny did try to set me on fire one day, but that was an isolated incident. The students who wore parole anklets so that the police could keep track of their whereabouts tended to stick to themselves. I did not ask about the acts that earned them their anklets. In general, I was less scared of them being in my classroom than I would have been to meet them on the street, a truth that is shameful to admit. No, what scared me were the ways in which our interactions confirmed biases in me that I did not want to see. One reason idealistic young people give for quitting teaching is that they don't like the person it is turning them into. Another way to look at it is that we don't like the person that teaching reveals us to be. Many of us have found that in order to keep teaching, we have to change. I did.

Teachers cursed in the hallways and in faculty meetings. It alarmed me even as my own language outside of school began to include lots of cursing, which I attributed as much to my increased levels of frustration as to the osmotic effect of hearing so much profanity. Words like *hood rat* and *gangbanger* and *tramp* appeared in my lexicon, words my students used with so little animosity that I occasionally used them myself to describe my students, though never to their faces. Perhaps I should clarify that this is not something I am proud of.

Some teachers cursed in front of the kids. My students told me they appreciated that I never did.

"So-and-so, they always be cursing at us. F-this and F-that," they told me. "That's not right!"

While I agreed with them, it was odd to me that some of the students with the foulest mouths were the most scandalized that their teachers cursed.

"What," I asked cautiously, "makes it okay for you to curse at school and not teachers?"

"They're at work!"

"We're teenagers."

"It's not right for us to curse, but it's worse when the teachers do it."

I agreed with this double standard. It *was* worse when the teachers cursed. No teacher who cursed could ever say *You can't say that in here* with any authority. Because I was interested in this issue, and because my students were interested, I began talking about cursing with my classes.

At the beginning of my second year, we talked about how coming to school is a student's job, and if it was wrong for teachers to curse at work, then it must be wrong for students as well. We talked about it being a sign of disrespect and hostility to curse at someone. We talked about cursing in the context of tone and slang. The students liked to talk about cursing almost as much as they liked to curse. It helped to talk overtly about these issues. I was no longer saying, "No cursing in here!" We were discussing ideas about language that were interesting to all of us; we were developing ground rules for our community. I began to glimpse how there could be functional pockets in a dysfunctional system, and how these pockets could be the saving grace in a life punctuated by chaos and violence and arbitrary uses of power. I tried to stop calling my students *hood rats*.

I began to differentiate between offensive cursing and inoffensive cursing in this culture where three-year-olds used the word *shit*. *Fucking* could be an adjective, or it could be a challenge. My students cursed as a way to make their language colorful, though I did try to point out to them via a sign on the wall that excessive profanity indicates a profound lack of vocabulary. They cursed to show frustration, or if they dropped something. I decided to settle for just making them aware that they were cursing in inappropriate places. It wasn't a sudden insight, but somehow I realized that what I wanted when a student cursed was recognition of the fact that it could be objectionable. I quit yelling and began raising my eyebrows when I heard cursing. Like magic, I began to get apologies. To stop and be silent, with eye contact, was so much more powerful than to reprimand.

Every time they cursed, I also required students to get a vocabulary word from a box. After finding the definition and writing a sentence, they tacked it up onto a bulletin board that functioned (in my mind, if not in reality) as a wall of shame. The students liked to make their classmates do vocab words and, so, listened for each other's cursing. Sometimes students would get up and extract a vocab word for their friend, and I wouldn't be involved at all. Sometimes I hadn't even heard the offending language, but I would always nod knowingly, and the kid with the dictionary would groan and hunker down. I wasn't mad anymore. It was sort of funny to all of us. The kids didn't even realize how tuned in they'd become to swearing. Most days, they did my work for me.

Offensive cursing was different. It required more than a vocabulary word exercise. It was hostile and malicious and directed at someone, either me or another student. It still occurred and had to be dealt with as defiance. I still had my stack of referral slips, and I still sometimes moved to the phone to call security. But I didn't let them see me mad. Even when I was boiling inside, I tried to look pleasant. I didn't take it out on the class as a whole. And somehow, this difference meant there was a lot less cursing in my classroom. The power dynamics shifted, so that if one student was out of line, it was she and I, rather than me against the whole class. By the end of my second year, it was rare for a student to curse at me. I tried to remember those first few weeks of teaching when I was called a bitch so many times each day that I would go home stunned that I was still standing. Now, if a student cursed at me, they had to go to the deans' office, and since it wasn't happening all that often, I could follow through on that threat. I called their houses. I separated students who cursed at each other, and sent the provoker out in the hall for a few minutes to chill out. When the rest of the class was working quietly, I would slip out to where he was prowling, pounding lockers, or sitting slumped over. I'd talk to him a bit, one-on-one. Sometimes all these students wanted was a little attention, some respect, a person on their side.

They just had really fucked-up ways of showing it.

I Thought I Was Ready

Sherri Wright

It was September 1968, and I was ready for the first day of school. I had left my apartment early and walked under a blue sky and a canopy of elm trees in front of the turn-of-the-century three-story houses that lined my street. I loved the front porches with blue-painted ceilings and lined-up rocking chairs. The condition of the houses varied: some were immaculate and stately with manicured lawns and others run-down and tenement-like. Many, like mine, were carved into student apartments with rows of mailboxes and bicycles on the front porches.

Central Elementary, a mammoth brownstone with a thick stone entryway arching over double doors at the top of a wide stone staircase, was just around the corner. Shrubs along the sidewalk were scruffy, and the grass was patchy. A chain-link fence enclosed a stark asphalt playground with one lonely monkey bar and a swing set. Overall the once-stately giant looked a little worn. If I'd been more aware, I might have noticed there were no wide driveways, no manicured lawns, no uniform houses, no neatly trimmed shrubs. I was not in the suburbs. Central was in the heart of Ithaca, New York, in a mostly poor neighborhood. Many of the students' families were on welfare.

Inside my classroom, I turned on the ceiling lights—since the sun would never reach my north-facing windows. There was a chill in the room but the atmosphere was cheery—orange and brown paper leaves on the large windows and construction paper apples on the bulletin board. I could smell the pungent red geraniums on the windowsill and the fresh wax on the old pine floors. I'd stacked twenty-six reading books and twenty-six arithmetic workbooks on the shelves. Twenty-six giant letters of the alphabet that I'd brought here from my classroom in Minnesota marched above the high chalkboard in the front of the room. Twenty-six metal desks with heavy wooden flip-up lids stood in five straight rows. On each desk, I'd taped the carefully printed name of a child I'd never seen. What would Artra look like, I wondered? Or Faith? I could picture a Scotty from my last class. I had no idea how well I would get to know the kid named Michael.

With a degree in education and one full year of teaching first graders in a suburb of Minneapolis, I knew how to teach reading, math, art, and science to eager little minds. In my crisp aqua linen sheath that came appropriately to my knees and my not-too-high patent leather heels, I waited in the doorway for my first graders to file in. A loud bell clanged and echoed into the high ceilings of the dim hallway. I heard the big double doors creak open. Immediately a charge of footsteps and a blast of loud voices burst into the hollow space. The little ones came toward me—some with parents, some with older siblings, a few alone. I was ready.

When I was growing up in Minnesota, first on a farm, then in a small town, and then finally in a suburb, my world was narrow, white, and middle class. Even at the university, students and faculty in the College of Education were primarily white. In our senior year, my colleagues and I all applied for teaching jobs in lily-white suburbs. We had no experience with diversity, and rumors about tough kids in poor inner-city schools stoked our fears. We wanted so desperately to be good teachers—and we did not want to jeopardize our first ventures into the real world. Consequently, I was elated when offered a contract to teach first grade in a good school in a suburb of Minneapolis before I'd even received my diploma. I loved teaching that first year. The kids were bright, eager to learn, and cooperative. They sat down at their desks, stopped talking when I flipped the light switch, and were reading thick books by Christmas. Their parents were mainly professionals—university faculty, lawyers, teachers—who supported their kids, participated in parent conferences, and chaperoned field trips.

Looking back now, I imagine I expected that I would keep teaching in a middle-class suburb until I decided to have children, and then I'd stay at home in that suburb, a contented mother with a husband supporting our family.

In 1967, my first year of teaching, I had been so absorbed in my new career that I wasn't focused on the racial tension roiling the country. I had recoiled at the news of the little black girls killed in the Birmingham church bombing, the black college students refused service at the Woolworth's lunch counter in North Carolina, and the Arkansas National Guard escorting black students into white schools. My church supported the Freedom Riders. I was horrified at images of fire hoses and police dogs turned violently on black demonstrators. I had applauded Martin Luther King Jr.'s "I Have a Dream" speech and I was hopeful at the enormous audience he had drawn. I knew what was going on, but it didn't really involve me—it seemed far away from my world. It all started to change when I was packing to go to Ithaca, where my husband was starting graduate school, and I heard that King had been killed in Memphis. Then the riots started—burning up black communities in Detroit, Cleveland, Newark, Washington, DC—even in North Minneapolis. I remember being in my kitchen packing boxes for our move and thinking it couldn't get worse when the radio blasted out news of Robert Kennedy's assassination. I was scared about how the world was changing, and I was moving far away from all of my family.

Nevertheless, I thought I was ready, and I had no way to know how unready I was when those twenty-six first graders walked into my classroom that first day. Tall and serious Artra, in a starched yellow dress and matching yellow ribbons tying five thick pigtails poking in five directions; tiny blond Donny, grasping his mother's hand; Margaret, shyly exposing a missing front tooth; Rose, with cheeks to match her name; and sweet, smiling Scotty, with dark eyes under long lashes. Tall and thin, Lynn followed her older sister, who motioned her through the door. Faith hid behind her mother, tears from her black eyes wetting her pink dress. A lanky kid whose name I didn't catch slid past me without a word and drifted to the back of the room.

As the rest of them came in, the noise and activity surprised me. *It's only the first day*, I thought. *Did they all know each other already?* Over the crescendo of voices, laughter, banging lunch boxes, and the bell clanging in the hallway, I politely asked them to sit down. (Don't try to outshout them—Methods 101.) Some sat and squeaked their desks open and shut a few times. Others moved around, chatted, picked things off shelves, and paid no attention to my "Good morning, boys and girls." I repeated myself, louder. I switched off the lights and tried again. Feeling my face flushing, and unsure of what to try next, I looked up at the clock.

Suddenly from the back of the room, "*Ow, ow, ow!*" Kids screamed, twisted around, jumped out of their seats, and ran to the back. Artra, eyes wide, face twisted in rage, had lifted her heavy metal desk up off the floor. *Crash! Thud!* She slammed it down, glaring at Scotty, narrowly missing his foot.

"Oh my God!" I raced to the back, cringing at the thought of what might come next.

Scotty was screaming and crying, "She tried to hit me! She tried to hit me!" I put a shaky hand on each of their shoulders, not sure of what Artra would do next—or what I would do about it. Still trembling, Artra shrugged me off with a heave of disgust, plunked down in her seat, and planted her arms across her desk. "Don't you touch my stuff."

Scotty's big brown eyes pleaded through tears for comfort. Going purely on impulse, I guided him back to his desk, never taking my eyes off Artra. For the first time the room went silent and the kids sat down—except for the lanky boy still wandering the room, bopping kids on the head and leaping out of reach before they could hit him back. He didn't speak or make eye contact. Kids yelped and hollered, "Michael, stop! Michael, no!" By now, Faith was clinging to my dress, crying softly. Donny sat frozen at his desk. Artra glared at me, hanging on to her desk as if someone were threatening to take it away. Twenty-five pairs of eyes watched me.

Unsure of what I was going to do until I got there, I walked over to Michael, grabbed him firmly by the shoulders, and led him to his desk.

Silently I sighed, relieved, when he sat down. Then I started moving. As fast as I could, I handed out fat pencils, crayons, workbooks. I asked a couple of kids to help pass out papers. Somehow, I blurted out rudimentary instructions for a picture worksheet. The kids started opening up crayon boxes and yelling questions, demanding my attention before they would start on their own. Some got out of their desks and wandered around. The lanky kid pulled out his lunch bag and started eating. It was just 9:30. My "teaching experience" had not included this decibel level or such chaos. I didn't know if I'd ever gain control. Over and over that day a voice in my head asked: *What have I gotten myself into?* I had been so smug just this morning. Now I wasn't sure I could survive through lunchtime, and I had signed a one-year contract.

At three o'clock, I sunk into a mini-chair in Joan's classroom next door. "My God, is it always like this?" I asked. I scanned her room. It looked even worse than mine. The desks were helter-skelter, the floor strewn with paper, crayons, lunch bags, food wrappers, and workbooks. In the corner, an easel dripped wet paint and brownish water. Brilliant finger paintings lined the windowsill and *N I K K I* was scrawled in crooked letters across the length of the chalkboard. Joan nodded. "It'll get better." She laughed as she shoved desks into rows and squatted in her fitted red jacket and black miniskirt to pick up paper. A small woman, Joan wore high-heeled shoes, oversized glasses, and a short angular haircut—uncommon in those hippie days. She had taught for ten years in Buffalo, but this was her first year at Central, so we had become fast friends in our week of teacher orientation.

"You're lucky. You got the good kids! They assigned the *behavior problems* to me." She sighed as she grabbed a sponge and started mopping up wet paint.

I walked home slowly, not seeing the tall trees or the old front porches with their blue ceilings and rocking chairs as I replayed the incidents of the day and thought about what I should have done. The problem was, I didn't know. I felt like I had failed.

"I've worked with kids all my life and never experienced such chaos, such disrespect, such anger. And they're only six years old," I wailed to my husband as I reached our third-floor apartment. He had started a graduate program at Cornell, and we were depending on my teaching income, so I knew I couldn't quit.

I braced myself each day I went back to Central. I was not the confident teacher who had fixed up this classroom that first day and thought she was so ready. I wondered if I could even hang on to this job. Would my principal support me in the chaos of my classroom? Every day I wondered how I would handle the next crisis. In desperation, I just worked to keep everyone busy—reading, math, science experiments, art projects, and chores: washing chalkboards, dusting erasers, cleaning paintbrushes, handing out papers, sharpening pencils, dumping the pencil sharpener, feeding the fish. I had to respond to their questions and their actions as soon as possible—especially to those with short fuses, like Artra. Eventually more of them sat at their desks and worked on their own. I focused on reading—reading to them and teaching them to read. I knew that reading gave kids a concrete skill and allowed them to work independently—to feel success. I just had to figure out how to get these kids to stay focused long enough to learn.

For the first two or three weeks, Michael refused to do any assignment. He wandered and muttered, "No, not me, I ain't" to any request. I did not know how to get him to participate. I just prayed he wouldn't hurt someone while I wasn't looking. One day as he was pulverizing another kid, I grabbed him by the waist. He squirmed, his long legs flailing and his arms trying to propel himself away. I held tight and finally, exasperated, sat down and pulled him onto my lap so I could continue working with a reading group. Very gradually, he quit struggling and I felt his tension release and his body melt into my lap. He sat still. Not a method I had learned in college, but after that whenever he bothered another kid I did the same thing. After a few sessions on my lap, Michael started mumbling answers as the kids sounded out words. One day he sauntered up and took a chair in the reading group. He opened his book, and after a few others had read, he sounded out a few words. Then a few more. For the first time I saw a shy smile skim his face and his eyes look right into mine. To this day, I can still feel the joy I experienced at the moment Michael realized that he could learn to read.

The classroom calmed substantially once Michael began working productively instead of hurting others. During that year, he took on tasks in the classroom—feeding the animals, sorting supplies, washing chalkboards, running errands to the office. I learned that Michael had three brothers and three sisters. They had no curfew, and the older children traveled in groups, often with their toddler sister tagging along. Their single mother worked at a discount store and came to school events on an irregular basis. Michael told me his father was in the army. And although he and his brothers and sisters all carried the same last name, a teacher told me they had six dads.

Over the next three years, Michael and his siblings would visit me regularly and bring me the neighborhood news. They would tell me when Freddie was hit by a car, when David was kicked out of the corner store, when their mother's boyfriend beat her up. They would tell me when they were in trouble with their teachers or when they'd been stopped by the police. I couldn't have known then that, years later, after I'd heard awful stories of drugs, alcohol, prostitution, and incarceration involving many former Central students, including some of Michael's brothers and sisters, Joan would send me an article from the *Ithaca Journal* with a photo of an adult Michael in New Orleans assisting with cleanup after Hurricane Katrina. The article said he worked for a community center in Ithaca. As an activities director, I think.

As I learned to know my students, I was able to see the little children beneath the hard protective shells they wore to survive the place where they happened to have been born. I discovered beautiful kids who loved to play, to laugh, to learn. Faith stopped crying, and little Donny started sharing stories about his dad who was a singer and had just cut an album. Even Artra, after I enlisted her sister to take notes home to their mother, turned from the angry girl of that first day to a cheerful and helpful student. She lived in a tall, unpainted house that I could see from my fire escape. Her mother and father both worked long shifts at a factory, but I remember how she always arrived in freshly starched dresses, talking loudly and laughing and smelling of pancakes. She never lost her spirit.

Ida, on the other hand, was never feisty. Arriving midyear from North Carolina, she wore a timid smile, stringy dark hair over her eyes, and limp, oversized dresses missing buttons and belts. She was a good reader and eager to please. I wondered about her mother when she sent Ida right back to school pale and weak after the nurse had sent her home sick. And then, one Saturday at a school carnival, Ida told me she'd hurt her finger. I lifted her dirty little hand to see an ugly bruised finger starting to swell. When the principal said I couldn't take her to a doctor, I walked her home. Ida led me to a run-down house that hadn't been painted in years. The front door swung wide open, so as I waited on the porch, I could see into a living room with worn wood floors and almost no furniture. I watched Ida run up the stairway calling her mother. After several minutes, a tall woman in a rumpled housedress and disheveled hair, looking like she had just gotten out of bed, slowly descended the stairs. She said hello and chatted pleasantly as if I were a neighbor stopping over for coffee. I told her Ida's finger might be broken and asked her to take her to the doctor, but she didn't even look at her daughter's hand, now puffed up like an oversized mushroom. She just nodded. I looked back at Ida and walked home feeling sick knowing that Ida's mother had no intention of taking her to a doctor. When I went to bed that night, I saw that dirty swollen hand with the purple bruise and Ida's sad eyes. The next day Ida came to my apartment, her finger wrapped in a bright white bandage, her hand swollen twice its normal size. Her mother had finally taken her to a doctor after she'd fallen and re-injured the hand. Ida was cheerful and happy. For the rest of the year, I asked myself how this little girl could be so optimistic, so cheerful, so eager to learn.

Not all Central parents were like Ida's mother. I would meet single mothers raising five or six kids who came to all of their kids' conferences and volunteered at school. I would see mothers working the cash register at Jamesway discount store and going on to a night shift at a factory. I would see older kids walking their siblings to school in the morning and fetching them in the afternoon when both parents worked. I wouldn't know what to say to mothers who told me to whip their kids if they didn't do their work. I would learn that almost every parent wanted their kids to learn to read, to succeed where they themselves had failed. They wanted their kids to get good jobs—to do better than they had.

I would see the tenacity of these kids as they faced discrimination—like Renee, a fifth grader who came to my apartment to work on a project. By the time I got down three flights to answer the door, Renee met me on the stairs. She said, "Mrs. B said you weren't home. She told me to go away. But I told her I knew you were home because you just invited me over." Renee had walked right in the front door, past Mrs. B, and up the steps. Mrs. B, my landlady, lived with her husband and daughter on the first floor of their big white frame house with two apartments on the second floor and our very large attic apartment on the third. She kept the house, yard, and gardens in pristine condition and gave us the recipe for the chicken cacciatore that wafted garlic fumes to our bedroom every Sunday morning. She had always been kind to us. She would tell me later she did not appreciate black kids hanging around her house. I'm ashamed to say that although I burned inside, I did not stand up to her. I would need to learn how to be as honest as this young girl to stand up for what I believed.

I would despair when I heard older colleagues complain, "Those black kids don't obey, don't respect teachers, don't achieve, don't do anything right. And they always start the fights." Some of us newer teachers tried to stand up for the kids but our opinions were discounted because we hadn't been there for fifteen or twenty years. The older teachers rolled their eyes, smiled through gritted teeth, and called us naive. They said we'd eventually learn about the real world. Indeed, I was naive. I wanted to learn, but not what they wanted to teach me.

These tough kids in this poor inner-city school showed me a world I had never experienced. These kids were "the little black boys and the little white boys" of Martin Luther King Jr.'s dream. They lived every day being disrespected because they were black or poor. They struggled to learn in an environment that judged them even before they showed up in the classroom. They wanted to do well, and perhaps because they were so young, they still hoped to succeed. I saw real children who had ability, who shouldered responsibilities beyond their years, and who showed incredible resiliency. They deserved to be respected and to be given the same opportunities automatically assumed by the middle-class kids I'd taught before.

These kids taught me that civil rights and equal rights were not abstract concepts—not just news stories happening far away. Discrimination would not go away just because I recognized it and said it was wrong. The strength and courage of these young kids made me want to do something—to work for changes, for opportunities, for kids.

I started to follow the civil rights movement at Cornell, where my husband was in grad school. I would learn that Cornell students had repeatedly asked the administration to explore equal opportunities for blacks. They had appealed peacefully for two years for an African American studies program. Frustrated with continual promises but no follow-through, a radical group took over the student union building; when they were attacked by a group of white students attempting to retake the building, they armed themselves with rifles. They made the national news. They scared students and faculty and administrators at Cornell. They occupied the student union, Willard Straight Hall, for several days, calling for meetings with the administration—now making demands rather than polite requests. The armed protest scared me, but the fact was that the students achieved success only after they protested—it was their only way to gain a voice in their education. I knew that I could never be part of an armed protest, but I needed to figure out what I could do in the environment I knew.

One thing never changed. I always knew that I wanted to work with or for children. I loved teaching. Now, I also knew that I wanted to stay in a diverse school. I wanted to try to make some difference for kids like these kids at Central whose potential I knew was great but whose opportunities were limited by forces beyond their young control. I learned that I liked living in a city. I liked the diversity, and I liked walking to school, to the corner store, to the drugstore, to the movie theater, to a restaurant, and I liked being in the neighborhood where my students lived.

I didn't know then that the day my daughter was born, the kids from Central Elementary would be the couriers announcing her arrival to the neighborhood. They would tromp up to our third-floor apartment. They would be her first guests. Her first friends. I didn't know that my *real-world* career for thirty years would be in a program labeled "Youth at Risk" whose goal, long after retirement, I can still recite from memory: *to provide the children and youth who live in high-risk environments the educational skills and competencies they need to live productive, self-fulfilling, and happy lives.*

On the last day of school, Donny rushed breathless into the classroom. "Did I pass? Did I pass? My mother said she'll whip me if I don't pass."

Donny did pass, and so did I. I learned more that year in first grade than in four years of college and in all of my previous life experiences combined. I signed on for another stint at Central, working half-time, so that I could go back to school. I knew then I wasn't ready.

Now, almost fifty years later, I watch teens protesting in the streets of Ferguson, Missouri, and Baltimore, Maryland. I hear black kids demanding justice, shouting, "Black lives matter!" In those kids I see the faces of my Ithaca students. I wonder how their teachers prepare, how they create classrooms where these kids feel respected and motivated to learn.

In the aftermath of school shootings at Columbine, Red Lake, and Sandy Hook, I wonder how teachers have the courage to go to school every day. How do they build safe environments for students within the context of police guards, entrance checks, and metal detectors?

As I watched news of the Baltimore mother who grabbed her son out of the rioting mob, hit him, and ordered him home, I remembered parents like Donny's mother, who told me to whip their kids if they misbehaved. I thought about the fear driving these mothers. In Ithaca at that time there were no guns in school, no guards, no police. Kids did not carry guns on the streets. Those innocent days in Ithaca now seem almost idyllic.

I wonder if I could ever be ready for a classroom today.

Lessons in the Dry Season

Sara Ackerman

I'm on a narrow dirt path in red rubber flip-flops and an embroidered muumuu I'd seen in a thrift store in Brooklyn and surmised was the type of garment one takes to Africa. I am standing entirely still, because ahead there is a troop of baboons. They remind me of rats, but huge, and viler. I try to remember where I read that baboons can rip off human digits with their teeth. Panicked and unsure of what else to do, I count silently in my head. One, two, three, holy crap, I think one just looked at me…456, 457…I'm going to be late for class. When I am well past six hundred, the baboons look up and scatter, like the cockroaches in my New York City apartment when I flipped on the light. But I am eight thousand miles away from East Thirteenth Street, and I can think of no real reason for it other than that Alexandra Fuller wrote this about Malawi: "It doesn't seem possible that there can be enough air for all the upturned mouths. The land bleeds red and eroding when it rains, staggering and sliding under the weight of all the prying, cultivating fingers." From the lonely, lamplit bed where I was curled when I read that, I looked back and forth between the page of my book and the room's only window, which revealed a scrap of fire escape against a gray New York afternoon. A gap where the window wouldn't close let the chill in, while the radiator blew bone-dry gasps of air in my face. From the street five stories below, I heard a thousand anonymous footsteps. I set down *Don't Let's Go to the Dogs Tonight*. Malawi sounded perfect.

As it was, I was in between gigs. I'd left my job teaching preschool on the Upper West Side during the white and wealthy toddler boom of the mid-2000s. The kids had hip names, hip allergies, West Indian nannies, and strollers that cost more than my rent. I had a gummy candy addiction, a freshly printed degree in "individualized study" plus a complementary mountain of debt, the bottom bunk, and a busted knee-shoulder combo from being hit by a car on my morning bike commute. Twice.

I lasted only a year in the classroom overlooking Central Park. I had been a nanny previously, and when my charge became old enough to attend preschool, his kind but crazy mother got me a job there, perhaps to act as a spy. The work, while intriguing, didn't pay the bills and was not part of the (nonexistent) plan. Besides, was I supposed to follow this toddler to college? I attempted to study dance therapy instead and add to my pile of student debt and bizarre degrees. I abandoned the idea, however, when it became clear that pursuing this career might require me to deal with other adults and talk about my feelings. Sticking to toddlers and toddler feelings seemed less likely to provoke the anxiety I don't want to talk about, so I applied to the graduate school of education at Harvard. Upon acceptance, my boss mazel-toved me with a vow to set me up with her nephew at MIT— whom she declared was "twenty-five and a half and perfect for you."

So now, in the space between Manhattan and Cambridge, I find myself in northern Malawi, working as a volunteer teacher for a small British charity discovered after five minutes of googling. They run environmental, education, and health-care projects in rural areas. They employ locals to run the projects but take on foreign volunteers, like teachers and nurses, to pitch in. I have three months, a teacher's summer, to do something I am not very clear about but assume I can do. My luggage contains two ill-advised muumuus, Howard Gardner's *Frames of Mind: The Theory of Multiple Intelligences*, a jar of artisanal peanut butter, a toothbrush, Dr. Bronner's Magic Soap (eighteen different uses!), and 150 pounds of books, toys, and educational materials to donate. I fly New York to Frankfurt, Frankfurt to Nairobi, Nairobi to Lusaka, and finally Lusaka to Lilongwe. From the capital, I board a minibus containing a wrench instead of a steering wheel and brown packing tape holding the bits of cracked windshield together. I have nine hours of back-row jolting to contemplate these amenities. At the roadblock that is my stop, the conductor launches my bags out of the window and instructs me to follow.

"Mwaya? Mwaya?" a dozen hyper children ask, taking my hands and my luggage down two miles of dirt road to the village by that name. A thirteen-year-old hoists a fifty-pound suitcase on her head. Her name, she tells me, is Mercy. My wheeled duffel bag halts in the soft sand and the other children pounce on it, pulling out boxes of puzzles and books, separating a cap from its pen, so each has something to carry. We arrive at the charity's headquarters, and I see scattered on the shore of Lake Malawi a handful of reed huts built on wooden platforms. The children deposit the luggage on the stairs of one. This is to be my home for the next three months. Miraculously there is plumbing, with a toilet block that contains a fire-heated shower and rafters where black mambas slither. In the center of everything is a tin-roofed, outdoor kitchen with a wood-burning stove sheltering a heap of cats. I stare at my surroundings with enormous eyes as a full moon dips into Lake Malawi and the air immediately chills. In my admittedly spotty research of the country, I noted Malawi's brutally hot summers, failing to realize that I would be in the Southern Hemisphere, and therefore in the dry season, also known as winter. I sleep that night, and every night in Malawi, in my doubled-up muumuus and airplane sweater, basically all of the clothes I have with me.

The next day I set out to Kachere Nursery School where I am assigned to teach. Mary and Rabecca, the teachers, are both waiting for me with big smiles and bigger pregnant bellies. Thirty-five children sit on concrete benches, waiting. Most are between the ages of two and five, but some babies are sent to school with older siblings, and some children are six and seven years old, their families unwilling to let them graduate because the preschools offer free meals.

The room erupts: "There are seven days, seven days, in a week! Sunday! Monday! Tuesday! Wednesday! Thursday! Friday! And Saturday!" The class chants the months, numbers, and alphabet letters.

Rabecca takes a bit of chalk no bigger than a grain of rice and presses it into the blackboard to draw a triangle.

"What is this?" Mary shouts.

Selena is chosen, and she stands in her plaid skirt and ragged sweater. "Circle," she answers.

"Is she right?" Mary shouts again.

"No!" shrieks the chorus of the thirty-four other students.

Tena is selected next. She is wearing a short, pale, organza dress with a chartreuse slip underneath, hanging down to her ankles. When she says, "Triangle," Mary and Rabecca both answer, "Well done!" The rest of the class mega-chants, "Wello done! Wello done! Sure! Keep it up!" All thumbs in the room flash up.

This, the jolly drill sergeant style of teaching and learning, continues for an indeterminate amount of time until the whole class rises while Mary and Rabecca hoist their pregnant bodies all over the room in unlikely motions, yelling, "Do as I do!" The children copy their antics, shouting doubly, triply loudly, "Don't worry!"

When the game ends, Mary turns to me and asks, "You have something to teach us today?"

Overwhelmed and terrified, I promise, "Tomorrow."

Rabecca declares: "Break time! Go for wee!"

"Go for wee! Go for wee!" the children reply, squatting in the courtyard or peeing against a tree. After we serve the children hot sugared tea, they run amok outside while the teachers are free to run errands. Mary wants to buy a samosa and Rabecca wants to go to the clinic for a checkup.

"Should I stay to mind the children?" I ask, as they put their arms around me and pull me out of the yard.

Mary fixes her eyes on me and says, "They are on break," as if the very presence of supervision would negate that fact. "This way is best," she continues, "because they are used to it."

I watch from afar. The children play with nails they find in the dirt and soccer balls made out of condoms and shreds of plastic bags.

They balance leaves on their heads, chase grasshoppers, and swing on a rope tied to a tree.

And so the days pass in this arc. Rote, enthusiastic chanting, toddlers served scalding beverages, and unsupervised mucking around. Rebecca stretches a *chitenge*, a traditional printed cloth, around her expanding belly. Mary becomes so enormous that the doctor suggests it may be twins. At unpredictable intervals, one or the other turns to me asking, "You have something to teach us, today?"

Most of my lessons are a failure. The children don't understand my English and my Chitonga is like the tiny *E*s at the bottom of the eye chart: minuscule and fuzzy. I can't figure out what concepts they have already mastered and what still needs to be taught. I stammer. I sweat. I rile the children up merely by possessing straight hair, pale skin, and a strange voice. I find that singing helps to bridge the gap between my abilities and what the students might need to know. "Head, Shoulders, Knees, and Toes" and "The Hokey Pokey" teach English body part vocabulary. "Open Shut Them" teaches verbs.

I organize a field trip to the clinic across the courtyard so the children can learn what doctors and nurses do. The teachers and medical workers comply with my suggestion, humoring me. Dr. Manda points at people in the waiting room and tells the children about the diseases and injuries that could befall them. He takes the class to an examining room where he tells them sometimes people die. We visit Margaret, the janitor, listlessly pushing a dry mop back and forth across the concrete floor. The field trip ends in Dr. Manda's office where he reads from his logbook. "Sam is a psychiatric patient," Dr. Manda begins. "He is mad. He could do anything at any time." The children stare with wide, wet eyes.

I bring out the toys I have brought from the States. I teach the children to stack blocks, match wooden animals, string beads into patterns, listen to books and look at the pictures on their pages. The school door has no lock, so Rebecca, who lives the closest, carries these things back and forth on her head every day. I ride in the back of a pickup truck one hundred kilometers to Mzuzu and buy even more stuff. There isn't much available in this small city, but I clean out the stores until my money is gone, buying five of everything, so each nursery school in the district can benefit.

Back at the rural lakeshore, the walks to Kachere are long, several kilometers each way. With each subsequent trip across the shore, the layers of footprints left by my red rubber flip-flops grow. I am constantly covered in flies. Children accompany me everywhere. "Give me money." "Give me pen." "Give me sweet," they chorus. "Give me condom," a seven-year-old boy named Blessing demands. "Excuse me?" I sputter. "I don't *have* a condom." Determined to make a new ball, Blessing proposes a trade: "You give me condom. I give you lemon." It's a good offer, and I want the lemon. However, I don't walk to and from the nursery school with a supply of birth control. Baboons make regular appearances for a while. Then the villagers, annoyed at the baboons' plundering, poison their banana plants. The baboons are gone. The bananas are inedible.

The primary education advisor (PEA) of the area has organized a training session for the nursery school teachers. Because teachers from all five preschools in the district will be in attendance, I have chosen this day to deliver the materials I purchased in Mzuzu. By the time the PEA arrives, a representative from each school has a pile of brightly colored, made-in-China plastic at her feet. The topic of the training is Teachers Using Locally Available Resources—and I have unwittingly provided the introduction to the lesson. "What's all this!" the PEA booms. He grabs the toy brooms from a pile and snorts, "We can make this from sisal." Next up are the plastic shapes. He silently cuts a star from a scrap of paper and tosses the plastic things aside. He picks up a soccer ball and shouts, "We don't need this! We make this from condoms!"

As the tirade dissipates, the teacher in front of me slowly tears open a condom wrapper with her teeth and hands the contents to her fussing toddler. He waves it in the air, stretches it between his chubby fists, puts it to his lips, and blows air into it. The spread of humiliation I experience is warm, like my insides are full of soup. I try not to look at the PEA, or the crap I bought, or the woman, her toddler, or her toddler's condom. I try not to look at Rabecca and Mary, both pregnant, both HIV positive.

I leave the training with my eyes pricked with tears. I have been forcing a pregnant lady to carry wooden blocks on her head. I gave out junk proudly, junk that I would not have used in my own classroom. I took kids on a field trip to a room where a guy had maybe died. I packed for the wrong season. I violated one of my most sacred principles of living in Africa: try not to screw up too much. It is said that writers should read more than they write. On that same path is the sign that says teachers should learn more than they teach. In this too, I have failed.

That night I sit under my mosquito net sucking peanut butter off the handle of my toothbrush and washing it down with Malawi gin, sold by single-shot servings in plastic packets. When I am sufficiently sugared and tipsy I head to the bathroom, swinging my headlamp into the rafters to check for snakes. I flip the toothbrush around, brush my teeth with Magic Soap, and for the sixtieth consecutive night, regret ever believing in its eighteen different uses. I should have packed a real tube of toothpaste. And two jars of peanut butter.

I drag myself to the school the next day, which is good, since Mary is now on maternity leave and Rabecca is out sick. Dr. Manda from the clinic next door interrupts my class, mid–Hokey Pokey, to say: "Esther, I need you to go sit under a tree outside and give vitamin A from UNICEF to all antenatal women and children under five." As judgmental questions like, "Why me?" and "Who will teach the children?" rise to my lips, I shut my mouth and don't open it for several minutes, not even to tell him that my name isn't Esther. I give the preschoolers their vitamins, and let them loose in the courtyard. I sit under the tree with bottles of pills, scanning the passersby for women with children under five.

UNICEF established a Child Wellness Week in Malawi, but Malawi seems to be only vaguely aware of this fact, hence my sudden recruitment. I look at the wooden crate of vitamins and see nothing to open the liquid-filled capsules with. After some consideration, I point this out to Dr. Manda. "Teeth," he replies. I tell the first mother in line to bite the capsule open, but I lack the Chitonga vocabulary for any of the appropriate words. She misunderstands my miming and swallows it. So not only do I spend the next several hours making babies cry by squishing their cheeks together to squirt vitamins down their throats, but I also bite the capsules open with my own teeth. When I run out of infant-dose capsules, I am told to squirt five drops of the adult capsules into the infants and use the same capsule on multiple infants until it is empty. I'm not convinced it is what UNICEF had in mind, but it seems to work.

I expand my Child Wellness Week strategy to my teaching. In other words, I stop asking questions. I no longer say things like: "Shouldn't only teachers sharpen the pencils (with razors)?" No longer do I ask: "Do we really need to burn this brush to start the school garden?" or, "Can we at least burn it away from this low-branched tree?" I stop asking because they aren't really questions.

I begin spending my afternoons in the *mbaola* workshop. *Mbaolas* are clay stoves that are more efficient and safer than open fires. They are made by a group of barefoot, braless, sparsely toothed women who spend their days, skirts hitched above their knees, singing and laughing and squatting in the dirt, covered in clay. *Mbaolas* are quite a labor-intensive and complicated endeavor, but the "*Mbaola* Mamas" teach me how to make clay pots, which can be used for cooking or storing water. The pots are shaped with bamboo, seed-pods, shells, and maize cobs. We etch designs with twigs and grasses and paint the pots with a special red clay. I am not very good at making Malawian pots, but if I am honest, I am also not very good at teaching Malawian nursery school. The former is easy to admit, and I am coming around to the latter.

Though they have names like Chorus and Garden, most of the *Mbaola* Mamas speak little to no English. One day, one of them asks me why I like *mbaolas* so much, and I answer, "Because it's nice here." "It's tranquil," I elaborate. No one understands the word *tranquil,* so I continue, "You know, tranquil, like tranquilizer? Like, ummm, Valium. You know Valium?" When Garden leans in to speak, I assume I have made a semblance of a point until she replies, "A man at Kachere is satanic. He has minibus. You know that man?" There is nothing to do with this non sequitur except to choke on my laughter until I spew it out. Laughing and crying, I try again and manage to say, "Making *mbaolas* is peaceful." Now it is their turn to dissolve into raucous laughter. In fact, they find the thought of peaceful clay stoves so completely hilarious that we are all laughing and crying on a big pile of clay.

That year, I went from winter to fall when I flew back to the United States for my graduate school orientation. After a stint at Harvard, I packed my degree, and the right clothes this time, and went back to Africa. I have spent most of the last decade here. My tax returns say I'm here teaching in international schools, but I spend the majority of my time falling in love. I fell in love with an economist, a rafting guide, a teacher, the Namibian sky, the Maluti Mountains, Kinshasa rainstorms on corrugated tin roofs, and the feeling of being slightly off balance at all times. I fell in love with crossing borders, the way tarmac peels away from the plane at takeoff, and the constant cracking open of my heart and my brain. I fell in love with fried plantains, boiled eggs with salt and hot pepper, injera, mangosteen, and the eight hours of a papaya's lifespan when it actually tastes good. I fell in love with teaching and learning and hundreds of children. Children in Lesotho who swung on the orphanage swings, toes pointed to the clouds, until the chains broke. Children in Congo whose parents hacked bigger rocks into smaller rocks in the gravel mines, who came to my picnic table in a church for a god I don't believe in to learn how to draw. Children in my classroom, from Sri Lanka, Denmark, Swaziland, the son of a prime minister, the daughter of a diamond dealer, the children of ambassadors, missionaries, and infectious-disease specialists. And there is my very own daughter, Congolese by birth, American by passport, Ethiopian by food preference, and persistently confused.

Leaving Malawi, after that initial journey to Africa, necessitated a long string of good-byes. But in my last week in the country, I also had the pleasure of meeting someone new. Mary gave birth to a beautiful girl and I visited their home to welcome baby Nephia. As I melted and squealed over the baby, Mary's six-year-old peeked shyly from behind a doorway. "Her name is Buchi," Mary told me. "It means she came at random."

Me too.

Nothing Gold Can Stay

A. V. Klotz

Late one winter afternoon, I submit to the ministrations of Ange, a lovely hairdresser who is doing my hair and makeup for my school's annual fundraising gala. Feeling the wet worm of eyeliner, I think about transformation. How is it that we become ourselves? I have been the one to do hair and makeup for kids in plays for thirty years, but this afternoon, I am being made up. Tonight, I need to look the part of headmistress, appear in role.

As a little girl instructing dolls and stuffed animals, I wished for a pair of Mrs. Beasley spectacles, which I imagined would confer wisdom. In my first teaching job, in a boarding school in Massachusetts, I put my hair up every day and wore high heels, terrified that my students would discern my youth, question my authority. Then, my costume confirmed my identity; helped me convince myself so I could convince others. Tonight's updo and makeup are the visible manifestations of my latest role, headmistress.

I have served as the head of Laurel School, a girls' school in Greater Cleveland, for a dozen years. But for more than two decades before this chapter, I taught theater to high school students at a private school in New York City and in the summer program that my boyfriend and close friend and I established when we were too young to know better. A darkened theater feels like home, like the space I am supposed to occupy. I still make plays with young children in my school, but I miss my high school students. I close my eyes and imagine the final dress rehearsal for *Hay Fever*, *Great Expectations*, *Front Porch*. At school, I am the head, an upper school English teacher, and the primary school drama specialist. No matter what else I am doing, though, I find my way to the darkened theater during every high school production. I cannot stay away.

Secretly, as a drama teacher, I always preferred dress rehearsal to the actual performance. During the final dress, I didn't have to hold my breath, to worry about the audience. I saw what the play would be, noted who had stretched, who was still afraid. I thought about what I would have done differently if we'd had more time. I scribbled in my notebook balanced on a music stand, clip light filtered and softened by a sheet of blue gel, thinking of all I hadn't gotten to: an adjustment to a costume, a stage picture that didn't work, all the tiny details that would allow the actors to be clearer, to allow the play to shine through, to find the love.

The August after I finished ninth grade, my brother died. A car accident. He had been away at boarding school for four years and was headed off to college at the end of the month. I loved him, looked up to him, wanted him to think I was cool, worthy. And then on a Monday afternoon, he was gone. No therapy in those days. Just the stiff-upper-lip WASP training that had served our family for generations. Until Mrs. Goppelt, an English teacher in the upper school, greeted me that September, marbled composition book in hand. She was not pitying or cloying, simply matter-of-fact.

"They couldn't schedule you for creative writing. Use this notebook. Write everything you feel. And there's a play at the boys' school, *Our Town*. Go audition."

I was cast in the pathetic role of Woman in the Balcony, but I read the lines for main characters Emily and Mrs. Webb when the actors missed rehearsals. I fell in love with the character of George, as Emily does in the play. When Emily died in childbirth, and then returned, in a magical scene, to her hometown of Grover's Corners on the day of her twelfth birthday, I wept. No one minded.

I wrote to Mrs. Goppelt and she wrote back every few weeks for three years. She saw me, knew what I needed, pointed the way.

Theater gave me purpose, gave me a new version of myself, a girl who went on without her brother.

I have been becoming a teacher for as long as I can remember, but it was in the theater that I discovered the alchemy of teaching, and realized that it is about love, first and always.

I went to college determined to teach English and theater. I liked school, felt at ease in the classroom. I knew this was what I wanted to do; I didn't even consider other options. I moved from being an actress to falling in love with directing. I taught creative dramatics in a housing project, student-taught at Hamden High in Connecticut, then took a job teaching English and theater in a coed prep school in Western Massachusetts. Living in a boys' hall, I hoped that when I came around the corner or heard the boys laughing, I might catch a hint of the kind of teenager my brother had been, that my time with these boys would help me know the boy who had been lost to me. Tears would unexpectedly rise, and I'd brush them away quickly. He had been in a boarding school for four years before he died. I was older now than he would ever be. I studied the students in my care with a sociologist's curiosity: *Is this what it is to be a teenager who doesn't have a dead brother?* And: *Is that the kind of preppy ice hockey player my brother would have been?* I was chasing memories, trying to bring the outlines of my missing brother into sharper focus. I was also relearning adolescence, since grief had numbed so much of me the first time around. At the same time, in the dorms, in the classrooms, in rehearsals, I was practicing being a grown-up, trying to be sure I was never one of *those* adults. The ones who patronize.

At the beginning, patient teenagers let me practice while I mistook teaching for telling what I knew. I used my college notes and lectured. In a class of new juniors, many of whom spoke English as a second language, I taught *Sir Gawain and the Green Knight*, *Tess of the d'Urbervilles*, Sophocles, Shakespeare. I talked a lot and marked up compositions with green and purple hieroglyphics. My students kindly laughed at my jokes. They *ooohed* when I, as Lady M from the Scottish Play, read "Come, thick night—" and all the lights went out in Stone Hall—accidental but thrilling! I directed plays, loving the work of building an ensemble, winning first prize in a high school drama festival with an all-female technical crew that busted the "only boys do tech" stereotype typical of the eighties.

And then, in 1984, Seth and Eleanor and I founded the Ensemble Theatre Community School (ETC). Seth was my boyfriend, a lighting designer fed up with the paradox that the more successful he was, the duller the plays he worked on became. Eleanor had produced all my college shows. She was steady, smart, practical, and understood the legal and financial aspects of a 501(c)(3). We had a vision and chutzpah. We loved theater; we loved kids. Why not combine the two? And so we began in Eagles Mere, Pennsylvania, a tiny town my family had spent summers in since 1912, where we rented a ramshackle Victorian house that had always been known as the Players' Lodge, and invited teenagers to come for the summer to make plays. On top of a mountain in Pennsylvania, in a newly built performance space called the DeWire Center, I became the version of my teacher self I recognize myself to be—a woman certain of her instincts, creative, brave, vulnerable, capable.

ETC was an intensive six-week summer theater program for highly motivated high school students—boys and girls from public and private schools, wealthy and poor, all races and faiths, from across the country. All kinds of kids who loved theater or thought they might. We worked seven days a week, from 8:00 a.m. until 11:00 p.m., divining that theater kids were hungry to learn and work and wanted to be immersed in making plays.

Six weeks of classes in acting, movement, and music. A children's theater show created from scratch in the first week to serve as an ensemble builder. Two full-length productions, performed in repertory; every student appearing onstage one night and working backstage the next. We told them, "Actors are more useful when they can stage-manage or run a soundboard." Community Responsibility Teams of faculty and students made meals, cleaned up afterward, kept the house and bathrooms clean, swept the porches, tidied our rehearsal spaces, weeded the garden—adults and adolescents side by side. Workshops gave our theater friends the chance to guest-teach, to see us in action, and to expand our offerings: neutral mask, Alexander technique, stage combat. We held classes in the Presbyterian church next door, in the Fire Hall (a large community room next to the fire engines), in the DeWire Center, on the green, in our barn. We were not glitzy; the kids who chose us wanted an intentional community. We were low tech and proud.

We didn't know that the rituals we established would last for twenty-seven summers, from 1984 until 2011, with a few years off when our daughters were tiny. Each summer began with trust walks, theater games on the town green on our first night, meeting in circles to share ideas, offer feedback, be together. Standing in a circle, we passed a ball slowly from person to person, learning Robert Frost's poem "Nothing Gold Can Stay" line by line, then word by word, then by heart—working together, loving language, feeling the power of our group.

Acting is about empathy, observation, cultivating generosity. Our training centered on establishing a connection, opening the conversations about what kind of person a student wants to be. It's ironic that putting on another persona is really a way of becoming more aware of who we are and who we want to be.

I taught acting through Shakespeare's sonnets. Each student was to memorize a sonnet before arriving. We whispered our sonnets, said them blowing bubbles, pulling on ropes, chasing each other, hurling paper balls, playing tag, and jumping up and down. Real emotions emerged—frustration, anger, love, fear, sadness. Some kids needed to be pushed, some cajoled. We worked to change what most kids knew about school, dropping judgment, offering support, encouraging risk, insisting on real communication.

After we watched an actor speak the text, I refused to allow a pat "I liked it" from the audience. "Say more," I'd push. "What worked? When didn't you believe her? Think. How did you feel watching her?"

The F-word—*fine*—I banned as bland, meaningless. "Feelings are to actors what colors are to artists. Expand your feeling vocabulary."

In the safe space of the Fire Hall, with dust motes floating in morning light, students began to dismantle their own walls. Those who wanted to "act" the lines learned that dropping the performance paradoxically rendered an actor more compelling. Real eye contact, real connection, real feelings.

"Love the words. Pull out the vowels. Luxuriate in the sounds. Say the first four lines using only the consonants. No vowels at all. Breathe. Trust."

From the start, I said to kids, "I am a drama teacher, not a therapist, but I know that feelings can't hurt you—they are just feelings, and the more energy we spend avoiding feelings, the less compelling our work is onstage." We talked a lot about bad acting, what I termed "acting with a capital A" or "schmacting." So often the work was about letting go of showing and simply doing.

I made up an assignment called an autodrama: in three minutes, share a one-act play of yourself, playing yourself, as yourself. We all did them toward the end of the program, one after the next—inside the Fire Hall or outside on a patch of wild oregano at the foot of the rickety fire escape. Each member of the company chose her own location, his own approach to self-revelation. "You set the risk factor," I reminded them. I remember Seth, by then my husband, once reciting in detail every car he had driven. We laughed at his literal "auto drama." Typically, the autodramas were more abstract, often very emotional. One summer, after a series of miscarriages, I leapt, reaching over and over again for a too high branch, so grateful to be teaching other people's children, so desperate for a baby of my own. At ETC, I learned to share my grief, and that vulnerability made me stronger. This was the lesson Mrs. Goppelt and the little notebook and *Our Town* had started teaching me a decade earlier. The difference was that I had become the teacher.

One summer a girl arrived who didn't want to be with us. I asked her how she had duped us. We had an interview process; she had sounded enthusiastic, but once she arrived, she was churlish, obnoxious. I told her she would need to leave, that she was draining our community with her negativity. Eyes down, she muttered, "They won't take me back."

I called Dad, far away in Alaska. He said, "No, she can't come here." Mom said, "Are you kidding? I'm busy. I don't want her here for six weeks."

I looked at her across my desk, the edge of the loud floral table-cloth slipping back to show the scarred wooden surface, and said, "You're right. They don't want you. But I've decided that we do. You will work harder than you wanted to work this summer, but you will matter to us. And what you do here you'll carry back with you into your life. So you can sag through the summer, feeling sorry for yourself because your parents are jerks, or you can give this place your all and know that you are not a tumbleweed—what you choose to do matters. It's always a choice. Your freedom is in your choice. But we are glad you are here."

Tears came. She was brittle, defensive, anguished. And, bit by bit, she committed, discovering in her role in a Lorca tragedy that she could give voice to grief and rage, that the greasy broiling pans in the sink could absorb her frustration, that building platforms during tech periods was something even a willowy creature could excel at, that everyone feels better knowing how to use a screw gun. She, spoiled and neglected, slowly emerged. At summer's end, I held her tightly, sad we had to let her return to her lonesomeness.

I learned how to teach as I chopped vegetables with students who had never been asked to lift a finger at home, or dealt with students who were too timid or too reckless on a tech crew. Watching Seth play basketball with Malcolm and Kevin on the tennis court after supper those warm July twilights, I understood who needed to learn to pass, who needed to take more risks, who always looked out for someone else. Theater, I realize years later, is only the medium. What I hope I teach is what it means to be your best self. I watched the kids all the time. Was the girl who always volunteered to do more than her share of the work offstage also overcompensating as an actress, trying to save a whole scene alone, her voice too shrill, her tempo too fast?

Did the boy who tried to shirk his community responsibilities also hide his face under his bangs and blame others for not knowing their lines? What was he afraid of? Kristina, able to improvise if we ran out of an ingredient for a recipe, showed that same ability onstage, saving the show when someone dropped a line. Did Drew hope I wouldn't notice if he'd sewn a hem crooked? I noticed: *Drew! Absolutely not. Take it out. Would you want to wear that?*

Mark came from Estella, a town near Eagles Mere. At dinner one night, when several New York City girls discussed the cruelty of hunting, he said matter-of-factly, "If I get a deer, my family eats for the winter. Ever see a herd of deer starving?" The girls were silent. "Ugly," he continued. "Sad and desperate." I felt tense, thinking I should somehow intervene. Different worlds were colliding over fish sticks and mac and cheese. Should I say something? After a beat, one of the girls said, "You know, I had never thought about it that way. Thank you." The magic, as Dar Williams says, is in the learning. Mark had never been in a play and he told us he had never actually finished a book. When we did our read-through of *Ethan Frome*, rehearsal ended before we had finished the script. "We can't stop here!" Mark exclaimed. "I need to know how it ends." The rest of the cast instantly sat back down and picked up their scripts. His wonder was contagious, their respect for him clear—here was a boy who was unabashedly authentic. At the play's final line, Mark heaved an enormous sigh. "It's so wrong," he lamented. Later that summer, he helped to papier-mâché the enormous tree into which Ethan and Maddie would crash. "It's gotta look good," he explained. "It really matters."

We left classes and rehearsals wrung out, but buoyed by the sense that we were all learning. Sometimes my exercises failed—gloriously, with no discovery or revelation. But then we started again, tried another tactic, improvised, worked to get unstuck. Every rehearsal period has an awkward adolescent phase—the play's no longer new or interesting. We'd stagger through rehearsals, hot, frustrated, irritated. And then a breakthrough, a scene played with truth and guts that reenergized the whole cast, restored my faith, set us back on course, showed us all what the play could be.

At unwinding, our ritual at the close of each long day, we arranged ourselves in the living room, strewn across mismatched couches, perched on the sideboard, taking in the group while eating popcorn or cheese slices. Sometimes we sang or went around the circle, with everyone sharing one observation about the day: "Tonight, we improvised in character for an hour; it was amazing," Bill offered. Or, "Tonight, Alixa and Melinda were incredible," Jed reflected. Support, space to breathe and risk. Time. The plays came together, no two processes ever identical.

In rehearsal for Brecht's *The Caucasian Chalk Circle*, Julia, playing Grusha, wondered what it would feel like to be responsible for an infant while climbing over a mountain. I handed her my six-month-old daughter and told Julia to carry her across the platforms of the unfinished set. She froze. I said, "You won't break her." And then she began to climb the flight of steps to the narrow bridge between two high platforms. I held my breath. They crossed. I exhaled.

"She's heavy," Julia said, returning the baby to me. "I was scared I'd drop her."

"Me, too."

"Then why did you let me carry her?"

"Because Grusha would be scared, too. Right?" Trust. Breathe. Love. Risk.

I took sonnet class to the tennis court. I tossed a basketball to my puzzled students. "Dribble to the foul line as you say your sonnet. Shoot on the couplet—if you make it, satisfaction; if you miss, frustration. Feel it. Guard your scene partner and make a dialogue out of your two sonnets—really play the game." Theater as a sport? Who knew? I didn't have an athletic bone in my body, but I saw the power of physical activity and a little healthy competition married to text. And it was hilarious, intoxicating fun.

Some of our kids had never before been asked to memorize huge chunks of text. They needed to know we wouldn't send them out onstage until they felt confident. When Norberto, playing King Creon in *Antigone*, finally understood what he was saying, his nobility appeared. When he carried his dead son, Haemon, onto the stage, real tears streaked his face. In his daily life in the Bronx, he knew what it was to lose a friend. It was not so great a leap from that reality to Sophocles.

At ETC, we set the bar high because it never occurred to us not to. "Make a new choice," I exhorted, cajoled, demanded, wheedled, teased, threatened. "Don't fall in love with a pattern. Be in the moment. The foundation of acting is the reality of doing. What are you doing?"

This was my work, too. Back in the English classroom in the girls' school in New York City, where I had moved after the first summer of ETC, I learned to reduce the amount of time I spent standing at the front of the room, lecturing. I took more risks, invited more collaboration, let go of needing to have the answers. I listened more, allowed smart mentors to give me feedback. I practiced my craft in classes and in quiet conversations with kids in the spaces in between. I was comfortable being in charge, having the final word. But almost always I invited others to advise or offer an opinion. I liked not doing everything by myself. I was becoming.

In theater, a series of mottoes and questions guide my teaching: *Dare to fail gloriously. Be in the moment. What are the given circumstances? What's your objective? Cheat out—open your body. Be available. Show, don't tell. Your freedom is in your choice. Don't try to re-create the moment; let it happen as if for the first time. No straight lines. Make big choices. Vary your inflections. Love the words. Float up your spine. Trust. Commit. Be with each other. You are never alone onstage.* So many of those phrases feel relevant, too, in my ninth-grade English class, in my leadership of my school—funny, how what we learn in one domain informs what we do elsewhere.

After a summer of rehearsal comes the time to share the play. In the basement of the DeWire Center, which we use as both a greenroom and a backstage area, opening night is scented with powder and hair-spray and deodorant and hair gel.

"Bring your own comb if you don't want the lice brush," I intone.

"Look up," I command, applying eyeliner and mascara.

"Look down," I murmur, adding shadow.

"Kiss my finger," I instruct, applying lip color.

"Push against my hand," I say, pinning a hairnet into place.

Standing behind an actress, looking at her in the mirror, I take her pulse. Is she scared, ready, cocky? What is required in this moment? One more note, suggestion, idea—can I make it safe enough for her to explore, experiment, even in production? That is the goal.

"Let's make a circle. I'm going to count you down into character. Draw the world of the play around you. Remember, you are never alone onstage."

I am in love with this ritual, with this cast, with this script, with this process. Thirty-three years into a career that includes administration, school leadership, writing scripts with kids, teaching English, being a college advisor, and directing high school plays, what I know is that teaching is about connection; when a student knows I see and value her—undisguised, authentic—then she can soar. I have learned to be more patient, to offer a plank when someone paints himself into a corner, to prize dignity, and to soften my sarcasm—it rarely helps. It doesn't always go right—there are kids with whom I don't connect. There are kids who aren't looking to trust an adult, kids for whom the power dynamic is too large a chasm to bridge, particularly when grades factor into the relationship. Some kids are too defensive to be honest. Sometimes, I am too defensive to be honest.

Theater is ephemeral. You rehearse and perform, and then that play is finished. I don't like watching videotapes of shows I've directed. Particular memories endure, moments strung like beads, glowing. I carry with me all those moments that helped me become a teacher.

On the last night of the program, we chant together "Nothing Gold Can Stay," the poem we mastered on the first night. The first lines go like this:

Nature's first green is gold,
Her hardest hue to hold
Her early leaf's a flower;
But only so an hour.

Kids grow up. I continue teaching. It is a glorious waterwheel. Many of our ETC kids are frozen in my mind's eye. I see them flushed with the thrill of having focused a light high up in the beams, or having made biscuits for the first time, or having nailed a Shakespearean sonnet.

I return to the present: I realize I am not in Eagles Mere rehearsing a play but sitting in Ange's chair, preparing to make my entrance in a few hours at Laurel School's February gala. I am the headmistress, the lead teacher in our school, not actually so different from my work at ETC except that instead of watching from the wings or from the empty platforms during dress rehearsal, tonight I will be center stage on behalf of a school it is my privilege to serve. It's good to shift perspective from time to time. I am a teacher: mother, wife, headmistress, writer, playwright, daughter, sister, too. But first, always, a teacher.

Order

Michael Copperman

Educational inequality in the United States is easy to define by numbers: the disparity in spending between the wealthiest and poorest districts is some $9,000 per student per year. By the age of nine, a child from a low-income area is, on average, four grade levels behind his or her peers in middle- and upper-income areas. That same nine-year-old child is already some seven times less likely to graduate from college than a child not born into poverty.

These are shocking statistics, but awareness of numbers doesn't create change. A new crisis regarding the failure of public education, oddly similar in substance to the previous one, is declared every few years, and for a time politicians hem and haw, reporters dust off Jonathan Kozol's *Savage Inequalities* and attest to its relevance, and educators find themselves for a moment the center of discussion, if only in light of their failings. Then the moment passes, the media moves on, and things continue as they were.

Teach for America is an organization dedicated to placing recent college graduates as teachers in under-resourced areas for two years. Its mission is to create a movement dedicated to the vision that one day, all children of this nation, regardless of the color of their skin or how much privilege they were born into, will have the opportunity to attain an excellent education. The program is exceptionally selective: typically, the acceptance rate is close to one applicant in twelve, a more competitive entry rate than most Ivy League schools can boast. In 2002, I applied and interviewed and was deemed an appropriate addition to the "movement."

My entire life, I'd excelled at everything I'd tried through absolute dedication. I grew up a doctor's kid in a sleepy college town with a good public education system, excelled equally in academics and the sport of wrestling through unrelenting hard work, and did well enough to gain admittance to Stanford. On "The Farm," I'd assumed an attitude common to those lucky enough to have the privilege of four years of self-exploration in the splendor of material and intellectual paradise: I believed that everything I wanted to accomplish was not only possible, but imminent, pending only my own realization of what exactly it was I aspired to do. Teach for America's heady rhetoric of realizing the American dream of equality, embodied in the goal "One Day, All Children," didn't sound unrealistically idealistic or grand, but of proper scale, given my assessment of my own potential and ability. Of course I could become the change I wanted to see in the world.

I trained for five weeks in Houston, and began my responsibilities as a fourth-grade teacher in the rural black public schools of the Mississippi Delta.

At first, I didn't know that Tevin would be a problem. Amid the tumult and clamor of my classroom, he didn't draw attention, a slim, handsome boy with long arms and a careful, almost elegant manner. It was his silence that first made me notice him: I asked him a direct question the second day, and he turned and pretended not to have heard. When I pressed, he smiled, bowed his head. When I called roll he'd raise his hand but say nothing, just flash his strange smile, which showed no teeth—the corners of his mouth turned up, but his gray eyes remained implacable and wary, framed beneath dark, thick eyebrows made all the more prominent by his translucent honey-gold skin that on a less fierce boy could have meant mockery for looking almost white. He could speak, and sometimes would answer a question with a few words, but mostly he smiled and looked away. It wasn't nervousness, but indirect disobedience: if he didn't care to do something, he ignored what was said, glanced away, and kept on as he liked.

As the fall wore on, he started to do exactly as he wanted. He wanted to throw spitballs, take other children's pencils and break them, and mock me behind my back. He liked to flick other children behind the ear, pinch them on the soft flesh of the upper arm, gleek saliva onto the back of an unsuspecting neck. He liked to make animal noises, to hoot and whistle and bark. He wrote the word *fuck* a hundred times when asked to write a five-sentence paragraph—complete with five periods and capitals to satisfy the assignment. "This isn't okay," I said, standing above him at his desk as he grinned unsettlingly and stared at the ceiling. Whenever I caught him acting up and tried to discipline him, he turned his head and smiled infuriatingly and refused to respond. The first time I sent him to the office, he returned tear-streaked, and I knew Assistant Principal Winston had given him licks. He stared at me through the rest of class with a disarming intensity.

I called the number for Tevin's home that night. "I'm Jackson Johnson," a gravelly, black voice said. "The boy stays with me and my daughter Lizy—we foster kids for the state. I'll come on in and speak to you, Mr. Copperman."

The next morning, Tevin walked through the door before the bell, smiling.

"Good morning, Tevin," I said.

He walked to the nearest empty desk and tipped it to the floor with a crash.

"What do you think you're doing?"

He tipped the next desk in the row, then the next. Children in his path fled as he tipped their desks with their papers and folders as well.

"Stop!" I yelled. He met my eyes for a moment and began on the next row. I started for him across the room, and he upended desks in my path and moved toward the door. I pushed desks aside, running now, but he was out the door and down the hall. "Go to the office!"

He turned, his face hard, and closed on me; he was easily my height, perhaps even a little taller. Then he jumped toward me. I flinched and stepped back. He grinned, nodded once, and made his way down the hall with a swaggering step that filled me with rage, and for a moment I thought to kick his jaunty feet out from under him. I started after him, remembered the other children, and turned back. In the classroom, everyone was talking at once. Half the desks lay on the floor, tipped on their sides and corners, some upside down with their legs in the air, and folders and papers were scattered across the floor. I quieted the children, set them to putting the desks upright, and called the office on the intercom. "Tevin Downs just turned my classroom upside down," I said when the secretary answered. "Then he ran out."

There was a long, static-filled pause, and the secretary said, "Tevin Downs is here, Mr. Copperman. He just come through the door."

I stood at the intercom. "Huh."

Two hours later, I received a note telling me Tevin had been sent home. On my free period, I went to the office and knocked at Mr. Winston's door, but he was out and Mrs. Burtonsen, the principal, was away at a conference in Biloxi. The secretary called me over with a crooked finger and leaned in. "That boy was wearing two pairs of pants," she whispered. "Guess he was grinning at Mr. Winston while he was getting whupped. Mr. Winston, he got worked up. Stomped out of here after Mr. Johnson come in to get the boy."

After school, I sat in the empty classroom, the dull sun of October filtering through the back windows in blocks of heatless light. Winston still hadn't returned. When there was a knock, I thought it might be him, and hurried to the door. Outside was a black man of about sixty, his hair gray and white. He leaned on a cane that was too short, his shoulders rounded and bent. "Must be you Mr. Copperman," he said. "Mr. Johnson. Tevin stay with me. You'd called yesterday for me to come in, and I thought with what-all today I'd better come in all the same." He smiled, revealing gapped teeth, and extended his free right hand. His grip was firm.

"Sir," I said.

Placing the tip of the cane with each step, he made his way to my desk.

I hurried to pull my chair around so he could sit. Thanking me, he settled to the seat. I went around the desk.

"So," I said.

"Yes, Lord," he said, and chuckled from the belly, deep laugh lines crinkling at his eyes. He had a kind face. "Guess you wasn't figuring on no boy like this one."

"So—there have been issues before?"

He shook his head. "This is his second or third foster placement this year. And I'm gone tell you the truth, Mr. Copperman—I don't know how long I can hold on. The boy been nothing but trouble at home, and he too fast for me, what with my leg. I can't catch him for to whup him."

I took all this in. "What do you know about him, his history?"

Mr. Johnson leaned back in his chair and frowned. "That lady from the district, the behavioral specialist, Ms. Watson, she ain't been to see you? She ain't told you nothing?"

I shook my head. I knew the behaviorist by sight only, a reed-thin white woman in her late thirties with a shock of red, frizzy hair and a wardrobe that seemed to consist solely of strangely patterned skirts with matching leggings. A couple of days a week she pulled a couple of my problem boys, including Tevin, out from class for "meetings"; they returned grinning, plastic toys and trinkets like yo-yos and playing cards clutched gleefully in hand, boasting about all she was "gone give" them next time. It was my impression she was bribing them with baubles, but then, I wasn't a specialist.

"Well. I don't know where to start. You better contact them folks. I just need you to know—I told Mr. Winston this too, when he was telling me I'd better not let the boy wear two pants or whatever all—I can't do nothing with him. I done what I can. I tell him this way ain't no way but a bad end. But he don't respect me. He don't respect nothing but a good whupping, and I can't catch him to lay a proper hand on him. He just smile at me and keep on."

I tried to think what to say about "laying a hand on him." "Did his social worker suggest any—other—methods for discipline?"

Mr. Johnson grinned. "Mr. Barker was the one told me a good whupping the only thing the boy respect. You should've seen that man make the boy jump."

I wanted to demand more. I looked at him with his hands folded earnestly over the head of his cane. "Thank you for the information," I said.

Later that week, I ran down the behavioral specialist on my break while the children were in PE. "I'm Mr. Copperman, a fourth-grade teacher. Can I speak to you for a moment about Tevin Downs?"

"Tevin? Oh my, yes, Tevin. He's a special case. Let's get to my office for privacy."

In the office, she shut the door and turned to face me. "How much do you know, Mr. Copperman?"

What Ms. Watson told me strained credulity. Tevin Downs had been born to an alcoholic, crack-addicted mother in Midnight, Mississippi, where he spent the first eight years of his life in shelters and tents and boxes on the streets or in the cotton fields. His mother had been unable to identify a father on his birth certificate. He begged and stole to survive, knew no personal hygiene, and had never celebrated a birthday—when he was taken as a ward of the state five years ago, he did not know how old he was. The experts felt fine starting him in school from the beginning: his physical development had been so stunted by malnourishment that he was still smaller at eight than the average kindergartner. As for his mental status and development, tests proved consistently inconclusive. One report indicated he had all the signs of fetal alcohol syndrome, and retained a number of "permanent, complicating behavioral accommodations to his early environment." The sole IQ test had concluded that his IQ was well above average. His academic records were limited—it seemed he hadn't, in fact, ever completed a full grade due to disciplinary issues at each school and foster placement, though the state had continued to move him up each year because of his age and lack of evident mental retardation. He was a thirteen-year-old fourth grader.

All of this was revealing, but it was not what stunned me. The whole time she spoke, Ms. Watson kept a white sheet of paper tucked between her fingers, lifted a little as if to heighten my interest and stress its import. At the end she held out the paper. "You never saw this here, remember."

The paper was the report of the forensic psychologist assigned to the incident that had made Tevin a ward of the state. The psychologist, after a dozen interviews, had regressed the eight-year-old to the night in question at the apartment of man named Dequarius Jones, who'd evidently been Tevin's mother's boyfriend. The boy had reluctantly entered the apartment, as he was scared of Mr. Jones. He'd called his mother's name, looked for her in the kitchen, the living room, and bedroom, had finally knocked on the bathroom door where he could see from the bottom that the light was on. He knocked, called, waited, and waited, found the courage to open the door. There was his mother, lying prone in the tub. All down her shoulders and chest and all over the white porcelain was blood from her throat, which had been slit open from clavicle to clavicle. Tevin had run to her, had shook her and shook her, crying and screaming, had even tried to lift her from the tub and get her somehow to her feet, so that when the police found him hours later, he was soaked in his mother's blood.

I read the transcript over and over, imagining Tevin in the washroom covered in blood—just him now. Alone. And I wished I could go to the boy and lead him away to rooms free of such horror and sorrow.

The next week, Tevin was back. He walked through the door moments before the bell and sat, his face blank, his gray eyes wary, waiting to see what I'd do. I kept an eye on him and taught the morning's lessons. Tevin never lifted his pencil, just sat there slouched. After a time, he began tapping the edge of the desk, less rhythmic than nervous, and I didn't ask him to stop. He began to whistle, a tuneless twittering, and I didn't say a word in the name of quiet. By the time the children were headed to PE, he was visibly agitated. When Tarvis let out a shout, crying, "Tevin pinch my neck," I pulled Tevin to the back of the line without comment and walked beside him the rest of the way. As I sent the children into the gym, I took Tevin's sleeve. "Come on."

He glanced at my fingers on his sleeve, smiled, and looked away, but he followed me back to the room, whistling so the notes echoed eerily through the empty hall. Back in the room, I straightened desks and wiped the board. It was a bright, humid morning, and though the air-conditioning unit spat cool through the room, the sun through the windows bounced stars of light from the legs of desks and the glossy posters on the wall. Tevin leaned uneasily against the door watching me and whistling louder and louder, pounding a beat to the door. I let him be until he stopped making noise and just stood.

Finally he spoke, his voice so quiet I couldn't make out the words over the mutter of the air-conditioning.

"What was that?"

"You ain't gone beat me," he said.

"No."

He smiled and said nothing. I held his gaze until he glanced away at the ceiling.

"You know, Tevin," I said gently, "it must be tough, being on your own. Moving all the time. Not having anyone to trust."

He was still staring at the ceiling.

I waited. In the hall, a class clattered past with a burst of echoing footfalls, then a broader silence as they were gone.

Suddenly, Tevin slammed his hands to the door, making me jump. He didn't smile or look away, but spoke directly to me. "You don't know me." He opened the door and walked out, didn't look back as I ordered him to stop. Finally, I called the office to tell them Tevin Downs had just left my class—and I didn't know where he was headed.

That afternoon as I went to sign out in the office, the secretary pointed to Mrs. Burtonsen's office. "She want to see you," she said. "'Bout that Downs boy."

I knocked at the heavy oak door and was admitted by Mrs. Burtonsen, with her generous smile, her gray hair pulled to tight curls with a fresh permanent.

"Mr. Copperman," she said. "How are you this afternoon?" She motioned for me to take a seat, went around the desk, and sat and leaned toward me. "This situation with Tevin Downs is troubling me," she said.

I nodded. "Did he leave the school grounds today?"

She brushed aside my question and kept speaking. "Mr. Winston cannot discipline the boy because he protects himself against punishment. Yet the boy clearly needs to be put in his place. His guardian tells me he cannot catch the boy to—punish him."

"Mr. Johnson told me the same thing. I saw about his mother, the streets of Midnight—"

"We are not really here to deal with his history, Mr. Copperman," Mrs. Burtonsen said gently. "That is beyond the bounds of what we can do. We are here to educate him. His guardian and his social worker, whom I spoke to today, both concur. The boy needs discipline. I have tried to speak to him, and as you've no doubt seen, he just turns his head and ignores you—he is deaf to reason. The question, then, becomes quite simple: Is there a man who can teach the boy real respect? Or will he be—unfit—for school here as he is thirteen years old, and by district guidelines, ought properly to already be resourced and at the middle school?"

In the silence that followed, I saw what Mrs. Burtonsen was asking: either I get the boy into shape somehow, through force of manhood or fist, or Promise-Upper would be done with him for good. Finally I cleared my throat. "Yes, ma'am, I suppose that's the question."

She took a deep breath, sighed, put a hand to my elbow across the desk. "All right then, Mr. Copperman. I just wanted to be sure you knew the situation. I'm glad we have an understanding."

We do not really, ma'am, I thought, as I shook her hand and fled the office.

The next day the air in the classroom was stale and still and warm— the air-conditioning unit had broken. By 8:00 a.m., the classroom was sweltering, and sweat poured down my face, wet circles of sweat appeared on the children's polo shirts, the scent of bodies thick through the room. Tevin's chair sat empty as I taught, and I couldn't pretend it wasn't a relief not to deal with him. My undershirt was soaked with sweat. I could hardly see the children through the sweat trickling into my eyes. Around ten, the door opened and Tevin Downs walked in grinning. He was wearing the wrong color uniform, his red Friday polo when today was only Wednesday.

"Hi, Tevin. Have a seat," I said.

He walked to the front of the room until he stood inches from me. He wasn't sweating, seemed cool and calm.

"Sit down," I repeated. "Now."

He met my eyes and stepped closer still, until his face was inches from mine, and spoke, his breath hot to my cheek. "No."

"Sit!"

"You can't make me do nothing."

"You will sit down now."

He hocked, a throaty sound, and then, as the children gasped, he spit on my face. Some of it was in my eye, the wet, warm mucus sliding down my cheek, and anger and instinct rose in me. I seized him by the collar, rage summoning the strength of the college wrestler I'd been, and half lifted him off his feet, kicking and fighting, to the door of the classroom, threw it open. "Get—out of my classroom," I said, and tossed him in a great arc into the hall.

He tumbled to the floor as the children gasped. It felt—good. I wiped the spittle from my face with a sleeve as the children gaped. Tevin sat up, astonished, slowly brushed his shirt clean as he looked up at me in the door. I waited for him to rise and come at me, for a sign of resentment, but instead he stood timidly, waited for me to move from the door to pass, shuffled quickly to his desk, and then, cheek to the desk, began the math worksheet he'd missed earlier in the morning. I looked about the room, and every child whose eyes had been on me turned down to the work there—for the moment, they were as scared of me as I was scared of myself.

As we sweated through the day, I saw in Tevin's subdued manner that his respect was authentic. I'd established dominance, the only order Tevin had ever known. And I felt ill with the knowledge that at the day's end, I'd tell Mrs. Burtonsen to resource the boy, to send him away—what he required, I couldn't afford to give.

Of those years in the Delta, much is gone, and what remains are moments and images and voices, all of it freighted with the burden of how I was a decade ago and all I imagined I could achieve. It is impossible now to touch the fever dream of changing the world one lesson at a time, undoing injustice by benchmark met and lessons learned, any more than I can regain the frustrated young man who once tossed a boy out the classroom door. Mostly now, even the children are hard to recall, faces retreating into shadow, voices receding to clamor. Mostly, that absence is a relief and that silence is a blessing—it means that finally, I can let go a little. Leave off the harrowing of conscience. Rest.

The Delta changed me. People speak of how idealism ought to be tempered by experience, and maybe they think it's a benign process: growing older, becoming wiser. They're wrong. You can't restore faith. I wouldn't have been teaching more than a decade now at the University of Oregon if it weren't for those two years in the Delta, would long ago have traded in my Stanford degree for a job with status and decent pay. Each day in my university classroom with eighteen-year-olds of low-income, diverse background, I see my Delta fourth graders grown up, and a part of me imagines that somehow I am speaking directly to the children for whom I wanted so much. Yet back in Mississippi, children I taught walk the dusty streets headed nowhere, and I don't have it in me to help them. It isn't work ethic I lack, but the courage to fail again—to fail to save a child who doesn't have a fighting chance.

Some nights I lie awake bargaining, trying to get back to the man I was before the Delta, and imagine the children, a world away in shacks on the wrong side of the tracks, hearing the bark of a stray dog, the far-off whistle of the train bound elsewhere, always elsewhere. I left them behind, and so cannot let go; and so, if I close my eyes, I can hear their voices:

C'mon and pitch it, Mr. C! Hey now! How you gone do me like that? That don't count as no strike!

What the capital of Ory-gun is, Mr. Copperman? Everybody live in a tree there, right?

How come you always got to talk so careful, Mr. C, all like, "Hello, my children, today is a day when we speak using all the words we have in our dictionary here"?

Mr. Copperman, how come you not black and you not white but you say you like Nas? Don't you got some Asian-person music or something so you ain't stealing folks' music?

Mr. C, I told my grandad 'bout how you was teaching me that ai-ki-doe after school so I can be tough, and he say, "Boy, that Chinaman may teach you the kar-aaa-te, but I still gone have the Car—aazy!" So is we gone learn the Car-aazy too?

But Mr. Copperman, how you know you don't like a Kool-Aid pickle if you ain't had none?

Oooowee! Look at he face—he don't like them pickles!

Mr. Copperman, this a poem I wrote for you. Roses are red, Violets is blue, You making a face like you stepped in poo.

Man, shoot! That ain't nothing. That like half a poem. Here a real poem: Roses is dead. And violets dead too. 'Cause I on fire, and this—
___—just burned you.

That ain't no poem—you can't use no swear words in no poem.

Mr. Copperman, is that a poem?

Mr. Copperman! Mr. Copperman! Mr. Copperman!

And they are with me again, clamoring to be heard, bright eyed, cheeks shiny, hair shaved close on the boys or braided to tight rows or pulled back clean in buns on the girls, their uniform polos starched and their khakis belted tight, sitting straight in "listening learning position" or slouching beneath their desks with arms crossed or buried in a beanbag chair or crouched deep in a kicker's stance at the plate on the kickball field or speaking while doing the heel-toe two-step at a sock hop beneath the strobing lights, arms and hands waving, faces upraised, demanding my attention in calling out, joking, declaiming, being absurd and serious and smart and so full of joy and anger and outrage and curiosity, such—kids.

And so it is: the farther I am from the Delta, the clearer I hear them. Perhaps this nearness is how the past clarifies as it recedes from reach, so that finally what is left is distilled, too perfect to bear. Those kids are, after all, no longer children but full-grown men and women who likely even have children of their own and jobs and aspirations and adult burdens now. They are no longer my charge, but they are with me as they were, their faces bright and voices loud. And because what happened then is inalterable, it is possible now to love them purely as they were, without the need to have them behave or achieve.

Perhaps that is why I have begun to forgive myself for having failed them—because maybe I didn't fail them after all, any more than they failed me. They were bright, good kids, beautiful in all they didn't know and all they wanted. The poverty that limited them could be ugly, but they were not. And while I could be ugly in my frustration and all the arrogant naïveté of youth, I was not such a bad teacher. Not as good as they deserved, but as good a teacher under the circumstances as I could manage. There was nothing wrong with me or wrong with them. We were a classroom, and, for a time, a sort of family.

Though there was so much trauma and trouble and loss along the way that for a decade I couldn't understand why I kept gazing back, mulling over what was gone, it finally is simple: I left a part of my heart in the Delta. Since I left, I've always held back a little, unwilling to risk everything again the way I did back when I didn't know you couldn't change the world through force of will or longing. A part of me will always remain with those kids, and I will always yearn to return to them, to be with them once more and hear the cadence of their voices, see their upturned, eager faces, and have time for just one more chapter read aloud, one more times table and one more lesson, one last chance to be there with them and so be whole again—to be once more, simply and only, *teacher*.

Ancient Beef Made Me a Teacher

Lori D. Ungemah

Dennis strolled purposefully over to Vincent's desk. No words were exchanged, but a cold glance of understanding passed between them. Vincent stood up silently and it began.

Dennis's first punch broke Vincent's nose. The cartilage both popped and cracked, a sound so distinct that I knew exactly what had happened the minute it happened. Ruby blood spurted from the center of Vincent's face and a rage filled his eyes. They punched, wrestled, and pushed while blood sprayed all over the desks, floor, walls, and bookshelf in the back of my classroom. Strange thoughts darted through my mind: *Blood is such a gorgeous color...It's practically sparkling...It sprays outward like those lawn sprinklers we ran through as kids...I cut my foot on that stupid yellow sprinkler...My skin tore off in the shape of a V, revealing a pinker, meatier foot underneath...*

The abruptness of this fight made it seem unreal. The stage had not been set as it usually was; there was no prologue, no introduction for the audience. Usually the boys circled each other in a rooster dance, their man-boy chests popping out as they murmured, "Son...son..." until the shit-talking started in earnest and a punch was thrown. But none of that had happened, and we all—my entire class of students and I—watched in disbelief as Dennis and Vincent pummeled each other with no sign of stopping.

Each fist met a brick wall of muscle and bone. These boys lifted weights; they were tall, and they were solid. Their age made them boys, but their bodies made them men. Each punch landed with a soft thud that must have hurt both the giver and the receiver. I had never before witnessed violence like this, and the sounds struck me. They were clear, distinct, and mesmerizing.

I'm not sure how long I stood there paralyzed. It felt like an eternity, but it was maybe a few simple seconds. Nothing registered except the sounds of the nose break and the punches, but they echoed around in my head in symphony with my random thoughts. When my vision started to focus, I saw that desks and chairs had been knocked over. My students were clustered in the front corner of the classroom, yelling at the fighters. I resurfaced from my underwater daze and snapped into action.

The fight had broken out on an otherwise unexceptional afternoon— fifth period of the first day in the spring semester, a sunny but chilly day in late January 2002. It was my second semester teaching high school after a year of teaching middle school in Bushwick, one of the most dangerous neighborhoods in Brooklyn. During that first year of teaching, teachers were required to leave the school building before dark, when it became unsafe for us to walk to the train or wait for a bus. My Bushwick colleagues and I had mostly come from middle-class, suburban backgrounds, and our administrators told us we did not have the street smarts necessary to navigate Bushwick at night. I did not argue with them. In contrast, the school where I now taught was situated in an expensive Brooklyn neighborhood known for its boutiques, restaurants, bars, and fancy strollers, but our students did not live in the school's neighborhood. The students commuted there via subway in an attempt to dodge their neighborhood-zoned high schools; they came from rough neighborhoods across Brooklyn: Fort Greene, Bed-Stuy, Coney Island, East New York, Crown Heights, Sunset Park, Flatbush, and Brownsville.

The monotone bell signaled that class had started. My eleventh-grade English 6 class settled into rows of desks, and as I scanned the room, I realized that I had taught most of these students last semester. Not only had I taught them, I also *knew* them. I had nuanced information: Juan liked to *moo* in the back of the room to annoy me, and I should ignore him; Dennis had a candy addiction and made many trips to the trash to toss the wrappers; Krystal and Sherrie were frenemies, and a daily read on their relationship was necessary before group work; Terrance did not like to read out loud and would shut down if called upon; Glenny and Jabiel were girlfriend and boyfriend, liked to touch constantly, and should not sit together. It felt powerful to have this knowledge about my students and ideas on how to use that knowledge. I felt I was finally becoming a teacher.

I even knew one of the new kids in my class—Vincent. He was a friendly young man whom I had met because we both frequented a pizza place on DeKalb Avenue near my boyfriend's apartment in Fort Greene. When getting a slice, Adam and I would often see Vincent, and, free of the shyness of many high school students, he would walk over to us with a warm smile on his face to shake Adam's hand and talk. Even though I had never been his teacher, he recognized me from school. He did this whether he was alone or with friends, and I admired the maturity he had to approach two adults in public. When Vincent walked into my classroom that afternoon, I was thrilled. I liked that kid already.

As the late bell rang, I assumed my position in front of the room, holding my lime-green clipboard with the New York City Board of Education Scantron sheet for attendance. I had a generic first-day-of-the-semester lesson planned, but that lesson would not happen. As I pulled the mechanical pencil out of my ponytail and prepared to call roll, Dennis was already moving across the room toward Vincent's desk. I had no idea that anything was beginning, but the events that followed would define my entire teaching career.

Suddenly I saw everything around me with a remarkable clarity. Sprinting into the hall, I yelled, "Mr. Joseph—*fight!*" and with a magical quickness, the tall, kind school safety agent from Trinidad was on my heels. Mr. Joseph called the students his sons and daughters; he hugged and high-fived them in the hall as he moved them to class. He was a stand-in father figure for many of them, but he had a job to do, too, and he did it well. Assessing the situation, he saw the still-fighting boys, the wrecked room, the blood—and he radioed for backup before moving toward the fight.

School safety agents rushed into my room and wedged themselves between the boys. Multiple agents on each body, they separated Dennis and Vincent, pinned them against my posters and maps on the back wall, and handcuffed them. Filled with adrenaline but unable to move, the boys spouted obscenities as they were pushed/pulled out of the room, wrestling against the handcuffs and the safety agents. Our principal had shown up at some point, and he whispered for me to dismiss my class to the cafeteria because the classroom was unsafe.

I herded the students toward the door and tried to maintain a modicum of composure. I was twenty-seven years old. I had been in New York City for two years. I had been teaching for a year and a half. I did not feel like a grown-up at that moment. I looked around, but nobody was going to comfort me because I was supposedly in charge. The blood stared at me from the back of the classroom.

"'Bye, Miss!" some said, blatantly gleeful that class had been cancelled. Others walked right past me with their eyes aglow and mouths dripping with gossip. In spite of my efforts to be the adult in the room, tears edged their way into the corners of my eyes, and my bottom lip began to quiver as I held the classroom door open for the students. I wasn't sure why I was about to cry, but I could feel something rise inside me and break the surface; it couldn't be stopped. The last half of the class saw the tears escape and stream down my cheeks before I could wipe them quickly away. They looked at me curiously. At that point I became the spectacle, the grand finale of a very entertaining ten minutes.

After the last student left I shut my classroom door and went over to my desk, my eyes drawn again and again to the blood in the back of the room. In the bottom right-hand drawer, tucked into an empty Café Bustelo coffee can, were several pairs of latex gloves in a Ziploc bag. At some point in my teacher training I had been told to keep latex gloves in my desk in case of blood, vomit, or other emergencies involving bodily fluids. Custodians were coming, but there was blood on my fabrics from West Africa that hung on the back wall, and I wanted to clean those myself. Determined to make my classroom mine again, I slid my large hands into the too-small gloves that smelled like condoms. Defeated by a surge of unrecognizable emotions, I lowered my head into my hands and cried.

Peter, the white-haired Irish custodian, opened my classroom door and found me sobbing at my desk into those latex gloves. He silently mopped the floor and cleaned the blood off the desks and bookshelves, replacing the metallic smell of violence with the familiar smell of bleach, as I sat at my desk and wept quietly until I could stop.

The next day, I was back in front of my fifth-period class. This is the beauty of teaching: you cannot hide from your students for long. You have less than twenty-four hours to get yourself together before you are faced with a classroom, all eyes on you. Dennis and Vincent had both been suspended, but the rest of the class trickled in, electrified by the memory of the fight and looking for telltale signs of blood and drama. Eventually, they settled into their seats, disappointed to find no evidence from the day before.

But there was one piece of evidence standing in front of them—me.

I resumed my position in front of the room with my lime-green clipboard and the New York City Board of Education Scantron sheet for attendance. I pulled a mechanical pencil from my ponytail and started to call the students' names. *We'll just pretend yesterday didn't happen,* I thought to myself. *I'll do yesterday's lesson today and then I'll just have to catch them up with the other three periods of English 6 by the end of the week, and then this will all be okay.* I ran down the list of names, my mind elsewhere, until I was interrupted by the booming sound of Hector's voice.

"Yo, Miss, you were *crying* yesterday! Did everyone see that? Ms. U was *crying* after the fight!" He laughed a full-belly laugh, threw his head back, and slapped his hand on his desk as if crying as a response to real-life violence were the most ridiculous thing he had ever seen.

I was puzzled by this response to my response, but then the entire class joined in. They laughed at me, heckled me, made fun of me. And even though Sherrie and Krystal tried to defend me and pleaded with the class to leave me alone, they were the definite minority.

I stood there unknowingly at a teaching crossroads. In that moment I could have swept Hector's comment under the metaphorical rug that hid the vast differences between me and my students, or I could open this possible Pandora's box of race, class, and privilege and let us dig around in it. Thankfully, I chose the latter, but I didn't choose it intentionally. I had no explicit goal of being schooled by my students, of making my classroom a place of equal exchange between students and teacher, of being my authentic self with them. These concepts, the foundation of my teaching practice today, were too big, too foreign, too unstructured for me to consider in those early years of teaching. Those years I was in survival mode; I was barely making it day by day, class by class, lesson by lesson. I was holding on for dear life.

I chose to engage my students in dialogue that day because I was tired. Actually, I was exhausted. I felt drained from the day before, and I didn't feel like pushing through my lesson. Maybe it was this fatigue that defused my new-teacher flight-or-flight mindset and allowed me to shift into low gear, but in retrospect it was the best pedagogical decision I ever made.

Too exhausted to wrestle the class into the day's lesson, I admitted to Hector that yes, I had cried yesterday. I told them that, in fact, I'd cried more after they left. I'd cried when I retold the story to the assistant principal, I'd cried again to my coworkers, I'd cried last night to my boyfriend, and I might just start crying *now* if we talked about it. The classroom shifted ever so slightly at this admission. The students, with earnest curiosity, wanted to know why the fight had upset me so much. They honestly didn't understand.

"Miss, why were you so upset?"

"Miss, it's just a fight—it's no big deal…"

"That stuff happens all the time."

The students' comments gave me pause. I thought back to the previous afternoon and evening and the many times I had retold the story of the fight. Each time it replayed in crystal-clear detail: the nose break, the blood, the feeling of watching a movie in slow motion, the blood, the realization that it was not a movie but real life, the blood, the boys being handcuffed and dragged from the room like criminals, the blood, and how my classroom had been designated "unsafe." It is still clear today, fourteen years later.

I answered my students' questions, still unable to put my feelings into words accurately, but trying: "Because I have never seen anything like that before in real life. I've only seen fights in movies, never in person! It was horrible—we heard Vincent's nose break! The blood! I could hear their punches! It was so violent! They're both such nice kids, why would they do that?"

I physically shuddered recalling it all. My voice got higher and higher as I rambled, ending with a screech on "*Why would they do that?*" They laughed at my dramatic exclamations, but as their laughter died down, they explained to me that Dennis and Vincent had fought over "ancient beef" related to one of their cousins, and then an onslaught of questions followed as they processed what I had said:

"You've never been in a fight?"

"You've never hit anyone? Nobody's ever hit you?"

"You've never seen anyone get beat up?"

"You haven't seen someone bleed like that?"

"You haven't *made* someone bleed like that?"

They stared at me in disbelief as I shook my head no again and again and again. It was truly unfathomable to them that I had never been personally engaged in fighting or violence—either as a perpetrator, a victim, or an innocent bystander.

They looked at me. I looked at them. And we seemed to understand at the exact same moment that our lives were even more different than we had initially thought. But now we were curious about each other. So we talked.

In my life I had been in one physical fight, but it wasn't something I told many people about; I was ashamed and embarrassed by it, but I decided to tell the story to my students in an effort to buy myself some common ground at this moment.

This fight had been with my sister. I was nineteen and she was sixteen. I don't remember what the fight was about—something stupid like a bathrobe—but the climax of the altercation was when she charged me, wielding a hammer—and I am pretty sure she would have used it. In some crazy intuitive move that I still can't explain, I kicked her in the face, broke her front tooth, and bloodied her mouth with my Birkenstock sandal. As she clutched her bleeding mouth, the hammer now on the carpeted floor of her bedroom, I yelled, "You're lucky I'm not wearing my Doc Martens!" without a modicum of remorse. En route to me with the hammer, my sister had pushed our handicapped father to the ground, and my mother had called the cops. I don't remember how the fight was resolved. Probably in the same way my family resolves all of our issues—we pretend they never happened.

The students were surprised and impressed with this story and even called my teeth-kicking move "ghetto" (which, I must admit, made me feel a little proud), but they then insisted that family fights didn't count as *real fights* because "everyone has them." Some students shared their bloody sibling fight stories, too, to prove that fistfights and face kicking were normal facets of family life. The fight with my sister had always haunted me and was—in my mind—a prime example of how dysfunctional my family was, but it wasn't legitimate in their books. They normalized it for me in about one minute, and I was at a loss for words. The shame I had carried with me for years about that fight evaporated ever so slightly, and with that came a sense of relief.

They asked for other examples of fighting in my life, but there were none.

When I admitted that I had never punched anyone, Juan and Wes offered to let me punch them for practice, because they were worried about my lack of skills. I demonstrated some of the fight moves that I had gleaned from watching Popeye cartoons, doing a rolling punch and threatening the air with a "knuckle sandwich" as they laughed. I politely told them that I could not punch them, even for self-defense practice. I also admitted that I had never been punched, in response to which many female students, including Krystal and Sherrie, offered a similar service: hitting me to "toughen me up." Again, I declined. But at this point their offers were making me laugh and the conversation flowed easily. I sat in a vacant student desk now—eye to eye with my students and talking. It was probably Dennis's desk, now that I think about it, because he always sat in the front of the room.

By now I had lived up to every stereotype they had of white girls from the suburbs, and I acknowledged this. We circled back to the topic of the Dennis and Vincent fight and how I had never witnessed violence like that before—ever. They were amazed. Truly stunned. Thrown.

"Man, I seen someone get pistol-whipped right outside my window!"

"You mean, you never seen anyone get shot?"

"You've never seen anyone punch anyone else before?"

"How *old* are you? Where are you *from*?"

"Miss, this happens in my 'hood all the time. I've been seeing this stuff since I was little kid."

The students went on about the violence they had seen in their lives, and I sat there numb as I listened to their stories. I could tell they were being honest because the conversation did not contain a smidge of one-upmanship. Everyone laid their truths on the table, and I could not believe the things I heard. They were recalling actions I had seen only in rated-R movies, yet their stories did not originate on a screen but from lived experience. My mind was blown.

I tried to explain to them why I found the fight so disturbing beyond the visceral nature of it. I wanted to get their take on the cycle of violence. "You know, guys, where does it end? Seriously. If it's okay for Dennis to break Vincent's nose this year, next year will someone cut someone else? And the year after that, will someone walk into the building with a gun and settle some 'ancient beef' that's been lingering between two students and their cousin? I mean, you guys will have graduated and be long gone, but I'll still be here. That freaks me out. Where does it stop?"

I thought my argument was logical, but they didn't buy it: that stuff wouldn't happen in our school. I mentioned the Columbine High School shooting, but the students continued to shake their heads and explained that school was different for them and that they were different from those guys in Littleton, Colorado. The class was unanimous in their stance, which was a rarity. That wouldn't happen here, they repeated. They were from that violence, the violence of guns and senseless killings; it was woven into the fabric of their neighborhoods and the housing projects that many of them lived in and the streets they called home, and because they lived and breathed it, they did not want that violence to seep into their school. No way. Not happening. As we say in Brooklyn, *fuggedaboutit.*

At this point the class was all talking at once. I was not convinced, but they were adamant. Hector got the class silent, cleared his throat, and tried to break it down for me. He talked to me like I was a child, but with gentleness and kindness. He said, "Miss, nobody's bringing a gun in here. We keep the street in the street."

I taught many of these students for eleventh-grade English and for their twelfth-grade English elective; they were my students for two years straight. This topic of conversation resurfaced from time to time and their stance was consistent. They taught me an urban student code of ethics that my students for the next ten years agreed with: keep the street in the street. Yes, they owned weapons. Some even admitted to owning guns. Many of them brought those weapons (knives, blades, box cutters, socks full of batteries or pennies) to school because they had to go to night school or work the late shift at their jobs and then return home to their dangerous neighborhoods. They both wanted and needed a form of protection. All students said they would never use those weapons in school because that was crossing the line. School was safe; it was sacred. No way, they repeated year after year, when I discussed physical violence in the classroom. Nobody who knew such violence at home would bring the same violence—of that level—into school.

Fist-fighting, sure. Guns, never.

I did not believe them that day in February of 2002. I found their words fascinating, and I knew they were telling me what they believed was the truth, but how could the line between street and school not blur? And yet, when I left that high school for a new job ten years later, I had never seen a fight with a weapon within our school walls, and I had seen some serious fights—altercations that made that day with Dennis and Vincent seem easy. I witnessed so much physical violence that I became inured to it. I no longer cried after fights; I cried instead at the deeper structural violence that permeated my students' lives: homeless shelters, poverty, foster care, hunger, dirty clothes, parents dead at remarkably young ages, gangs, drugs, addiction. I cried for problems that couldn't be resolved with a few punches, some blood, a bottle of bleach, and a one-week suspension.

The longer I taught, the more I noticed patterns to these fights, too. Fights happened at routine times every year, such as before report card distribution, before Thanksgiving and Christmas, before standardized tests. Fighting no longer seemed mysterious or foreign to me. School shootings continued to happen across the country, but they never seemed to happen in an inner-city school.

One time a student did bring a gun to school. It was the fall semester of 2006; I remember clearly because I was in the early weeks of my pregnancy with my daughter. Our building went on lockdown during second period as a SWAT team entered to confront the student with the gun. No one knew what was happening at the time, and a flurry of text messages on the students' phones only clouded the matter. Later in the day, at the faculty meeting, we got the real story: a somewhat sweet young man had brought his first gun to school to show off, in an attempt to look "gangsta." The gun was nestled in his gym bag, snugly wrapped in his smelly gym clothes. When he offered a peek of it to a student in first period, another student saw and told the teacher after class. If you know anything about inner-city students, snitching is not okay—ever. The adage goes: *Snitches get stiches and end up in ditches.* The fact that one student snitched on another student who brought a gun to school, even though the gun was obviously for bragging rights and there was no intention of using it, was evidence to me that maybe, years before, Hector had been right.

It took over a decade of convincing, but now I believe him.

That day after Dennis and Vincent fought, I sat and talked with my class for the forty-two-minute period. No lesson was taught, but so much was learned. We ended class knowing each other a little better, and with that knowledge we trusted each other a little more, and with that trust we risked a bit more together in class, and in those risks, I think we all grew as readers, writers, thinkers, and people. And it was that day that taught me the value in knowing my students and letting them know me. Today, I pause lessons when conversations need to happen; I insert opportunities into lessons for truth-telling to emerge; I talk to my students more and more and more about their lives, ideas, and learning, and it is always, always worth the time.

I am still close with those students, the class of 2003 from that public high school in Brooklyn, New York. They will forever be my original teachers, and I owe much of my teaching philosophy today to Dennis and Vincent for having "ancient beef" over a cousin, to the blood that still stains my African fabric with almost invisible brown freckles, to Hector who had no problem calling me out on my crying, to the class that engaged me in the first real conversation I had with my students, and to some crazy moment of grace brought on by new-teacher exhaustion when I chose to listen as my students told me about their lives and opened up my life to them as well.

In my teaching practice today, I do not shirk from the difficult conversations. I seek out moments to find common ground and build understanding. I find it easy to love people who are different from me, as long as we can talk about those differences. I want to tell the truth and hear the truth at all costs. I learned from that class that I wanted to be this kind of person, and teaching them helped me develop into a better version of me. Becoming a teacher was, essentially, becoming myself after years of struggling to figure out who, exactly, I wanted that to be.

Inside the Labyrinth

Kristin Leclaire

As a high school English teacher, I am the ultimate translator. For thirteen years, I have translated the scratches of sophomore boys into essays about Daedalus's maze and Icarus's fall. I translate eye rolls into old breakups and new infatuations. I translate, with a giggle, a group work evaluation that states, "This project sucked. Largely because one of our members was incontinent" (this in response to a question about the group's overall *competence*). I translate the dreamy run-on sentences of a sixteen-year-old boy pining away for a girl with "the face of an angle." I write, "Best to measure that kind of beauty with a protractor" in the margins of his three-page memoir. Until recently, my students' essays centered on first loves, or friend fights, or mild, sports-related injuries. I'd smile at the way their words gathered and exposed their innocent longings: to be seen, to be lost, to be found. My purple grading pen would hover above the labyrinth of their teenage desires, trying to trace a meaningful path.

Lately, however, I've been translating nervous glances to the lock on the classroom door. I interpret quiet questions about when our library will reopen. I teach at Arapahoe High School, and we are still disoriented from Friday, December 13, 2013, the day Karl Pierson, a senior boy, punctured our school with his shotgun. With the numbers of several classrooms he intended to shoot up inked on his forearms, he walked into the school shortly after lunch, killed one of our senior girls in the trophy hallway, and headed to the library to hunt down Tracy Murphy, our head librarian and debate coach, who had recently cut him from the team. When he couldn't find Tracy, he open-fired on the circulation desk, set off a homemade bomb, and shot himself between the bookshelves. The rest of the school huddled in silent classroom corners.

All hallway noises are now suspicious. Our students' ears resonate with his gunshots, and each time someone shuts a locker too hard, my students' glances ask, "Are we safe?" So I test the door handle, right before returning to our discussion of Steinbeck, with a little nod they translate as, "Yes, you are safe. I will keep you safe." This never used to be part of my job.

When I was in elementary school, my teachers calmly prepared me for natural disasters. For tornado drills, I'd buddy up with another squirming kid, and the alarm could barely be heard over the giggling, shuffling tides of kids released from their classrooms. The teachers would somehow tame us into neat lines, and we'd sit with our heads between our knees, bony elbows protecting vulnerable necks. For fire drills, we'd quietly march through the doors and shiver in the winter sunlight. For earthquake drills, we'd ball up under our desks. I'd make my body as small as possible, hardening my back and arms into a shell in case the walls burned down, or the ceiling was ripped off, or the very foundation of the school shook loose. Of course, these events felt impossible. The school would shelter us like a dad, protecting us from the outside world. Ten minutes later we'd all be back in our seats, coloring in our math workbooks and thinking about lunch.

Schools now add lockdown drills to their routine precautions. Twice a year, students across America silently get up from their desks when the principal announces on the loudspeaker for the teachers to "initiate lockdown procedures." Even preschoolers practice lockdowns. Teachers sweep their students into the darkest corner of the classroom, turning off lights and hushing chitchat to make the classroom look and sound empty. If there is a gunman looking in our classroom window, we explain to our students, we want him to think there's nobody in here. It reminds me of the scene in *Jurassic Park* when the children stand perfectly still, and the *Tyrannosaurus rex* moves past them, unaware that they are right there, crouched and trembling.

Arapahoe High School's physical location reflects this intersection of vulnerability and protection. A one-story brick building, it nestles in a quiet corner of Littleton, Colorado; it's framed on two sides by busy streets prone to traffic accidents, and on its other two sides lie neatly mowed fields for football, soccer, softball, and marching band. Built in the 1960s, Arapahoe has a dozen doors to the outside world, unlike many post-Columbine school buildings, which have only one primary entrance. Arapahoe is about a fifteen-minute drive from Columbine High School, and our sports teams often play them in our pre- or post-season. We're less than a half hour away from the shopping center where the Aurora theater shootings occurred, and many Arapahoe students know somebody who was there that terrible night. Even before Karl Pierson barged into the trophy hallway at 12:30 on Friday the thirteenth and started shooting, we'd practiced lockdown drills diligently, because we were close neighbors to tragedy. We failed, however, to practice running for our lives, hands on our heads, through hallways distorted by hundreds of masked SWAT team members shouting and clutching the kinds of guns we'd seen only in video games. But in those years between Columbine and our own school shooting, we believed, like the children in *Jurassic Park*, that the predator would move right past us if we pretended it wasn't there. If we kept our heads down, the tornado would retreat, the earthquake would settle, and the fire would be a false alarm. This belief didn't come from arrogance or negligence; it was simply based on what we knew to be true.

In our old Arapahoe library, we'd walk through the glass doors, past the Arapahoe Indian statue watching over us, and into an alphabetical display of new hardback books with shiny protective covers and spines not yet broken. Each year, I'd make extra trips to the library in the last week of October, partly to peruse the annual pumpkin contest, partly to help myself to the candy corn and hot apple cider that Louisa, the librarian's assistant, laid out for us teachers in the back. Louisa wore black cat and orange pumpkin sweaters on Halloween and jingle bell earrings in December. When I jammed the copy machine, she'd rip out the paper tray with a deep sigh, but her voice was low and the soft crinkles reaching out from her eyes and lips gave her a permanent grandmother smile. Next to the buzzing copy machine, wafts of cinnamon steam curled out of the silver urn she'd brought for the cider.

Everyone and everything in the library was buzzing; long-haired girls clacking out their business presentations on the old Dells, two boys from my third hour doing algebra homework and sneaking Doritos from their backpacks, the Spanish teacher chatting with the head librarian, Tracy, while hacking away flashcards on the paper cutter. It was the buzz of energy, of things getting checked off to-do lists. It was a lullaby on Mondays, a hymn on Fridays.

If school was my generation's safe haven, then the library was its most sheltered space. It was protective and protected. Immune to classroom drama and hallway bullies, it was the sacred place of singsongy story time and round carpets, the place where we fell in love with our teachers and lost our first teeth, where walls were made of books and "READ" posters. As the teacher turned each page, we'd lean in, and lean in a little more until we could breathe her right in. We'd swing from one bold print word to another like they were monkey bars. We could sit with bare legs sprawled on a steam-cleaned carpet, tongues poking out and backs relaxed into bows.

As a little girl growing up in Old Arlington, a leafy suburb of Columbus, Ohio, in the 1980s, I'd spend the summer wandering the infinite bookcases of our white-pillared neighborhood library. While my friends attended morning mass and Jewish summer camp, I rode my bike under the green canopies of tree-lined, asphalt roads where old Ohio farms had transformed into red-bricked suburban homes with circle driveways. The Tremont Library rested in a sleepy neighborhood, its fire lane often occupied by moms in tennis skirts and gold earrings, dropping off their kids' books on the way to swim meets.

I'd stroll through the glass doors and approach the chestnut altar of the old card catalogue. I loved sliding out those smooth, narrow drawers, each card inside neatly charting the facts of a book's life. The cards were closely packed, and I grazed their tops with the palm of my hand as though I were stroking the soft bumps of my cat's spine. The space shuttle *Challenger* had exploded, I'd failed my fraction test, my best friend was already sporting a training bra, and my piano teacher had taught me the word *mediocre* by using it to describe my talent, but here at the Tremont Library, the Dewey Decimal system ruled all. Here, the world made sense.

After this brief worship, I'd head for the mystery shelf in the young adult room, past the Nancy Drews and right to the Trixie Beldens. Trixie was a bold, curly-haired girl who solved mysterious misdeeds in her small town's caves and manors. The scariest moments were only scary enough to keep me reading, and the climax of each story quickly resolved into a sensible ending: the ghost was just a peeved maid, the vampire a disgruntled heir, and the monster an angry boy.

I touched each book, fingering diamond-printed dust jackets and pages edged with red ink, and stared back at Trixie's wide, doll-like eyes on the peeling 1950s covers. I'd pull out the story I wanted, check it out with the library card in my jeans pocket, and ride home with it in my backpack. With our orange cat curled up on my tan feet and a pretzel rod dangling from my lips, I'd turn pages until the tomboy-ish Trixie's hands were mine. The dankness of the haunted mansion dampened the skin on my arms. The clues—a frayed photo, tidbits of overheard conversation, shadowy sightings—were laid out before me, and I assembled them like a puzzle. Each mystery was solved. Good people got shiny medals while villains often turned out not to be villains at all. And Trixie and I saw it all coming from a mile away. There were no press releases, no SWAT team with masks and guns ordering us to "get your hands on your heads and fucking RUN." There were no fifteen-year-olds so terrified that they ran out of their shoes, their naked feet sinking into the dirty snow.

If Trixie were here with me, would her wide eyes find clarity in this madness? The two of us could lift up her wooden-handled magnifying glass and examine the evidence, all of it spattered among the police report, my memory, and retold stories. Help me, Trixie, translate these fragments:

Fact 1: Karl Pierson dropped off his fifteen-year-old sister at the same entrance he'd stalk through later that day, nodding his blond head when she said, "I'll see you after school" before closing the door.

Fact 2: Claire Davis, a sleek-haired senior who loved horses, watched Karl barge through the glass doors, shotgun in his marked-up hands. She asked him, "What are you doing, Karl?" He answered her with three shots.

Fact 3: In the English office, I put down my hot chocolate, logged into my computer, and heard three bangs from the barrel of a gun: black, hollow *O*s swallowing the hallways.

Fact 4: I crouched behind someone else's desk, my phone across the office, out of arm's reach, along with the rest of my former life. I used another teacher's phone to send a text to my husband: "This is Kristin. There has been a shooting at Arapahoe. I am OK." I didn't believe a word of it.

Fact 5: Max and Trent, two tall boys from my third-hour class, were eating and scratching out homework in the library when Karl entered, yelling, "Where the fuck is Murphy?" Bandoliers crossed his chest, and shells fell to the floor as he shot at the front desk. His fantasy of murdering Tracy Murphy slipped away.

Fact 6: Max, one of my tall sophomore boys, bolted from the library. When he reached the trophy hall, he paused at the puddle of blood next to Claire, who now lay facedown like a dropped doll.

Fact 7: Karl, after piercing the checkout desk with bullets and blackening the shelves with a homemade bomb, shot himself between shelves of e. e. cummings and Robert Frost.

Fact 8: Louisa, the librarian's assistant with jingle bell earrings, stood just outside the King Soopers supermarket we'd been evacuated to, gripping an empty cart. She didn't seem to hear me until I asked, "Did you see what happened in the library?" She nodded slowly, like a sleepwalker, brown eyes locked on something invisible to me.

Fact 9: The next day, students shivered in the cold, stuffing Styrofoam cups into a chain-link fence to spell out "Warrior Strong"—our school's motto—before the candlelight vigil for Claire, who slept in a nearby hospital in critical condition.

Fact 10: Between the snow and Christmas lights, my department chair sent us a text on the darkest evening of the year. Claire was dead. The vigil hadn't worked.

Fact 11: When the crime scene tape came down a week later, teachers returned to the building for their cell phones, purses, and cars. The classrooms were just as we left them, except empty. Desks in neat rows of six held handouts and dead phones. The counselors had taken the liberty of closing the students' binders and books, and I wondered if Karl had died with his eyes open or closed.

Fact 12: Karl's mom, with gentle, shaky hands, pulled out my chair for me as I tried not to picture Karl in their now half-empty home, still partially decorated from Christmas. I was there to tutor the sister he'd left behind. I hadn't known their family before the shooting, but I figured the least I could do was help her through English 10. I wonder now if I was really extending this olive branch to myself, to forgive Karl by seeing him as someone's big brother. Instead, my nightmares intensified.

Fact 13: Warm stickiness seeped from my temple into my pillow, turning from blood to tears as I woke up with Karl's body in my mind. He was still smoking from the gunshot, blood soaking into the library's floor.

—

I walked back into the Arapahoe High School library yesterday after being shut out for six months. Even its windows were blacked over, like mirrors cloaked in mourning, as its insides endured evisceration. It's not open yet to students, but the other teachers and I have been encouraged to walk through and make peace with it. Most things have found their new places. The old carpet, rubbed from fifty years of soles, is gone. It and its bloodstains were ripped out before the memorial services took place. The new carpet's fibers are stiff and bright. Not a footprint to be found. The stuffed chairs have gone, too, and pencil marks from decades of daydreaming boys and girls have been erased. The countertops are so black and sleek that everything seems to slide right off them, and the chairs are hard. I don't know where to sit down.

In our new library, the evidence has been painted over, recarpeted, and sanded away. Now, I walk into a clean space of flat screens, TVs with scrolling announcements, and surge-protected outlets. The surviving books have migrated from the walls of the library to its heart. Small worlds still beat in between their covers, and I hear them even in the buzz of the high-tech group study rooms. Windows have replaced burned library shelves, and student volunteers shuffle old books onto new shelves. I'm not quite sure where to walk. Each time I turn, I bump into a glass wall.

There's one familiar corner: the glass case housing our Arapaho Indian statue. After the shooting, members of the Arapaho Indian tribe performed a cleansing of our library and the hallway where Claire was shot. The ceremony was private, but afterward I could smell the sweetness of burning sage in the spots most concentrated with death. I wondered if the tribal elders had stepped into the library to find Karl's ghost standing in the corner, the rage on his face slacked into confusion. He'd turned the library into a purgatory. I hoped that the sweeping motions of the ceremonial feathers, fanning the sage higher and higher, had brushed his death off the book jackets and into the air outside.

Standing next to the new circulation desk, I try to imagine the student council girls and the basketball boys strolling into this library, backpacks full of Spanish homework, Shakespeare plays, and energy drinks in tall black cans. I picture my sophomore boys typing their essays on laptops, giving them only a cursory glance before sharing them with me. Just down the hall with our office door wide open, other English teachers and I might find our way back to each other by reading aloud the funniest errors in our students' stories. Before the shooting, my desk mate liked to inform me that teenagers don't care to be "taken for granite," and I'd reply by wondering why so many seniors plan to spend the next four years in some kind of "collage." She'd always win, though, by asking me, "Who doesn't enjoy a soft, genital breeze from time to time?"

But my favorite, my very favorite, was the young memoirist who recently responded to a metaphor exercise with this sentence: "I am the clam before the storm."

I imagine my memoirist typing sentences like this one in the new library when it opens to students next week. She will chat, perhaps, with some student council kids at a high table in the library's café as school announcements scroll on the screen above her head. Throwing her bag on the ground, she'll stretch her arms into a sleepy yawn. I can see the rest of the kids in the new library lounging too, arms thrown over the backs of chairs like they're sitting in their own living rooms. As she and her friends laugh and type homework and eat cookies from the school store, the air around them will quiver and lighten. The silent eye of the storm will pass into something noisier, and she will mistakenly trade her "calm" for a "clam." Sometimes, lovely things come from mistakes. She will close her laptop case, open her plan book, and cross off *Get ready for tomorrow* with a wavy blue line.

My hand hovering above the checkout counter, I picture that tiny clam shivering on the foamy edge of the shore. I think of the clam as I feel my way back into the library. Heavy clouds move in, swallowing patches of blue sky with roars of thunder and singeing the ground with arrows of lightning. Nothing sounds or feels quite the same after the gunshots, and I move by groping, grasping, slumping against dead ends, rerouting. That clam could be washed out to the deep at any moment, uprooted and taken for a ride. Yet there it is, wobbling between the wet thickness of the sand and the disorienting rip of the tide, holding on even though there is little to hold on to.

I press my thumb onto the new circulation desk, softening the counter with my fingerprint. It forms a silvery spiderweb or a delicate compass, depending on how the light translates it.

Unsaid

Shannon LeBlanc

On February 10, 2015, Craig Stephen Hicks entered a Chapel Hill condominium and shot and killed three Muslims. The victims were Deah Shaddy Barakat, age twenty-three; his wife, Yusor Mohammad Abu-Salha, age twenty-one; and her sister, Razan Moham-mad Abu-Salha, age nineteen. In the days that followed, the public learned that Hicks might have murdered the three young Muslims over an ongoing parking dispute, but North Carolina authorities were still trying to decide if the murders could be labeled as a hate crime. Muslim and non-Muslim communities in the United States and around the world turned to social media and posted the hashtag #MuslimLivesMatter—a rallying cry for a group of people that had experienced so much loss and hatred and violence.

By then, I had been a teacher at the Nur Islamic School of Louisville, Kentucky, for seven months. I was a recent transplant from Boston, where I had spent the majority of my twenties living in a series of overpriced, drafty apartments while working at mind-numbing cubicle jobs. Days spent in the artificial glow of computer screens made me evaluate my career goals and, in 2011, I began a three-year master in fine arts in the creative writing nonfiction program at Emerson College.

Although Boston was a city I loved, it began to frustrate me during my last year of graduate school. The twitch to leave emerged as a small thought one windy January night and then evolved into a series of questions I contemplated on crowded subway commutes:

Did I really want to try to make it in a city that made me consistently feel as though I were swimming in anonymity? Could I really elevate my career in a place where PhD students were hunched over tables at every coffee house? The previous summer, I'd helped a friend beginning a PhD program at the University of Louisville. I'd helped her settle into her new place, and I'd instantly liked the sunny, laid-back city with a thriving food-and-drink scene, plentiful parking, friendly residents, and affordable housing. Before I walked across the stage to receive my master's degree in May of 2014, I'd decided to move to Louisville. That summer, I scoured the Internet for positions there and applied to any job that even remotely fit my skill set and credentials.

Initially, I didn't expect the offer to teach middle school English language arts at a small, religious, private K–8 school in Louisville. The Craigslist ad was concisely worded, yet had an implied sense of urgency: the 2014–15 academic year would begin in three weeks. Although the posting stated that candidates were required to have two years of previous teaching experience, I applied, and was surprised when I received an email for an initial Skype interview; I was even more surprised when the principal of the school revealed that it was an Islamic school.

I'd expected a Christian-based private school, especially because I recalled seeing many churches when I'd helped my friend with her move—but an Islamic school intrigued me. I'd had few prior interactions with Muslims, with the exception of the GRE math tutor I'd found advertising in The Coop in Harvard Square. My tutor, a then-PhD student from Iraq who spoke with a thick Arabic accent, calmly tried to help me conquer the math I never quite understood in high school, but after our six weeks of tutoring were complete and I received a decent score on the math portion of the GRE, I never saw him again.

On a Skype interview, I spoke with the principal, a Muslim originally from Russia who had converted at age eighteen, and the academic dean, a Muslim originally from the Philippines. They described a diverse group of students, some of whom had been born into the religion, while others belonged to families that had converted. They told me that many of their students spoke multiple languages, that some were refugees who had fled conflicts in Africa and the Middle East, and that around 85 percent of the student body was at or below the poverty line. The more we talked, the more my curiosity and excitement grew. The school encouraged its students through holistic methods: an educational philosophy based on personal, social, intellectual, and spiritual growth and learning attained through connecting to nature, the surrounding community, and humanitarian values. Also, the school enrolled around 120 students in kindergarten through eighth grade, and my largest class would have only twelve students. Even before the interview ended with an invitation to visit the school as a prospective employee, I'd begun constructing lesson plans.

A week later, I flew to Louisville and taught a lesson focusing on sensory details. A group of ten or so middle school students had been asked by the principal and academic dean to come to the school on that insufferably humid August afternoon to help judge my performance. At the end of the forty-five minutes, as a reward for sacrificing one of the last of their summer afternoons, I offered the students hard candies, unaware that it was Ramadan and that most Muslims were fasting. One student kindly explained that they could take the candy, but couldn't eat it until they broke fast after sundown. I was mortified, and stared at the tile floor with blazing cheeks as I packed my bag.

When the principal asked me to come to her office, I figured she'd tell me to educate myself more on Islam before I decided I wanted to teach at the school. I nearly fell into a large potted plant when she smiled, complimented my lesson, and offered me the position. In a week, I'd either sold or donated most of my larger belongings. The rest I packed floor to ceiling in my car, and then I drove the fourteen hours from Boston to Louisville.

Each day after attending staff orientation, I crashed on a borrowed air mattress in my friend's apartment. As a new staff member, and just one of a handful of non-Muslims, I scribbled notes about

Islam during an hour-long PowerPoint presentation during the first day of orientation. A week later, I began my first year of teaching, and gradually became accustomed to lesson planning, the hectic pace of the typical school day, and the trials of managing three classes of students with varying degrees of behavioral and learning differences. I began to feel more comfortable in front of a classroom; however, seven months later, I couldn't answer the barrage of questions from my seventh-grade students the day after the shootings in North Carolina.

My seventh graders were understandably upset and wanted to discuss the shootings and the national and international response, but we were in the midst of a unit on journalism. Their editorials were due the next day, and I was frustrated by their constant chattering and their inability to focus—and our schedule, as always, was running a day or two behind what I'd planned. Instead of having a conversation about their feelings as Muslims, enabling them to enter a larger discourse concerning their religion and culture and the world's view of both, or giving the students a free-writing exercise where they could detail and develop their feelings of confusion and sadness, I snapped: I yelled at them and said that they needed to focus on their writing and classwork when they were in English class—regardless of what was happening in the outside world. Immediately, the room quieted; hot shame singed my cheeks. As someone who's written about her own religious wanderings and curiosities as part of her master's thesis, and as someone who's used writing to grapple with difficult thoughts, contrasting opinions, and intense emotions, I should have encouraged my students to do the same. These were twelve- and thirteen-year-olds, an age group often disregarded by society as lazy, self-absorbed teenagers. Since they were Muslims, another layer was added to this stereotypical view. My students—all born after 9/11—struggled to understand why the world often could not accept or trust their culture and beliefs and religion. They'd asked me for the opportunity for self-expression. Rather than providing an outlet, I'd silenced them.

I'm not a Muslim, yet I teach in an Islamic school. I don't practice a religion—and although I was raised Roman Catholic, I left the church as a young teenager because I couldn't accept Christianity, and all of its creeds and dogmas, as absolute. But I chose to work at an Islamic school because I wanted to learn more about a religion and a people that, as I see it, have been so shrouded in negative news reports that many people still associate them, regardless of generation, with terrorist acts that occurred nearly fifteen years earlier. I wanted to see another religion, one I had little knowledge about before I accepted the job at an Islamic school. Naively, I assumed that my students wouldn't be as conflicted by their religion as I had been as a young teenager.

The day after the shooting, however, I started to understand that Islam, like the Christian faith I'd been raised in, could be just as complicated to accept. When my students asked questions I'd never be able to answer about an event that I—like them—couldn't fully grasp, I knew they desired to understand more than why Hicks shot three Muslim youths. My students wanted to know why, if this world was fair, and if these three young Muslims were devout, intelligent, and caring people, they had died in such a senseless, violent way. All around the classroom, I heard a refrain: *Why over a stupid parking spot? Why did they die so young? Why Muslims again and again and again?*

At 1:20 p.m., my seventh-grade class convened for afternoon prayer, and we all removed our shoes, leaving a row of footwear of varying colors and sizes against the wall outside the classroom. I led the seventh graders across linoleum floors that spread cold through thin cotton socks, past rows of lockers and binders and books and backpacks strewn on the floor, past storage rooms filled with vacuums and cleaning supplies and frayed brooms, to the *masjid* attached to the school. I prepared myself to ask for quiet, but it was already silent. Usually, the seventh graders talked about anything and everything: their favorite songs—even though the school holds the strict view that mainstream music is *haram*; their plans for the weekend; a difficult math test; a sale at the local mall. I've joked that my seventh graders talk so much that they must continue while sleeping, but, on this afternoon, they were unusually somber while we traveled through the hallways and into the *masjid*, where the boys and girls separated into different praying areas.

With my back resting against a wall on the women's prayer side, I listened as Arabic words echoed around me. A weak ray of winter sun extended inside, brightening spots in the gold patterns etched into the dark red carpet. The students and staff formed neat lines like every Muslim across the world, facing Mecca and the *ka'aba,* the site of the first house of worship originally built by Adam and reconstructed by Abraham and his son, Ishmael. I watched from a short distance away as the imam on the men's side led prayer: mismatched socks peeking out from the students' long navy blue skirts and cropped pants, the swish of cloth, and shuffling of uniformed bodies as the students and staff and community members worshipped together.

Muslims pray five times a day: once before sunrise, at midday, then in late afternoon, again in early evening, and finally in the late evening. Prayers are recited in Arabic, and although I can now recognize the melodic sound leaving the imam's lips and the movements associated with each tone, I still cannot understand the meaning and I doubt I ever will.

One day after the shootings, I thought about cultural isolation as I watched my students pray—as I had done every weekday afternoon for the past seven months. Their religion dictated routine, but the world they lived in was filled with confusion and chaos, with xenophobia and hate, ignited years before many of them were alive. In Louisville, friendly strangers in grocery store lines and in gym classes initiated conversations by asking where I worked. When I answered, these people usually seemed surprised because they hadn't realized there was even a Muslim community in Louisville, never mind two Islamic schools. Many were confused as to why I wasn't wearing a hijab until

I explained I wasn't Muslim. Although no one directly told me they were against Islam or Muslims, the narrowed looks and the abrupt end to these conversations spoke volumes. On one hand, the intolerance I perceived from some locals was especially jarring because I'd never experienced religious prejudice before. On the other hand, I knew many Muslims had experienced worse, especially given what I knew of many students' stories: dictators and regimented governments and religious extremists and terrorists groups had pushed many of their families out of their homelands and across countries and oceans to the United States and our school, where they tried to maintain their culture in a Western community that was both afraid and misinformed. As an educator, I was supposed to be a negotiator for my middle schoolers, an outsider who could both instruct and learn along with them, even if our lessons were vastly different.

I taught my students about five-paragraph essay organization and thesis statements, and they taught me about Islam and its five pillars. While I taught them vocabulary words, they politely (and often) corrected my butchered pronunciation of their names. When I explained story structure and conflict and theme, they explained Arabic words and meanings and tried not to laugh and tease me when I attempted to recite the words. My favorite phrase is *yalla,* and I often use it to hurry students when they are dawdling in hallways or classrooms. Once, my female seventh graders made me a hijab out of a colorful winter scarf, and we all agreed that my oval-shaped head was not suited to that particular style.

In the *masjid* that day, I realized how wrong I had been to stop my students the previous class period, and I began to unfold the past seven months: I was an outsider without a hijab or *abaya,* who had no knowledge of the Quran or the Arabic language and no belief in Islam and its twenty-five prophets. Before moving to Louisville from Boston, I had had few interactions with Islam and Muslims, and the first two months of teaching had been disorientating. The names of my coworkers and students stuck to the back of my throat, Islamic prayers confused me because the words had no English connotations that I could decipher, and the random Arabic words that floated down the hallway to my classroom made me feel as though I were visiting a foreign country and not teaching in a school in Kentucky. When I had students read aloud during English class, they asked about word meanings that I naively assumed they'd know—like *hymnal*, because in my childhood, I'd pawed through one every Sunday while I sat on a cold, wooden church pew.

I had and have my doubts about the religion and its practices, as I know I'd have with any organized religion, but I choose to observe instead of judge. When I accepted the teaching position, I thought that I might not belong at the school, that my coworkers and students' parents might distrust me in ways similar to how I saw Westerners distrusting them because they practice a religion that's not Christian based; I never expected acceptance. Despite my internal worries, the students and community welcomed me, addressing me with a "hello" instead of the typical Muslim greeting, *assalamu alaikum*. My coworkers offered to help with setting up my apartment in Louisville, parents greeted me with a smile every morning when they dropped off their sleepy-eyed children, and my Muslim coworkers patiently answered my numerous questions about Islam. In class, when it was needed, my students have explained aspects of Islam and I explained aspects of Christianity, and then we moved on, differences and similarities acknowledged and respected.

But as an English teacher who had made the seventh graders write until they complained of cramped fingers, I'd disregarded them when they wanted to truly express themselves. They had asked me for a moment to harness their words, map confusion, and flesh out narratives, yet I had been afraid to deviate from the Common Core curriculum; I hadn't yet realized that the best lessons were the ones that weren't plotted into a week's worth of stopping points on the road to understanding: the pre-assessment, the daily lessons, the class activities, the standardized test. I'd ignored the holistic mission statement and had been too focused on the standards to give students the room to breathe and explore and grow. Months earlier, I'd begun teaching with the idea that if I could help one student express him or herself through writing, then I'd done a decent job. Nine students had asked me for that opportunity, and I'd failed myself; worse, I'd failed them.

Next to me in the back of the women's prayer side, two adult Muslim teachers who were not praying whispered about the shootings.

"I can't stop thinking about it," one said. "It's repeating in my mind."

The other one nodded in agreement. "I keep looking at the door, afraid someone will walk in here."

The three of us stared at the door leading to the outside world, and I thought of the violence that occurred when I was in seventh grade: six days after I celebrated my thirteenth birthday, the Columbine High School massacre ushered the issue of school violence, and subsequently school safety, into the discourse of American education. In the years that followed, the next generation of students, educators, and administrators became accustomed to locked doors that required codes or identification cards to enter, conversations in the classroom about school shootings, which seemed to increase in frequency every year, and school shooter and bomb drills that became as customary as fire drills. I acclimated to zero-tolerance policies, the threat of school violence from insiders and outsiders, as well as the discussion and preparation for said violence, but I never felt like it could walk through a door and threaten a lesson, a prayer.

While staring at the doors leading to the parking lot and the adjacent plot of grass the students used for recess, I suddenly felt aware of a reality that I hadn't experienced before working at a Muslim school: there were people who would inflict violence against children who were learning the tenets of their faith, against a culture continually branded as terrorists and extremists after 9/11 and other attacks, against a religion whose etymology was derived from the word *salem*, or peace. For the first time, I understood the fear my students must have felt every time they left their homes wearing traditional hijabs, *abayas*, *thobs*, or *koffis*. For my students and their families, to openly express their faith was to make themselves open targets for hate.

Both teachers met my eyes, as if acknowledging a space for my thoughts and opinions. I didn't know how to explain that I felt as though I had no right complaining, no right joining a conversation about what had happened the previous day in North Carolina, because I had the privilege of never living in a society that hated me or my beliefs to the extent where I feared for my life or the lives of my friends and family. My two coworkers had acknowledged me as their equal, but I wasn't. I said nothing.

In September of 2015, another Louisville mosque a short distance from the school's was spray-painted with colorful words that darkly pronounced "Arabic is the language of Nazis"; "Moslems—leave Jews alone!"; "This is for France" (likely a reference to the *Charlie Hebdo* office attack of January 2015; the subsequent attacks in Paris wouldn't occur for another two months). Louisville mayor Greg Fischer asked residents to help paint over the graffiti, saying to the throngs of people that gathered at the mosque, "Extremism of any kind will not be tolerated in our city and in our country." By then, seven months after the North Carolina shooting, I'd acquired a basic understanding of how to reply to my students' questions about hate and intolerance, how to navigate my response to the ways the world reacted to Islam and Muslims.

Back in the classroom after prayer, I watched my students tie their frayed shoelaces, and I told them to place their editorials in their writing folders, which I then collected among a sea of bewildered looks. When I instructed the students to take out a blank piece of paper, one student stared at me before asking why we weren't finishing our assignment. In a way, I understood the question: we'd been diligently working on our papers for a week, and I'd told them right before prayer to focus on our class assignments above all, as if this class were more important than the feelings stirred by an act of violence against a group that had been already been victimized so many times in the past years.

I scanned the classroom before telling the students that I wanted them to write letters to the families of the three Muslim students who were killed. I explained to the students that I'd learned that the Muslim community was a kind, welcoming community, and that these families needed that community and its support. It didn't matter, I emphasized, that they were in Kentucky and that the families were in North Carolina. It didn't matter that they were close to a decade younger than the three deceased young Muslims or that the families of the deceased didn't know them. What mattered, I told my students, was that they were part of a community and had voices within that community. What mattered the most was that those families knew they weren't alone.

And my students, the ones who incessantly chattered through class every day, fell silent. They hunched over notebook paper and scratched out and erased words and mumbled lines to themselves. They didn't consider their friends' thoughts or ask me how to spell a word or even so much as complain. They worked so diligently that when class was over, I had to gently remind a few that they could finish their letters for homework that night.

My students wrote pages and pages, and I mailed their letters to both families. The words are beautifully forgiving, humbling, inspiring, and loving. Not one student blamed Craig Stephen Hicks or expressed rage toward him. A few students urged forgiveness, and one explained that the family had to be brave, even in the throes of grief, and especially in a world that was very anti-Muslim. If the families accepted and showed their tears, my student explained, then the world would witness their strength.

Two days after the shootings in North Carolina, one of the seventh graders approached my desk before class began, grinned, and gave me a handwritten note that read: *Ms. Shannon, thanks for yelling at us and teaching us to be better people.* I silently vowed to yell less, and then I hung the note on the wall next to my desk. I look at it frequently, especially during days filled with frustration because there are more students who haven't completed their homework than those who have, or the students are unmotivated, loud, or disrespectful. I look at that note when I want to quit and find a job with fewer headaches and less stress, shorter hours and paid overtime, and better salary and benefits. But when I see those words scrawled on lined notebook paper, I think: *I'm not doing the teaching; I'm the one being taught. Better people. They are becoming better people.*

I used to find faith in my belief that words have the power to shape, change, and impact lives, yet that conviction feels unfounded and naive now because my understanding is constantly shifting and molding each day. Whenever class ends and the students rush out into the hall in a wave of books and binders, laughing with friends or complaining about homework, I canvass the empty classroom and the chairs scattered around long tables, and I begin collecting the forgotten pencils and crumpled notebook paper, the words written in loops and slants and blocks, and I think that there are still so many words left to learn and even more that have remained unsaid.

Trust Fall

Leslie Hill

The spring sunshine nearly blinds me as I balance precariously, standing on the edge of the picnic table, while eight grade-nine students and my colleague, Paul, shout encouragement. I like to be in control, not a bad thing in a teacher, and at this moment I'm afraid. My "family" group stands in two rows on the ground behind me, hands locked around the wrists of the person opposite them.

"Fall, Leslie. Don't be scared. Sir and me will catch you where you're widest."

I'm supposed to fall backward into their outstretched arms. It's the last of eight group-building exercises on our first afternoon together at this outdoor education center. I've survived all the others, the problem-solving tasks, the group coordination projects, even the uncomfortably intimate moment of two teachers and eight students teetering together on one large tree stump. But I'm failing the trust test. I'm no longer sure I like groups.

I glance back and down. From this height they all look small. Even Paul is slightly shorter than I am, and I bet he weighs less. I feel panicky, although everyone else landed safely, including Jackie, the tall, heavy girl from my school. She meets my eyes and says: "You can do it, Miss. You caught me; I'm not going to let you fall." I grit my teeth; it's time to die trying.

I turn back to face the sun, stand ramrod straight as instructed, shut my eyes, and topple like a pine tree. When I open my eyes, I'm wrapped in arms and the faces above me are smiling. They stand me on my shaky legs. After a few seconds, I begin to breathe again and smile back.

———

Students from ninety-seven different countries attended the seven high schools in Toronto's inner-city borough of York in 1977. Racial tensions seethed just below the surface and sometimes boiled over. It probably didn't help that the teaching staff were generally white and middle class, like me. As an experiment, the board of education decided to try a five-day residential anti-racist leadership program, situated at their outdoor education center some sixty miles outside the city. Each school sent five students and one teacher. Despite the high cost of the program, its early success persuaded the administration to fund it twice a year: once in the fall, once in spring. The hope was that an ongoing seed group of ten students per year in each school would defuse racial tensions before they blew up.

In the spring of 1981 the principal of my high school suggested that I "volunteer" to be the staff advisor for the next Pine River Multicultural Leadership Program. I knew little about the program then, but I knew when I was being set up. I narrowed my eyes. "Why me?"

"You're young, you're single, you still have energy. You've been teaching what—ten years?"

"Nine. So you think I should take on a bunch of kids from seven schools, twenty-four hours a day, for five days?"

"Sure. They're the cream. Leadership material, high grades. Those are the ones who go on this program. And there are other staff members there; you're hardly alone. Besides, I think you can learn something."

"What?"

But at that moment the secretary stuck her head into the office to say the police were there and could he come. Police arrivals were not unusual in my high school, but it definitely meant the end of the conversation.

I headed off to my next class: thirty grade-ten students, restless with hormones and springtime, and less than receptive to studying poetry. They shredded one of my favorite poems in fifteen minutes flat. Too late I remembered that I had resolved never to teach poems I really liked.

"Come on, Miss, when you gonna give this poetry shit a rest?" said Joe, a thin, pimply boy, whom I found reading a *Muscle & Fitness* magazine underneath his desk instead of "This Was My Brother." "Hey, don't take that!" he pleaded. "It's my future! *Miss!*"

"Can't we read poetry outside?" grumbled Carlotta, the girl behind him, gazing out to the field where a boys' physical education class was playing baseball. "I'm sure I'd appreciate it more in the sunshine. It's spring, Miss. Don't you have any heart?"

"No. Now, write me either a paragraph or a poem, about a hero in your own life. Try to make the reader, me, *feel* why your subject is a hero. A page in length. Due tomorrow."

The inevitable wail of protest swelled, then ebbed.

"No, I *didn't* say it had to be a poem. It *can* be a poem. But try to use some of the poetic devices we've been discussing. You've got fifteen minutes to start it. *Yes*, Glenford, of course it's for marks. You wouldn't do it otherwise."

By the time they exited, pushing and shoving to escape, I had a headache, and the prospect of doing something completely different for a week felt attractive.

I said yes to the Pine River Multicultural Leadership Program.

Later I would ask myself how a control freak like me ended up in a situation where she's not a leader at all, just one more vulnerable member of a group, but the truth is I didn't do the research. I walked in and got blindsided.

Did the principal really believe I'd learn from the week? Perhaps. But I imagine he chose me because he thought I was a good teacher, dependable, professional, hard working. I thought I was a good teacher too. I was thirty-one, and I still liked my job after nine years in a tough school, where the student population was more than two thousand, two-thirds male, 70 percent immigrant. It never occurred to me that my comfort zone with students depended on barriers and boundaries.

The program was not for several weeks, but the next week, there was a staff orientation meeting one day after school, at the board of education office. Eight of us clutched coffees around the table; Paul Sutton was the only person I knew. Paul had taught at my school for a couple of years before he'd been promoted to another school. I didn't know him well; in fact I'd never noticed how blue his eyes were.

"The program will involve both indoor discussion groups and outdoor activities. You'll be involved in both, but the Pine River teachers will run the outdoor parts," said Rod McColl, who organized and ran the week. "We begin with group building in 'families,' each one a mix of kids from the seven different schools, and discuss race and racism later in the week. We know that ignoring the racial tension doesn't work, so this program is an alternative approach. I look forward to your input afterward. Of course," he added, "it's good professional development for staff too."

I wondered about the professional development aspect for a moment, as he handed out the manuals, and then forgot it. I didn't teach grade nine, and now I had only three weeks to find five students of varying ethnic backgrounds, leadership ability, and academic strength, get their permission forms in, and organize lesson plans for the classes I'd be leaving behind me.

The two biggest cultural groups in my own school were Italian and Caribbean students and they didn't coexist easily. But there was also tension between different Asian groups, between Caribbean and East Indian, Caribbean and African, and Ethiopian and Eritrean students, even the few Serbs and Croatians in the system. Teachers weren't immune to charges of racism either.

My focus had always been narrower, more pragmatic. Did my students, regardless of race and gender, understand the skills required and the materials covered? Measurable objectives. Outcome-based learning. Those were my concerns.

———

Stuffed partridge, red-winged blackbirds, flickers, blue jays, and crows stare glassily down from the walls surrounding the four long tables of staff and students, who've been divided into "family" groups of eight or nine students. It's lunchtime. I rode up on the bus this morning with the students in near silence and it's still unnaturally quiet, thirty-five kids and thirteen teachers and only the scrape of forks on plates and the clink of a glass here and there. The kids don't know each other or us yet and everyone is wary. Paul sits across the table and two seats down from me. We're both new to the program but we're teamed as the "parents" of this family. He looks as if he can cope. Maria, the girl next to me, tries to fork up noodles, sprays tomato sauce over the table, and mutters, "Spaghetti is no kinda meal to eat with strangers."

"What animal or bird would you be if you could choose, and why?" Paul says to our group of eight that night. He is leading the first of our indoor group exercises.

Our family meeting place is the center area of the boys' dorm between the washroom and the bedrooms. No chairs. The floor is hard, the carpet a shabby brown. There's a draft from the bedrooms and a faint smell of urine from the washroom.

Carol, a round-faced Jamaican girl, squirms and complains until one of the others leans absent-mindedly into her and then she settles. When it's her turn she says she wants to be a koala bear because they look so cuddly and everyone likes them. I feel an unexpected rush of tenderness and a prickling behind my eyes.

The Pine River outdoor education teacher leads us on a night hike. He carries the only flashlight; he wants these city slickers to experience the dark. Stars pepper the night sky. The kids giggle, shriek, and jostle each other as we feel our way along the gravel road that weaves through forest, fields, hills, and valleys of this two-hundred-acre property. I drop back to the tail end of the group, hoping for less noise. A tall boy I haven't met glides like a shadow nearby. As we emerge from the woods I catch a glimpse of his grim expression in the starlight.

"Are you okay?" I ask.

"Okay, yes. But this—I am used to the dark but not the noise." He pauses. "My family comes from Afghanistan. We walked for many nights like this to escape the fighting, always at night, only when there was no moon. Hid in the day. If we had been caught we would have been shot. I saw people who were. It took more than a month. This—hike—makes me remember."

I don't say much while the kids eat their evening snack and retreat to the dorms. I'm too tired, too overwhelmed. Paul pours me a cup of tea and sits across the table from me while we wait for lights-out.

"I wonder about Jackie," he says. "One of yours, right? She's so heavy. And so watchful. I wasn't sure we'd catch her on the trust fall."

I hadn't been either. "Jackie will be okay. It's Tony who's going to drive me crazy. He's got the attention span of…of…"

"A flea. I know. I brought him." I grin at his rueful expression.

"Carol complains a lot," I say.

"Yeah, but she really responds to being touched, have you noticed? It doesn't seem to matter who, but she needs a hug or a shoulder rub or even a punch on the arm, especially at the beginning of an activity."

"Touched!"

He looks at me. "It's not a big thing. There was a lot of physical contact this afternoon."

"I know but…" I feel exhausted. Touch *is* a big thing. I never touch students. Actually I rarely touch anyone unless it's a boyfriend. And as I haven't had a date in four years, not since I decided independence was better than my fiancé's emotional abuse, touch is huge.

"Have a cookie."

I eat one and feel comforted. "It's just—all this is so personal. I'm not used to it," I say. In my classroom, a desk and a pile of marking stand between me and thirty students who call me Miss. I know about their writing skills and their classroom behavior, but nothing more. I've never really wanted to know more. This—I'm not sure I can cope. How many people here have had the kind of experiences the boy from Afghanistan talked about tonight? Not me. I've been physically safe my whole life. How can I contribute anything to this program?

Later that night I lie awake on my narrow bunk bed in the staff cabin. If I've been too sheltered to lead a group here, should I even be teaching in an inner-city school?

I'm awake for a long time.

Maybe it's lack of sleep that leaves me fighting back tears in our family group the next morning. I'm leading the "significant person" exercise: identify someone who is important to you and say why. My significant person is my mother, who died three years ago. I'm confident in my choice until I get to why. Then my voice falters without warning. I'm horrified. My real-life family lives in a no-cry zone. Even death isn't considered sufficient cause for a public display of tears. I'd rather die than break down now in front of students. My neck and jaw tighten. I mutter how supportive my mother was. I don't want to admit that I overlooked her and hero-worshipped my father. In the void left by her death I saw at last that she was the heart of the family. My father married someone else within months, while the rest of us grieved. One or two kids look oddly at me, as if they know they're only hearing a fraction of the truth.

Paul's significant person is his father, who came to all his sports games when he was young, even though they don't talk a lot these days. The boys gravitate toward Paul and I can see why. He's much more relaxed and easygoing than I am. The kids mostly choose friends as significant people, although Maria says softly that her grandmother is important because she loves her more than anyone else does.

By lunchtime I'm exhausted, but I enjoy the afternoon outdoor work project. Paul and I are just members of the group; we're not in charge. The task is to build a bridge across a small trout stream deep in the woods so people don't disturb the trout eggs. As we work it's easy to pick out the leaders, the distracted ones, the thinkers, the complainers in our family. Paul is right about Carol; when Marcos grabs her arm and smiles at her she stops complaining and starts to work. The smallest boy, Randy, is clearly a leader; he's bright, practical, and the others listen to him.

The woods are full of trilliums, shining like stars in the grass.

The next day the focus shifts to racism. Paul leads the exercise. We're asked to identify a moment in which we've experienced discrimination, on any basis, sex, race, body type, age. We need to describe the situation and say how we feel about it. Fortunately we only have time to talk about a few. I have no example—none—and I'm ashamed. Teachers are supposed to be experts, but everyone in this group knows more about obstacles and survival than I do. Even Paul experienced a lot of discrimination in Japan, where he taught English for four years. But it's Carol's story that stands out for me, Carol with her round face and glowing smile, her need for love.

"This guy phoned my house by accident last fall, a wrong number, and we started to talk. We laughed and joked and later he phoned me on purpose." They got along so well they decided to meet at a McDonald's halfway between their schools. It's a sweet story. Then she pauses and I remember this is about discrimination. My shoulders hunch involuntarily.

"I saw him standing outside as soon as I got off the bus. I smiled and said, 'Hi, I'm Carol.' He stared at me, said he was waiting for a white girl." When she reminded him how they got there, he said he'd made a mistake and took off.

"I felt real bad." Her voice dwindles. "We got along so well on the phone."

There is silence. Joey looks stricken, Randy stony faced. Maria puts her arm around Carol's shoulder. Tony stares at the floor. I bite my lips to stop their trembling.

The noise at dinner the third night makes my head throb. Kids are laughing and cheerful and talking nonstop. I'm fretting about tonight's exercise, "strength bombardment." Rod McColl said it's the most powerful of the small group leadership exercises. Each person gets two minutes to identify his or her own strengths, and then everyone else in the group gives the person one piece of positive feedback. I'm leading it; Paul is doing the timing. I can't decide whether to ask for a volunteer or choose the first person myself. Paul is comfortable with either, he says. But what if no one is willing to start? What if kids can't name strengths or aren't willing to give positive feedback? What if all that happens is silence?

The boys' dorm now smells of dirty socks as well as urine. No one complains. I explain the exercise, we take a few minutes to think about our strengths, and I tell Randy to start. He glares at me and his lips tighten into a stubborn line.

"I'm timing now," Paul says. And we sit, in silence, for two terrible minutes. Randy refuses to open his mouth. This is a disaster; I sit still but inwardly I'm writhing. When Paul signals the time, I draw a deep breath and begin the feedback.

"I guess I shouldn't have put that pressure on you, Randy. I'm sorry." His eyes widen. "I chose you because I think you have a lot of leadership skill and you've shown it over the last two days. Like the way you directed the group in the work project yesterday, cutting up logs for the bridge over the stream. You got everyone organized and working well. I was impressed."

Randy looks skeptical but turns his eyes to the next person. They all give feedback, some articulate, some not, but they seem genuine. Randy refuses my offer of additional time but he doesn't look angry anymore. He chooses the next person, Maria, who actually speaks. Again the feedback flows in. Maybe it's going to be okay.

When it's Jackie's turn, she looks around the circle. "I'm fat. I know that's not a strength but in my school if you're fat you've only got two choices: go under, give up, and drop out or get stronger and survive.

That's me. Strong and a survivor." She says her teacher recommended her for the program because she is smart and a leader, even though she knows no one in her class wants a fat leader. Her strength shines through her vulnerability and without warning I'm crying, tears spilling helplessly down my cheeks.

After the feedback she picks me to go next. My tears have stopped but words have deserted me. I've been so worried about how they'll cope I haven't thought about my own strengths. For a long moment I'm as silent as Randy. When I begin I'm no longer sure that what I'm saying is true.

"I'm articulate, thoughtful, good at expressing myself." Speech dries up. I grope for more. "I'm positive. I work hard at my job and I like what I do, and—and who I work with, students and teachers both." The silence is unnerving. Two minutes is longer than I had any idea of. Sweat prickles my armpits.

"I'm a good organizer." My face is hot. I look over at Paul. Surely the time is up. He smiles placidly back at me.

"I'm an honest person." Another agonizing silence.

"Time," Paul says. My shoulders slump in relief.

Around me kids lean forward, ready to give me feedback. Carol says she always feels better when I give her a shoulder rub. Randy has never had a teacher apologize to him before. "That's good, Miss, that you can do that." Tony likes my sense of humor. Jackie thinks I'm very sympathetic because I listen "like you're really there, you know?" I feel such shame I can hardly meet their eyes. I'd barely made it through the trust fall. Then it's Paul's turn. He looks at me from across the circle and my heart starts to thud so loudly the whole group must hear it.

"I feel that you are more committed to this week than any of us, that you really want the program to be a success and all of us to get a lot out of it," he says slowly. "I love how much you care."

For a moment I stop breathing. Roles and barriers dissolve, the silence vibrates, the drab colors shimmer.

Another teacher takes my place on the bus to supervise the return trip Friday afternoon. We wave the students off with tears and hugs and shouts. For a few minutes we revel in the quiet, then Paul and I put our bags into his car and hug Rod McColl and the other staff good-bye.

I look back as we turn out of the gravel road, away from the Pine River Center, and see the pine and cedar trees swim together, hiding the entrance. There will be follow-up meetings in the city but it won't be the same.

We are quiet on the way home, both exhausted from the wakeful nights and full days. When I see the layer of dirty, dun-colored air hanging over Toronto I want to turn back.

As Paul wheels his car into my driveway I blurt out, "Would you like to stay and have supper with me? It will just be something out of the freezer but…it would be so nice if you stay." He looks over at me as the car stops.

"I can't," he says, and I think my heart will break. "I'm just too tired to be any kind of company. Can I take a rain check?"

"Of course." I look away so he won't see my eyes. He reaches over and takes my hand.

"I want to see you again. I'm just too tired now."

I risk a glance. He's looking steadily back at me, not smiling. As if he means it. A moment later he passes me my suitcase, gives me a quick hug, and he's gone. I watch his car disappear before I turn to face the doorway of my house, a place that's been a much-needed refuge ever since my mother's death and my father's remarriage. Now it feels—empty. I can't imagine returning to school on Monday. Eventually I find my key and unlock the door.

I spend the weekend alone, trying to make sense of this new world. Teaching has got to mean more than a love of the subject, or a commitment to hard work. Can I really deal with the emotional realities of students' lives when they cross over academic lines? What about boundaries? Can I stay present emotionally as well as intellectually, see students as complete people, not just bodies in desks? Do I still think the structure of a sentence is what's most important when an

Afghani boy relives a long, danger-filled trek through mountains or a girl grieves over a potential relationship lost because she is black? Can I stay tough in the classroom once I've learned more about my students?

I will have left teaching before I understand that it's my own emotional chaos that demands control to feel safe. Right now my heart feels split open. Do I trust that Paul will phone me? Do I trust myself to be real at work, to come into the classroom with openness and compassion and acceptance? Do I trust the students enough to be that vulnerable?

I'll have to try.

Joe

Jane Bernstein

In the fall of 1980, while waiting on line to use a portable toilet at the start of the New York City Marathon, I met the man who convinced me to teach a writing workshop at my house. It was a frigid morning, and I was passing the time bouncing on my toes, hugging myself, and chatting with strangers. The day before, I'd moved from my longtime home in New York City to a New Jersey town near my husband's workplace, where I knew no one, and I was feeling jittery, inside and out. So when I found out that the interesting man waiting with me on the Port-o-San line was practically my neighbor, it seemed an amazing piece of luck.

It was a long wait for the race to begin, and we had plenty of time to talk. That was how I learned that Paul was a psychiatrist who'd co-written a guide to physical fitness with a friend named Joe. While I was dancing in place on that frigid morning, I must have told him I'd published a novel and had taught part-time at Rutgers-Newark for two years. I suppose I also confessed that I didn't know anyone in the town where I'd just moved, because he said he had a great group of runner friends and encouraged me to call when I got home.

I did call, and we ran together a week or so after the race—and for the next ten years. Paul had other reasons for urging me to contact him. He wanted to learn how to write in a more personal way about his childhood in Newark. His friend Joe had also been looking for someone to help him with his writing. Joe had been in an Italian prison camp during World War II and for a decade had been working on a manuscript about his experiences. Paul was sure there were plenty of others who wanted to learn more about writing. He asked if I'd consider teaching at my house.

I no longer recall how much time passed between that icy morning in Staten Island and when I agreed to Paul's suggestion. I can't remember what I charged or whether I provided refreshments. There was only the surprise of realizing that I'd missed teaching. Though I'd loved my students, all of them first-generation college-goers, I'd never thought of myself as a teacher and had viewed the Rutgers job as a way to subsidize my writing. When my daughter was born the year before, I hadn't considered teaching elsewhere. Not until Paul's proposition.

The second surprise was how easy it was to round up a few other students. Two were spouses of men who worked at Bell Labs, as my husband did. Sam, the owner of a nearby bookstore, brought a couple of local people. Glen, my former student at Rutgers, took the train in from Hoboken. And then there were Paul and Joe.

I remember meeting Joe that first night: a tall, trim man in a sport jacket, thin hair swept straight back. He was soft-spoken, and stooped, as if to make himself less of a presence. I remember him sitting with the others on chairs I'd bought at garage sales, in a room the realtor had called the "solarium" when she showed us this charmless old house, the only one we could afford in this tony suburb of New York. Joe listened intently to whatever was read aloud. Polite. Reserved. Sam the bookstore owner asked in private if Joe was a minister.

I must have known Joe's last name by then—Frelinghuysen. It was a name nearly everyone who lived in New Jersey had heard. Frelinghuysen was the name of a major thoroughfare in Newark, a middle school in Morristown, and an arboretum in Morris County, where Joe's forebears had settled in the 1700s. A Frelinghuysen had been an officer in the army under George Washington and a member of the New Jersey Convention that had ratified the Federal Constitution, and there had been Frelinghuysens in public service and the military in nearly every generation. According to a *Washington Post* list of American political dynasties, the Frelinghuysens came in seventh place, just below the Bush family.

Before Joe asked if I'd help him with his manuscript, I'd heard pieces of his story from Paul during our long runs. Joe had been a captain in the army when he'd been captured by the Germans in North Africa and taken to prison camps in Italy, where for ten months he lived on scraps of food. He tried to escape and failed, taught himself basic Italian, and adhered to a strict exercise schedule. He believed that discipline, keeping physically fit, was the reason he'd survived. On his third escape attempt, he and another American soldier managed to get free. They hid in the forest for weeks, racing from enemy fire, close to starvation. A family of Italian farmers, "peasants," Paul called them, risked their lives by feeding and sheltering the American soldiers. After the war, Joe returned to the small town in Italy where the family had lived. When their daughter and her husband expressed interest in immigrating to the United States, Joe brought them over. He supported them financially, helping them settle in New Jersey, finding work for the husband, initially in his family's dairy business, staying in close touch.

Paul was the one who told me of Joe's generosity. Joe never told me this part of his story—and he never spoke about it in the workshop. When he sat with the others, a good-natured group of beginners, he listened to their stories and brought nothing of his own. I don't remember when he asked if I'd work privately with him or exactly why I agreed, though I suppose I said yes because I liked Joe and was attracted by his openness and receptivity. He gave me his manuscript to read. Then he began to come to my house an hour or so before the others gathered in the solarium.

I can still see us, sitting side by side at my husband's desk in the small room he used as an office before our second daughter was born. Joe in a sweater and sport jacket: tall, lean, attentive, nearing seventy. He sits in a Danish office chair on casters. His manuscript is open on the desk, lit by twin lamps that clamped onto either side of the oak desktop. Typewritten—because this is still the era of landline telephones and typewritten manuscripts. And there I am beside him. I'm thirty-one or thirty-two years old, dark hair, turtleneck, jeans, holey socks: all my socks have holes from the splintery pine floor in the attic, where I write.

I am inexperienced, raw, compared to Joe. Young. His faith in me feels touching or naive. What have I done to deserve it? Run a couple of marathons, published a novel and some newspaper articles. Yes, I taught at Rutgers, but as a part-timer, officially a "coadjutant instructor of journalism and mass media," a position I'd fallen into without training or prior experience, and was astonished to find I liked, since in my twenties I'd been set against teaching and motherhood, which I'd viewed as default activities for women of limited horizons. And now, while I sit beside this man who trusts me to help him with his war story, my little girl is in the bathtub, singing "Baby Beluga" with her dad, and I am feeling the hole in my sock and wondering what I might say to Joe and how I might phrase it.

The sentences that fill the pages of his manuscript are flawlessly constructed: Joe majored in English at Princeton. He knows Latin, knows the formal rules of grammar, which I don't. When Joe came home from his wartime ordeal, his wife bought him a Dictaphone and had him record his story, so the pages are rich in specific detail. And yet there is a deadness in his descriptions of the troop maneuvers, the land and weather, the physical effort he exerted, the people in his midst, who for all their scowling, squinting, grunting, and muttering, never come alive. Nor does he, on these pages.

Joe is the most respectful person I have ever encountered. I've seen this in the writing group. I've seen it in the way he backs up when my little girl toddles in, with no glimmer of impatience at being interrupted. I can feel it in the way he trusts me. It's easy being kind to Joe; the challenge is being candid. To falsely praise this work denies him the chance to rewrite it effectively. It's disrespectful.

I am certain that Joe has no interest in telling a story of derring-do. He doesn't think of himself as a hero. Whatever has driven him to work on his manuscript for a decade is deeper and more complex, although I cannot say what it is, nor can he. The title of his work in progress includes the word *survival,* so I know he wants to write about his ordeal. Yet he seems to lack the language to tell such a story. Sometimes I think he has no access to what I would call an interior life.

Each time I ask what it was like—to go without food, to scrabble alone in the woods—he points to his sentences, as if together we might crack them open and find what they lack.

I try a different angle: It's a survival story, isn't it? I ask.

Yes.

To tell a story about your trials and how you emerged intact means going beneath the surface. You want to give your reader the chance to experience what you did, to be in your skin. Do you agree?

Yes, he says. This is his intention.

What did you *feel* when you were running through the woods at night? You're hearing enemy gunfire. Can you put yourself back at a particular moment? Was it day? Night? Had you eaten anything? Had a drink? From what source? Did you worry the water might be bad?

The first year I taught at Rutgers my classes were standard journalism courses of that era—headline writing, copyediting, reporting. Nothing seemed more important than pressing the fundamentals upon my students, making sure they understood craft. Craft was still my focus when I was able to teach a fiction workshop the following year. Although I borrowed techniques and styles from my favorite teachers in graduate school, I still felt it was my job to teach them about scenes and dialogue and point of view, to look at stories as if we were mechanics opening the hood to check out a car. With Joe, it was different. Even though I could not have said it at the time, at the heart of our discussions was how to get humanness on the page in all its complexity.

I remember saying: Your wife was pregnant when you parted. Did she come to mind? When you were alone in the forest, did you write letters to her in your head? Dream of the past or the future? Your friend, the soldier who helped you escape. He wrenched his knee and urged you to leave him behind and flee alone. Where were you when he first asked? What made you finally agree? What did you feel when you left without him?

And Joe, turning the pages of the manuscript, showing me his sentences: *I hated leaving Dick. Deserting a friend went against the grain.* Asking: Isn't that what I say right here?

I scan the passages on the page and hesitate, worrying that I'm demanding that Joe pull something from memory that he never experienced. When we're apart, I ask myself in shame: Who am I? What audacity to prod him to think and write in a way that's alien to his culture, to his whole way of being. It feels mean-spirited. It makes me dread meeting with him.

Then the next week we're again sitting together at my husband's desk, and something Joe says makes me aware of the shadows of a story not yet written: a man raised in a family with a proud military tradition, haunted by his "failures" as an officer; a man who feels responsible for his own capture, guilty for having left his injured friend behind; a man who was irritable and impatient in his hunger and fear, flawed, frightened, human. I feel sure this is the reason he's kept at this task for so long, that he's driven by all the unpleasant, inchoate *stuff* inside him, and so I push a little, thinking I can help him shape it into a story. I ask questions, try to take him back in time. He listens. Turns the pages of the manuscript, points to a paragraph and waits.

Once, at the end of one of these sessions, Joe looks up at me and says: "I think of you as 'teacher.'"

Teacher. As if I were Annie Sullivan and he were Helen Keller.

When I pull back from this image of the two of us hunched over Joe's typewritten manuscript, out of this room, this house, this town, right out into the world of disco and Pac-Man and Ronald Reagan, I am reminded that our time together was in an era before public confession, before "the age of memoir." A few memoirs were on the shelves, written for the most part by writers or dignitaries in their waning years. Joe had read some of these books. He'd also read and admired *The Naked and the Dead* and *From Here to Eternity*. But this was not yet a time when private figures and celebrities had begun to reveal the kinds of intimate details once considered too personal to air, to let strangers read candid aspects of ordinary and extraordinary human life. Frailty was not yet out of the closet. Joe and I sat together before there were public conversations about PTSD—before the traumas suffered in war were even called PTSD, although there were other names for the most profound of the psychological repercussions some returning soldiers experienced.

When Joe and I sat together, I thought of myself as a fiction writer. I never imagined writing a memoir. Then again, I had never imagined having a child or teaching. I saw my role as helping Joe write a gripping story that would bring me into his past, so I could feel what it had been like to be captured by the Germans, to wake in a prison camp, to starve, to devise the means to keep his sanity. Often I believed this was what Joe wanted, too. But his perfectly constructed sentences were so devoid of immediacy that I had no sense of his life as it was then lived.

I find myself wondering: If there were other voices besides mine, would it have helped Joe tell his story in a deeper way? If he'd read memoirs by other soldiers who'd returned home, shaken and irritable, full of stories that would not recede, would he then be able to render his tale in a different way?

I quit. I stopped meeting with Joe one-on-one because I had nothing more to offer him. For a long time, this is what I believed, so when I thought of Joe, which I often did, sadness and regret rose up. I'd failed and then I'd quit. I'd been presumptuous to keep demanding from this lovely man the kind of story *I* wanted to read, when in the end it was never what he had intended to write.

Now, going over the dates, I see that this version of events is a little harsh. During this period of time, I was struggling to complete a second novel, co-writing a screenplay, taking care of my little girl. When I look at a calendar, I realize that I must have been pregnant when I quit working with Joe, since my second daughter, Rachel, was born in the fall of 1983. She was not a healthy baby: after her arrival, her physical and intellectual disabilities took much of my attention and altered everything in my family's life and in the life we had imagined for her. So maybe I hadn't quit in such a petulant way.

Also: Joe and I stayed in touch after we stopped working together. I remember a long conversation with him, during which he defined *courage* as "grace under pressure." I also remember running a 10K race in Morris County with Paul, then driving to Joe's and having lunch in the dining room of his grand old house, with its portraits of forebears on the walls. Joe's wife came by to greet us, and I shrank in my chair, feeling sweaty and self-conscious in a singlet and tiny running shorts. It reminded me how comfortable I'd always felt with Joe. His good manners did not hide any judgment. This was the way it had been when we'd sat together in my shabby house, Joe beside me, listening.

Over the next years, Joe continued to work on his manuscript. He'd found someone else to help, a man who taught at a local community college. I tried to work on my manuscript, too, but after Rachel's birth, the novel I'd promised my editor vanished along with all of its characters. My agent suggested I write a "nonfiction book" about parenting a child with disabilities. At first I said no. I did not think I had the inclination or ability to write such a book. But her suggestion sparked an urge to write about the life that was now mine, so different from the one I'd had before. I had not seen such a life depicted elsewhere. So I began to draft a story that I now see was much like the one I wanted Joe to write: a story about daily life during a tumultuous time. It wasn't called a memoir when it was accepted for publication, since that was not yet a marketing tool, but that's what it was.

Two years after my book, *Loving Rachel*, was released, a small press in Kansas accepted Joe's manuscript. By then he'd been working on it for twenty years. In March 1991, a writer with an interest in military history reviewed *Passages to Freedom* in the *New York Times Book Review*, calling it "an exciting tale of physical and moral courage put to the severest of tests."

The book wasn't so different from Joe's manuscript as I remembered it, although I could see the effort Joe had expended weaving into the narrative a few paragraphs about his family's illustrious military past, and a sentence here and there that hinted at the "bitter strains" of being separated from his wife, the anguish he felt as a prisoner when reminders of his family and home rose, despite his attempts to push them from his thoughts. Several grainy photographs gave the book an extra dimension.

In an "Author's Note," Joe explained that his intention had been to write a personal story, not a military book. "The human side always seems to be involved in questions from young people…who ask… 'What was it like to be caught up in those disasters? How did you feel?' I have tried very hard here to answer such questions, though at times being frank and honest with myself proved painful indeed."

I must have congratulated Joe on his achievement. It seems impossible to imagine I neglected calling him or writing a note, but I have no recollection of doing either. I'd like to believe that this memory was overshadowed by other events in my life: the month before the *New York Times* review of Joe's book, I'd accepted a teaching position at Carnegie Mellon University, and soon after, I moved to Pittsburgh to join the creative writing program there. But I can't say for certain. I recall Paul telling me Joe was "disappointed" to hear I was moving to Pennsylvania, a reaction I understood, given his family's unbroken history in New Jersey.

I made a life in Pittsburgh. Over the next years, I raised my kids, wrote as much as I could, ran. I learned to love hills. I became a teacher. I taught for the pleasure of sharing what moved or delighted me, and to open my students to a range of literature and film they hadn't encountered. I taught for the chance to mentor students in their own artistic pursuits. We still talked about craft, but craft as the means to get to the heart, and not the heart itself.

Sometimes I worked independently with a student, and while sitting together, going over a manuscript and talking about the challenge of getting life to rise up from the sentences, Joe came to mind. I thought of his trust in me and his determination. Whenever I was asked about memorable students, Joe was the person I named first. Sometimes, while running, I composed a letter telling him some of this. The letters stayed in my head.

Then one Sunday in late December 2005, I picked up the *New York Times Magazine* to read their turn-of-the-year feature, "The Lives They Led." Among the one-page stories that marked the passing of notable people whose merits or exploits were often not widely known, was a story about Joe. That was how I found out he had died at ninety-three.

"He was prodded to his feet by rifle barrels. This was northern Tunisia, Nov. 29, 1942. Just after midnight, following faulty intelligence, he had led his men into enemy territory." This is how Sara Corbett's gripping narrative begins. "Now he stood surrounded, trembling, sickened by the gravity of his mistake. A German sergeant jammed a pistol into Joe Frelinghuysen's gut and joked that he'd been easier to catch than a rabbit."

Corbett's story is terse and vivid, and tells of Joe's "self-recrimination," and his difficult homecoming, "snappish, disoriented." It relates Joe's postwar return to Italy, that he'd found the family that had sheltered him and helped the younger generation emigrate. "Some soldiers put war behind them, and others live it forever," Corbett wrote. "Joe Frelinghuysen wanted only to make amends."

I remembered sitting with Joe, his manuscript on the desk and the shadow story I sometimes believed was in his grasp. Then these words, written by someone else, echoed in my mind. Self-recrimination. The desire to make amends.

I found Joe's book the other day in a section of my bookshelf reserved for books written by people dear to me. The glue had hardened, and when I opened the cover, all the pages came loose. I had forgotten the inscription: "For Jane, with many thanks for your assistance with this book. It was sometimes stern, but always brilliant and honest. I loved the workshop and the tutoring, and shall always be grateful, especially for our friendship. With much love, Joe. July 1990."

I tried to focus on his kind words about our friendship. I tried to focus on the closing: "Love, Joe." But these words, "sometimes stern," filled me with regret, and made me wonder if I had been too harsh. There was so much I did not know—as a teacher, a mother, a writer. I never told him I enjoyed our time together, never told him how much I learned from him. He was the student who showed me that to teach writing is so much more than teaching craft. I never said, could not have said at the time, how surprised and undeserving I felt of his respect. *I think of you as "teacher."*

Since reading of his death, I've wanted to write about my time with Joe. Years have passed, and the need has not lessened. I suppose the need to revisit the past is a necessary trait for all memoirists, but I'm also driven by self-recrimination, by the desire to make amends, whether or not I've done harm. My own fervent, impossible desire is not only to enter the world we left behind, but to relive it, this time with forbearance and grace, as if eventually I'll meet the impossible standards I set for myself. Maybe in this way, Joe and I are alike.

Teaching for America

Kate Ver Ploeg

It is already 11:00 p.m. Sticky and sweating, I sit in my underwear on my bare living room floor, every window thrown wide. Paper handouts encircle me within arm's length: readings lists, writing prompts, best practices, templates, models, suggestions. I have not had time to buy a desk. Three weeks since moving to the southern tip of Texas, two weeks after the start of school, I have only just bought a bed.

America *needs* you, they told me. Its students are *waiting*. Yes, I thought, yes. I'd graduated valedictorian of my New Hampshire high school class; I'd maintained a perfect college GPA. I believed in education, social service, the right to achieve. When Teach for America hired me at the close of my senior year of college, I believed I could make a difference. I was twenty-three.

In the close heat of my bungalow, I prop my head up, elbows next to my laptop balanced on a board between two chairs. I scan, I search, I click. Cheery, personified pencils smile next to lists of nouns. Punctuation flutters under falling autumn leaves—the period, the exclamation point, the maple leaf, the question mark. I stare again at the single typed sheet next to my computer, titled "English as a Second Language II Curriculum." This is what Veterans Middle School has handed me for guidance. *Nouns*, it lists. *Verbs. Reading Comprehension.* Web page after web page listing link after link. Christopher Columbus sails his three ships into seas of prepositions; Pilgrims doff their buckled hats to explanations of subjects and predicates. Read a Pilgrim story, answer Pilgrim questions, make a Pilgrim hat. How about a five-fingered turkey?

How about the alphabet? I think, realizing, sickened, that my students will not be able even to read the directions. I search out preschool curricula. *A* stands for apple; caterpillars crawl over *C*. Cherubic white toddlers cavort. I think of Javier, my sixteen-year-old eighth grader who struggles to read even in Spanish. No, I think, no. No, no, no.

I expected this to be difficult. I expected my students to be reading below grade level. I did not expect this: on the reading diagnostic I handed out the first week to my intermediate-level class of sixth through eighth graders, four of my twelve students scored "Frustrated" on the pre-K reading passage. Two merely stared at me blankly.

My five weeks of summer training with Teach for America focused on how to improve middle school, not elementary, reading levels and manage classroom disruptions. Make it fun, advised my trainers, who were barely older than me. Read aloud. Use proximity. Incentives. They did not explain how to teach reading from the beginning, and my memory of learning to read is only one: I sat at a curved, bean-shaped table and held a book open before me. There were pictures of animals in winter. I was five. I do not know how to teach a teenager to read for the first time, let alone read in a language he can barely speak.

I look again at the clock. Quarter of midnight. I imagine myself walking into that clean, white classroom tomorrow morning, my students staring at me, waiting—I start to cry. Panicked, exhausted, I imagine a hole opening in the floor next to me. I throw myself down. I don't sink. Sitting up, I blink to focus through my tears. I keep searching.

My alarm will ring me awake in five hours.

Here in the heart of the Rio Grande Valley, orange groves and Rio Star grapefruit trees stand in neat, hazy rows, squeezed by acres of slick asphalt still smelling like tar. They line up beside Highway 89, strung with shiny new Super Walmart and Super Target and Best Buy stores, each the size of a cold city block without windows. Air-conditioning units hum and drip. Beyond this thin, commercialized strip, each evening falls quiet, almost like the New Hampshire woods where I grew up. But here forests are groves, and hills are highway overpasses. Houses are one story, not two, with concrete walls, not clapboard, and parched patches of dirt for yards.

Here in Donna, Texas, home of the Donna High Redskins, nearly everyone is Hispanic. Arriving from Mexico, many have built their homes with what is cheap and available, mixing concrete with corrugated fiberglass and brick, tacking on rooms as families grow with each generation.

I arrived alone. Among Teach for America's twenty-five regions, the Texas-Mexico border was my second choice. Teaching middle school ESL, however, was not. I had imagined teaching high school English—Shakespeare, poetry, conversations about books and ideas. I'd majored in English literature. Two weeks before the start of the school year, I was told: Donna, Veterans Middle School, ESL. I was told I had to accept.

Although Donna is a town of merely fifteen thousand, it boasts five elementary schools and three middle schools, all of which feed into one high school. Nearly half of Donna's residents are younger than eighteen years old. Few earn college degrees. Many more people live uncounted in Donna's *colonias*, impromptu border settlements where plumbing is nonexistent and water trucked in. Everywhere in the Valley, insulation and basements seem less necessary than cinder block stilts. When the rain comes, the fields and roads north and south of the highway turn to mud.

Daniel walked to the store, I write on the empty whiteboard. I underline *Daniel* and circle *walked*—subject, predicate.

Chairs scrape, papers shuffle. My students wait, some looming over their desks like adults masquerading as children, others dangling their feet. Sixth, seventh, and eighth graders, they range in age from eleven to sixteen. This is English as a Second Language, Level II. This is Donna, Texas, 2006. This is me: skinny, short, white. One year out of college.

Turning around, I tap the board with my marker. "Subject." I point. "Predicate." Because these were on the list to teach and I have no idea how people learn to speak English.

I cannot determine the cause of my students' blank stares: Are they bored, confused, shy, or do we lack a common vocabulary? The English words they utter are few and never in entire sentences. And the Spanish I studied in high school, like the *río* two miles south of us, seems to have trickled to an impractical memory.

My stomach feels cold and metallic. The glossy walls glare under the fluorescent lights. I reach for the textbook. "Let's try reading," I say, holding the pages open to a passage about the New York City subway system. I thrust the book toward my students—the way I remember my kindergarten teacher doing for me. "Page five." I tap my finger at the page number and wiggle five fingers.

Squeezed into his desk, shoulders hunched, Ricardo hulks over Esme. He pokes her. She squeals. He laughs loudly, childlike. She hits him.

"Esme! Ricardo!"

I walk over to stand beside them like Teach for America demonstrated during summer training. I begin to read aloud slowly, trying to enunciate, then stop.

"Who would like to read next?" I ask. "Daniel?"

The small, stooped boy before me, so quick to jump from his seat, looks trapped. His eyes bulge like his nickname, *Sapo*—Frog. He looses a frantic stream of Spanish that I cannot understand. Everyone laughs but me. I feel desperate.

"Ricardo?"

Vocal and large, Ricardo is an easy target. Even as I ask, I suspect that this passage about New York's subway is too difficult, too *foreign*, but I have nothing else.

"Ricardo, please read."

When he finally begins, his voice croaks and he trips over words like *the* and *with*, as well as *subway* and *borough*. I prompt nearly every word, and with each falter, I feel increasingly tense, but I am afraid to embarrass him by asking him to stop. Finally, we reach the end of the paragraph. Ricardo wads up a piece of paper and chucks it across the room. His younger brother laughs and ducks. Daniel screams. Chatter rises.

"Let's read the next paragraph together," I call. "Ready? Daniel! Ricardo! Ready? Jonathan, stop!"

Someone, probably the secretary, has taped colored leaves to the window of the school's main office. A pumpkin sits on the front counter. I think of home, where I imagine my family, like a picture from a calendar, picking apples under a crisp blue sky. Here, humidity hangs like a blanket. Temperatures still push 100 degrees, and even in the middle of the night, I kick off the bedsheets.

I wait my turn to sign out for the day. More autumn leaves have been sprinkled around the vase of fabric flowers on the low table next to me. A small, striped loveseat sits under a framed pastel print. The room might look homey, except for the bright white cinder blocks and shiny linoleum floor.

I flip the signature-filled page—Garcia, Hinojosa, Ortiz, Reyna. I am one of very few white teachers here at Veterans Middle School. More than a thousand students, sixth through eighth grade, attend Veterans, but I have seen only one who does not look Hispanic.

School day finished, the front office buzzes with the kind of energy that surges only after students leave. Instead, I have a feeling of curling into myself, of tucking my edges into shadow, and disappearing. I am only trying to survive.

"Ms. Ver Ploeg, how's it going?"

Veterans' principal crows this greeting louder than he should, louder than I'd like, joking, self-satisfied, happy to be done. Mr. Villanueva is a small, compact man. He gels his thinning hair, likes to flirt, and keeps an uneasy but tenacious grip on power.

I intend to say that it's fine, that I am managing, that I am a good teacher. Instead, my shoulders drop; my face sags. "They won't listen to me."

Mr. Villanueva pauses his energetic strutting. "Why didn't you say something?" he yells. I feel acutely aware of the other teachers present, the assistant principal, the dean of instruction. "Which period is the worst?"

I hesitate. I did not expect immediate, direct action. I did not expect to say anything. I am suddenly uneasy about pointing a finger.

"Those kids." He shakes his head. He means those ESL kids, those border-hopping children with spotty school attendance and minimal language skills and those legal residents with low academic success, those needing special education and those on medication and those not sufficiently proficient in English to test for special needs diagnosis, all who have repeatedly failed to pass the state exam, all of whom the school wishes would disappear during testing time, *those* kids. My students. "They don't know how to behave."

"It's period one, isn't it?" he asks, identifying my ESL II class, my lowest-level learners, the students who barely speak English, few of whom are literate even in Spanish. I feel protective of their inabilities. But no, they do not listen to me. They do not do their work. I feel like a failure.

"I'll send over Sergeant Garcia tomorrow." Then he turns, slaps a hand on the counter. "Ms. Escobedo, what are you doing this evening?"

I mumble my thanks. Sergeant Garcia runs Veterans' Junior ROTC program. A muscular man with a quiet voice, he squeezes into civilian clothes only on teacher workshop days. I've heard he is a father. Several days after I confess to Mr. Villanueva, Sergeant Garcia walks into my classroom.

"On your feet!"

Sergeant Garcia's back is drill sergeant straight, his legs splayed. He is the tallest in the room.

My students stumble to their feet. They are awkward, slow; they are surprised.

"Now!"

"Have you been disrespecting Ms. Ver Ploeg?" Sergeant Garcia shouts, and I wince. He pronounces my name as it's spelled—"Ploeg," he yells, with a long *o*, rather than "Ploog."

"You, Ricardo! Daniel! Stand up straight! I hear you don't do your work! You don't listen! You goof around!"

He yells at my students, who are also his students (because Junior ROTC pulls my students and dismisses the honor roll students, college-bound, to band practice and sports). Our students stare at the floor, at each other, at me, everywhere but at the yelling sergeant. I stand near my desk in the corner and force myself not to stare at the floor. I wish I were anywhere but here. We are all silent.

Ricardo, taller than I am; his younger brother, Jonathan; Javier, sixteen, with his spiked hair and a preschooler's vocabulary; Esme, petite and cherubic; Itzel, thin, angry, cautious; Daniel. When Sergeant Garcia yells questions, they mumble their responses, and the sergeant shouts at them to speak up.

He turns to me. Though his size is imposing, his face is soft and he has kind eyes. "Who are the troublemakers?"

I freeze. I wish I could say: *This is a mistake. I made a mistake. Don't bother. I'm sorry.* But I do not want to make this man look foolish. My students turn to stare at me, too, waiting, their expressions wary and small. They look like children. They are children.

I lift my hand weakly and point.

Ricardo, I mumble. Jonathan. Itzel, Esme, Javier. The class and the sergeant wait. When I point to Daniel, he spins around, sags, and throws his head back: "Ay, Miss!"

"Line up!"

I shrink where I stand beside my desk in the corner and watch them go, all but a couple, shuffling out in a line behind the barking sergeant to sprint suicide drills on the track, again and again and again.

I will want to apologize to them—to Ricardo and Jonathan and Javier, Itzel, Esme, and Daniel—for pointing the finger and also for not knowing how to help. For being as bewildered and frustrated and confused as they are. I will try to salvage what little authority I think I still have.

The sun has not yet risen; the air is still cool. The Valley's sky spreads weakly purple before it fades to blue. In Veterans' parking lot, I pull into a space. My car softly shudders off; a clank, a drip, a drop; it's quiet. I step out and tug my canvas bag, heavy with papers and binders, onto my shoulder. When I reach for my lunch, the bag swings down, pulling me forward. I try to push it around to my back and straighten up. I pause.

Fields stretch around me. An early breeze blows. The soft furrows breathe celery, maybe carrots. It must be harvest time again. Sometimes, I think, it is so peaceful here.

"Hey," a teacher yells into the rush of students flooding from class. "Hey!"

The teacher yells at Ricardo, who as far as I can tell has done nothing more than walk out of my classroom and into the hall.

"That boy," he says to me, shaking his head in mild disgust. "*Un payaso.*"

A clown. I stare at Ricardo pushing into the crowd. He wears the seventh grade's navy polo shirt, but even the eighth graders seem to swirl around and below him. He looks back as if he knows we're talking about him and smirks.

Un payaso. For a moment, I want to fight for him, this lumbering thirteen-year-old (maybe fourteen) who barely squeezes into his desk and acts more intent on poking Daniel than learning vocabulary. I want to prove to this teacher, so casually dismissive, that Ricardo is as smart and capable as his own students.

Instead, I turn and walk back into my room, past the poster I've taped above my nameplate, the one I found left behind by last year's tenant: "This is a new day, with new hopes and new dreams." I shut the door.

Before I arrived in Donna, I'd imagined myself as Edward James Olmos in *Stand and Deliver*, as Robin Williams in *Dead Poets Society*. Yet when the movie *Freedom Writers* comes out three months after I begin teaching, I refuse to watch it. "It's a good movie," my friends tell me. "You'll like it. That teacher struggles, too," they add, sensing the root of my hesitation. "She's just like you."

But I don't see it. I imagine Hilary Swank playing the attractive and righteous young teacher and I feel angry: her inevitable, uplifting Hollywood success infuriates me. It doesn't end that way in real life, I think. It's not that easy. We don't all get to play the hero.

I close the door on the last few students running to lunch and turn out the lights. Through the one window in the far wall, the sun burns again in a pale blue sky. Outside, the temperature will be in the nineties.

In the absence of fluorescent humming and a roomful of middle schoolers, I lay my cheek against the cool cinder block walls, still unmarked by graffiti or chipped paint. For a moment I contemplate lying on the uncracked linoleum floor. I know I should bring my lunch to the teachers' room; it's only next door. Instead, I walk to my desk and press play on the small CD player behind my desk. A guitar strums, a plaintive twang eases me into my chair. I have only this one CD. Despite the many I keep at home, I will never remember to bring another.

I put my head down on my desk and close my eyes. I am too tired to eat.

Mayans in East Oakland

Anne Raeff

In May of 2012 my partner Lori and I returned to San Francisco from a two-year stint in North Carolina, where Lori had been the visiting writer at UNC Chapel Hill. When we moved to North Carolina, I had just finished a particularly difficult year at a charter school where many of the students were involved with gangs and had little faith in their abilities and the future. This had not been my first time working in a difficult school, but the hopelessness and violence had gotten to me and I was exhausted. Wanting a break from teaching, I found a job as a server in a fifth-rate Chinese restaurant. This job gave me the flexibility I needed to focus on my writing, but the meager tips and $2.03-an-hour wages were not enough to keep us afloat, so we arrived back home in San Francisco broke.

I needed to get a real job fast, but it wasn't easy getting settled again. For the fall semester I took a position at a private school as a long-term substitute Spanish teacher. I loved teaching at the private school. The students were eager to learn, sophisticated, hardworking, and optimistic about the future and their ability to make the world a better place. I hoped that the teacher on maternity leave for whom I was subbing would realize that she was so in love with her baby that she would not be able to leave it and return to work, but that didn't happen. No one left that school. The teachers worked there until they died, like Supreme Court judges. So at the end of the semester I had to scramble again. Because there was an increase in immigrants coming into California after the holidays, the Newcomer Program at Fremont High School in East Oakland needed another English language development teacher to handle the surge in enrollment for the spring semester. I applied for the job and got it.

Every morning, I was up at 5:00 a.m. so that I could go for a run, get ready, leave the house by 6:45, and walk the fifteen minutes to the Balboa Park BART station in San Francisco, where I took the Fremont or Dublin/Pleasanton train to the Fruitvale station in East Oakland. From there, I walked another twenty minutes to Fremont High School. When I told my friends that I had taken a new job in Fruitvale, they responded with warnings about the neighborhood. "I would drive," they said. "There are shootings there all the time." They sent me links to articles about the woman who was killed by a stray bullet at eight o'clock in the morning. But I dreaded wasting time and energy in commuter traffic more than I worried about the possibility of stray bullets, so I took the train.

From the start I enjoyed the walk from the BART station to the school along Fruitvale's bustling main street, International Boulevard. Already at seven thirty, one could smell the sauces cooking at the taquerías, there was a line at the Mexican bakery, and the *pupusa* and fruit trucks were doing a brisk business. Even the hookers were at their posts at the corner across from the freeway exit, although I never saw anyone paying them any attention. I soon became an International Boulevard regular and exchanged "good mornings" and pleasantries while waiting for the light to change with the other regulars—parents walking their children to school, the man who swept the sidewalks.

There was nothing charming or welcoming, however, about Fremont High School. The building was surrounded by a fifteen-foot-high barbed-wire fence. A guard was posted at the front gate at all times, and seven full-time security officers patrolled the grounds. The fence and guards were not there to keep people out but rather to keep the students in. The buildings were dilapidated and covered with graffiti. The windows were barred, as were the doors, the lockers banged up and dented. There was rarely toilet paper in the bathrooms, and if there was, it was strewn all over the floor. After lunch, the halls and patios were covered with paper plates and half-eaten pizzas, apple cores and purposely squished oranges. When it was windy, napkins flew about, keeping low like ghosts of birds who had died a violent death.

Within the walls of Fremont High School, nestled amid all of the garbage and cursing and the ubiquitous odor of marijuana, was the Newcomer Program. The newcomers at Fremont High School were recent immigrants, mostly from Central America—Guatemala, El Salvador, and Honduras—with a sprinkling of Mexican, Chinese, Vietnamese, and Yemeni students. They took separate, sheltered classes until their English was good enough for them to be mainstreamed, so they were also sheltered from the bad behavior of the American students and were, for the most part, respectful, though many of them had not attended school much in their native countries and were unfamiliar with classroom routines. I had to teach them how to look up at me when I was talking. "One, two, three, look at me," I would say, and they had to put down their pencils and look at me. At first I felt silly saying such things, but they did not laugh. They put down their pencils, looked up, and waited. "Pay attention to Miss," the more mature ones would say to the ones who were not.

In the beginning, when I looked out at them gripping their pencils like first graders, straining to understand, it was difficult to imagine how they had ever managed to come all this way from their villages. Many of the Central American kids had made the journey to the United States on their own in order to join their parents, who had left them in the care of grandparents or aunts and uncles to seek their fortunes in the North. These students hardly remembered their parents, but when a grandmother died or an aunt got remarried and the new husband didn't want them in the house, they came north. Their parents sent them the money for the *coyotes* and the journey, but they had to figure it out for themselves. They had to cross the border into Mexico without getting caught and then travel all the way through Mexico, and cross another border without getting caught. One of my Honduran students, a sixteen-year-old who did not even know the alphabet when he started at Fremont High School and whom I taught how to read in Spanish during lunch and after school, had spent a month locked up in a cellar in Mexico with his friends, waiting for the *coyote* to fetch them. During that month they never saw the light of day. They slept in their clothes on the bare floor without blankets. Once a day someone brought them leftover scraps of food.

Some of my students had tried to cross two or three times before they made it. When they were caught on the Mexican side, they were put on a bus and sent back to their countries. When they were caught on the American side, they got sent to a youth detention center, where they waited while their families went through the necessary legal procedures to get them out. These centers are located all over the country—in Michigan, Oklahoma, Texas, New Mexico. Those who ended up in Michigan saw snow for the first time. My students all had positive memories of their time in the detention centers. Life was simple there. They had their duties—dishwashing, cleaning up the dorms—and they had to attend English classes. The counselors took them ice-skating and swimming. They remembered the names of all of the counselors. Some of the counselors didn't speak Spanish, but they laughed a lot. When everything was finally arranged, their parents paid for them to fly to Oakland. Their ears felt strange when the plane took off and landed, but they weren't scared.

This was in 2012, before the dramatic increase in young people crossing the border led to overcrowding and mistreatment at the detention centers. Still, I was surprised to learn that they had been treated well there. I knew that at detention centers for adults, detainees had died because they were denied necessary health care and were often incarcerated for months, even years, without being permitted to contact their families or a lawyer.

"I'm glad they were nice to you," I said. "It makes me feel better about my country."

"If I had to do it again, I would. I learned a lot from this experience," Julia, who was from El Salvador, said.

In addition to teaching Spanish language arts for Spanish speakers, I taught a double-block introductory, bilingual humanities class. The class was intended to teach the students basic facts about the world, improve their literacy in Spanish, and supplement their English language development class. Most of the students in the humanities class were Mam-speaking Mayans from Guatemala. Almost all of the Mam-speaking students were from the same highland town of Todos Santos Cuchumatán in the department of Huehuetenango. Before they moved to the United States, the families of most of the *todosanteros*, as people from their town were called, had been coffee growers. After the harvest they had to guard the coffee beans night and day to protect them from bandits. When they transported the bags of coffee beans to market, they had to be armed, or bandits would take everything. People died protecting their coffee. Because of the increasing violence and a string of natural disasters, Guatemalans were granted temporary protected status when applying for visas to enter the United States—hence the surge in Guatemalan immigrants in Oakland.

When they arrived in my classroom they did not know that there were planets or that the earth revolved around the sun. They did not know that the world was divided into continents. They did not know the difference between a city and a state and a country. They knew that they were in California, but they didn't quite understand the difference between California and Oakland. When I asked them the name of the department that Todos Santos was in, they were not able to tell me.

The Mayan students spoke Spanish at varying levels of proficiency. The few who had had the opportunity to go to school beyond the second or third grade spoke quite well, though they tended to regularize irregular verbs, saying *poní* instead of *puse*, similar to the way that young children in English say *buyed* instead of *bought*. They also disregarded noun gender, saying, for example, *el mesa* rather than *la mesa*. Mam, which is their native tongue, they referred to as *un dialecto*, even though it is a Mayan language and completely unrelated to Spanish. When we started the semester, they did not know that their ancestors had crossed the Bering Strait from Asia into North America, and they had only a vague sense that somehow they were connected to the Mayans who built the ancient city of Tikal, which they had seen only in photographs. They did not know about the Spanish

Conquest, nor did they know of the existence of Spaniards or Spain. They thought that Guatemala had always been Guatemala and that both Spanish and Mam had always been spoken there.

Later, after they'd learned about the Big Bang and that there were planets and that the earth was spinning and revolved around the sun, and after they understood the difference between cities and states and countries, I decided that we should take all this new knowledge and do a project. Before they could do the research and make PowerPoints, I had to teach them first how to use computers. I taught them the words *click, double click, screen, save, open, cut, paste, Google*. We practiced opening and closing documents, saving them, pasting images onto PowerPoint slides, searching for photographs on Google. They learned quickly, and, soon enough, some of the boys figured out how to find photographs of scantily clad women on the Internet.

For the project, I chose several countries to research. One was Peru; they learned about llamas and the Incas and Machu Picchu. When I showed them photographs of indigenous people in Peru, they did not find them familiar. "What about the clothes? Don't they look similar to the *huipiles* you wear?" I asked.

"The colors are not the same," they said.

"Not the same but similar, don't you think?"

They shook their heads.

Elías and Mercedes researched Egypt. They were in the core group of students who had completed elementary school and were fluent in Spanish. When they were looking up images for the religion of Egypt, they came across pictures of the ancient Egyptian gods. "What are these?" Elías asked.

"Gods," I said.

"What are gods?" he asked.

"Like the Mayans used to have. They have a god of the sun and of the moon and of the dead," I explained, pulling up images of Osiris and Amon as I spoke.

"So there used to be many gods, not just one?" he asked.

"People used to *believe* in many gods," I said.

"But when did they decide to have only one God?"

I explained again that there were different religions and that some people believed in many gods while others believed in one God.

He nodded. "Thank you, Miss," he said, but I could tell he was still confused.

The group that was studying China learned about Buddhism and reincarnation. When they presented the concept of reincarnation to the class, the students didn't understand. I explained, as I had with Elías, about different beliefs and how there were many people in the world who did not believe in Jesus or heaven. "Religion is about belief, but can we know for sure that God exists?" I asked.

"Yes, we can," Marta said. "I know that when I pray to God, he is listening because my prayers are answered."

"But other people pray to different gods and they feel that their prayers are answered too," I said.

"This is very interesting. I will have to think about it," Marta said, and I knew she would.

Most of my students belonged to Protestant evangelical churches. During the dictatorship and civil war that lasted almost forty years (from 1960 to 1996), the Guatemalan government had brought in fiercely anticommunist Protestant evangelical missionaries to counter the effects of Catholic parish priests, many of whom were advocates of liberation theology and regarded as supporters of the guerrillas and communism. Although they attended church regularly and were definitely Christian, the Mayan students were also not dogmatic or closed-minded. In fact, they were open to learning and thinking about anything, no matter how different it was from what they were familiar with. By contrast, many of the Salvadorans, Hondurans, Mexicans, and Ladino (*mestizo*) Guatemalans in the Newcomer Program seemed not as curious and eager to learn as the Mayan students, though they knew more about the world—not much more, but perhaps just enough to make them aware of their position in it, I conjectured, and perhaps to feel angry and ashamed of their ignorance.

Overall, the Mayan students had a hunger for learning that one does not often encounter. Whether this was due to the depth of their ignorance and to their previously limited contact with the modern world, I do not know, but I do know that they were as willing to incorporate the existence of other religions and gods into their worldview as they were to accept the existence of the seven continents or the concept that the Big Bang started the universe. Similarly, when, after much explanation, they finally understood what it meant that I was a lesbian, they could not understand why, if Lori and I loved each other and had been together over twenty years, we were not allowed to marry.

It was their openness and sense of wonder that kept me going, that pulled me ever more deeply into my work at Fremont High, despite the fact that I was often frustrated by the lack of resources and general dysfunction of the school and often got tired of teaching the basics. I was a high school teacher, after all, not an elementary school teacher. I was not used to teaching students how to follow simple instructions or constantly having to remind the boys not to touch the girls. Once when I said, "Save a tree. Don't waste paper," they asked me, "What do trees have to do with paper?" I had to go all the way to the beginning to show them how paper was made and to teach them about deforestation in the Amazon. They had never heard of the Amazon, so I had to backtrack again. I felt as though I was always backtracking, although I understood that what we were really doing was moving slowly forward, building.

Each time I discovered a gap in their knowledge, I created a project. When I discovered that they assumed that cars and trains and planes and buses had always existed, we did a project on transportation. I showed them the clips of Neil Armstrong walking on the moon, and they learned about Laika the dog, one of the first passengers in space. They were impressed with Laika's journey, though they did not think it was right to send her into space when she wouldn't be able to survive. Still, even after finishing their project on transportation, my students had a hard time keeping straight that trains were invented before cars and cars before rockets. They had difficulty conceptualizing that for millennia, until the nineteenth century, human beings lived without electricity, without cars and engines. For them the nineteenth century was simply a long time ago, as was the sixteenth century, when El Capitán Pedro de Alvarado y Contreras began the brutal conquest of what is today known as Guatemala. In fact, any time before their birth in the mid-1990s was, for them, simply very long ago.

They did not know about their home country's civil war. Their parents and grandparents never talked about it, so they did not know that two hundred thousand Guatemalans had died or that the state of Huehuetenango and their villages in the municipality of Todos Santos were some of the hardest hit areas. They did not know that they were the survivors of a genocide.

Toward the end of the semester I showed them the movie *El Norte*, which is about the experiences of a brother and sister who escape from their village in Guatemala after it is attacked by the military and head to *el Norte*. After a harrowing border crossing, they end up trying to make a living in Los Angeles, but the film ends with the death of the sister. They did not know which of the twenty-one Mayan languages the brother and sister in the movie were speaking, but it was not Mam. They loved the parts in the movie when the brother and sister pretended to be Mexican by saying *chingado*, a ubiquitous Mexican curse, every other word. When the protagonists were attacked by rats in the sewage tunnel as they crossed under the border, even the boys gasped.

Afterward, we had one of our discussions. We put the desks in a circle and I sat down with them. I told them to put everything away, even their pencils. I reminded them about good listening, about looking at the person who was speaking, about raising one's hand if one wanted to speak. We practiced these good listening skills before we began. We talked first about immigration. A few of the boys recounted their experiences crossing the border into the United States and walking through the desert. "All we ate was chicken for three days," one of them said.

"No bread or tortillas?" I asked.

"No, just chicken."

Rolando and Marta said earnestly that they had been lucky. They had filed for and been given temporary protected status and had traveled to the United States by airplane with their parents.

I asked them whether Todos Santos looked like the village in the movie. "That is what it used to look like," they said. "Now it is different."

"How is it different?" I asked.

"There are new houses and cars," they explained.

They asked when the war in Guatemala took place. This was the first time that they had wanted to know a date. "From the 1960s to the 1990s," I explained. "When your parents were young."

"Why did the soldiers kill the people?" they asked.

"Why do you think?" I asked.

"This is what I don't understand," Elías said.

About a month into the semester, long before this discussion, I had created a presentation for them about my own family's history. I had begun the presentation by explaining that my family is Jewish, and I explained who and what Jews are. I showed them Israel on the map. They already knew their continents by then. I explained that Jesus and Moses were Jewish. Next, I showed them photographs of my grandparents and parents, and of my grandmother's passport with the swastika on the cover. They did not shiver when they saw the swastika, since they did not know what it represented. I showed them images from the concentration camps. They looked at the pictures without comment, in complete silence. I explained that everyone in my mother's family except my grandparents, my uncle, my mother, one of my grandmother's two sisters, and my grandfather's brother died in Auschwitz. When I finished the presentation, they asked me the same question they would later ask about *El Norte*. "But why did they kill your family?"

I tried to explain. "Because they were different. They had a different religion."

"But that is not a reason."

"No, it isn't," I said.

So when the question got asked again about *El Norte*, I helped them articulate what had happened in the movie, which begins when government soldiers attack a village because the *campesinos* have been organizing to fight against exploitation in the coffee fields.

"Why do rich people not want to share a little bit with poor people?" they asked, and so we talked about greed. They said that they would rather be poor than greedy, rather be poor than killers.

I told them that my mother used to say something similar: "It is better to have been among the victims than to be a murderer."

They agreed.

At this time, the trial of General Efraín Ríos Montt, former president of Guatemala, was in the news a lot, so after we watched *El Norte*, I wrote a simple lesson in English about the trial and Ríos Montt's role in the massacre in El Quiché. They had not heard about Ríos Montt or about the trial. One of the Mexican students suggested that he should be executed for what he did, but the Mayan students did not agree. "Only God has the right to kill," they said.

"So what should be his punishment?" I asked.

"He should have to stay in prison for the rest of his life."

I asked whether they thought it was sometimes necessary to take up arms to fight against a government that is unjust.

"It is not good to have blood on one's hands," the Mayan students said.

"What if someone kills your family? Would you kill them?"

"No," they said. "It is not good to have blood on one's hands."

I wondered whether there would come a time when they would be angry about the genocide of their people that has been going on for over five hundred years. I wondered whether learning more about their history would eventually change the way they think of their lives.

Before getting to know these students, I had never questioned the need to know about the past. I grew up knee-deep in it: the daughter not only of refugees from the Holocaust, but also of a historian. I believed that it was our duty to study the past, just as my ancestors believed that it was their duty to study Talmud. I believed that George Santayana's famous line, "those who cannot remember the past are condemned to repeat it," was irrevocably true.

Now as we talked about the historical events that had created the present-day conditions that caused them to leave their native land and end up in my classroom in a dysfunctional school in a crime-ridden neighborhood of East Oakland, I saw a group of brave young people who had traded in the familiar for the unknown, who trusted me and appreciated whatever it was that I chose to teach them. They, like me, were the children of the victims of war and genocide. Their grandparents and parents, aunts and uncles had witnessed and experienced the worst forms of brutality. Yet neither their families nor mine had given up. Their families had rebuilt their villages and brought children into the world, and those children were in front of me now. They had lived all these years without knowing about the rings around Saturn or that their ancestors had made their way slowly from Central Asia across the coldness of Siberia and the ice blocks of the Bering Strait to the highlands of Guatemala. They certainly had known nothing about my ancestors, who had been slaves in Egypt and ended up in Europe, where they had survived pogroms and poverty and finally fled one last time to the other side of the world. Now we were all there together. We had all survived, and I could only hope that their futures here would be better than their pasts, and that, whatever the future held for them, they would preserve their dignity and their sense of wonder.

What we didn't know at the time was that I would be leaving them. A few weeks after this discussion, the director of the Newcomer Program would inform me that although they had hoped to be able to make my position permanent, there was no money to keep me on. It would take yet another year before I finally found a permanent position at a charter school in East Palo Alto. My students in East Palo Alto are also refugees from the violence of Central America and Mexico. They too have been robbed by *coyotes* and crossed the desert on foot to come here, to this country, to this school, to my classroom, where they discuss the significance of dreams and why Saturn ate his children, and ponder the mystery of the Big Bang that set everything in motion and is propelling us all to our futures.

Jiao Wo (Teach Me)

Caitlin Dwyer

The dean had a heart attack a few weeks after he was assaulted with a baseball bat.

At least I think it was a few weeks; the first month at the American International High School runs together like watercolors on rice paper: blurry streaks, images more Rorschach than clear scene. I recall the cool, dry air; the way the track emptied out after final bell and blue-gold mountains rose in the distance, hazy and immense; the cloying Chinese pop song blasted over the loudspeakers each morning for calisthenics and a school yard full of kids in uniforms waving their arms and bobbing in tune. I recall the smell of the takeout noodles, spicy and sour. I recall sitting at my cubicle and flipping through a GED textbook, wondering how to teach fourteen-year-old Chinese freshmen from a rural southern province about critical thinking and commas and democracy and beer pong.

It happened during the second week of school. The students in his class were supposed to be looking at a social studies text. In a classroom bare of any decoration except a large, laminated map of the United States, with a blackboard covered in the names of cities and wars and kings the students had never heard of, the dean had noticed a student playing with a Rubik's Cube. Our school was modeled after English preparatory schools, so the dean expected the markers of such an institution: straight-creased pant legs and striped sweaters and lively debates. He had, instead, some sullen teenagers who rarely understood his lessons. The young man with the puzzle had already been labeled a "problem kid"—hair falling over his face, distracted in class, texting under his desk. When the dean requested that the student put the cube away, the student refused. The dean snatched the puzzle from his fingers and left.

Leaning against his desk in the teacher's office, the dean cursed under his breath, looking for a spot to stash the Rubik's Cube. A moment later, the same student stomped into the office, his face crumpled in anger. There were a few gym supplies in the corner—a soccer ball, a basketball, two badminton rackets. The student picked up a baseball bat, gripped it hard in both hands, lifted it over his head, and ran for the dean.

I was one of the two other people in the room. Luckily, the second person was Sam, a six-foot-three former basketball player. Both of us leaped toward the attacking student. I clung to the end of the bat with all my weight, but Sam just put the kid in a bear hug and lifted him out of the room. The dean, breathing heavily, cheeks red as raw bacon, collapsed against the desk.

I had lived in China for a year when I was recruited as the writing teacher for a new preparatory school in Yunnan, a mountainous, multi-ethnic province near Tibet and Myanmar. Intended to capitalize on the growing interest of young, affluent Chinese in studying for university abroad, the school had the potential to be gigantically profitable. As the pioneering first staff, our job was to teach our specialty disciplines, so we were given leeway in the classroom. *Leeway* meant that the school had not yet established a guiding curriculum; they left it to us to invent our way through the first semester.

During the previous year, I had been working as a college writing teacher in a nearby province. Living abroad with my boyfriend was an adventure, and I was developing a successful side career as a travel writer. I had always dreamed of living someplace with Romance languages, siestas, and opulent cheeses; instead, after traveling around the world, I had landed in China sort of accidentally. I had stayed because of the well-paying jobs for foreigners, and because my boyfriend was enthusiastically learning Chinese. After a year, however, I was still illiterate, bewildered by the language, the crowds, the utter foreignness of it all.

The first week of school, we all struggled. Aside from the dean, there were five foreigners: myself; my boyfriend, Hank; a seasoned expat couple from Kansas named Sarah and Patrick; and a Dutch science teacher who arrived late after losing all his money in Laos. Three young Chinese teachers filled out the teaching staff: Amanda, a tiny woman with a fierce love of language who taught writing with me; Sam, the basketball player with huge arms and a gentle, acne-scarred face; and Lee, who always wore black and whose dream was to be a forensic investigator. The Chinese teachers—and many of our sixty students—used Americanized names at school, a common practice in China. Leading the charge was our boss—a no-nonsense Chinese businesswoman—and her first-in-command, a portly, blustery British man in his forties: the academic dean.

The dean wore a suit every day and sweated through it by five o'clock. He spoke in broad, all-encompassing statements about the state of Chinese education. Since we were all new, he tried to make us feel as comfortable as possible. Primarily, in his mind, that involved comfort food, so he invited us to the home he shared with his wife, another Chinese businesswoman he'd met in England, and served us Scotch and cheese and crackers and bacon. He seemed fairly at home in a foreign country—loudly proclaiming things in broken Chinese, gesticulating with the exasperated privilege of a white man abroad. But in his meals, we saw the underlying desperation of a man who was eating his way back home.

All the foreigners, barring the Dutch guy, had lived in China before, but no one had taught in a school like this: a brand-new, rigorous, English-immersion prep school. There was a strange disconnect between the image we wanted to project—the bold sallying forth into rigorous intellectual exploration—with the reality of the situation. The school was in a rented space, the third floor of a local elementary and middle school. Located in a newly constructed golf community on the outskirts of Kunming, a big southern city, it felt utterly distant from everything. The streets were clean and empty, occasionally patrolled by a guard in a golf cart. We lived in spacious, sterile dormitory rooms across the road. We didn't have any science equipment, and we taught our academic subjects out of the Macmillan GED test-preparation book. None of our students spoke more than rudimentary English. Many of them had flunked the high school entrance exams in their own school systems and had come to us in desperation—their parents were hoping that America could rehabilitate their kids.

The first day, I handed each student a word written on a scrap of paper and had them stand up and group themselves by parts of speech. Standing awkwardly next to their new classmates, holding the words *apple* and *car* and *run* and *study* and *sit down* and *beautiful* scrawled in Magic Marker, they peered at each other, squinting at the words. Someone asked me what *verb* meant. When I told them to sit down, I had to model it by sitting down in my own chair and waiting patiently for them to follow.

The dean never quite recovered from the baseball bat incident. A few weeks later, he had the first of several heart attacks. It was minor, and after recuperating at home he attempted to come back to work. He had a second attack, this one larger. By November he had flown back to England for bypass surgery, and we had no academic manager, no staff support, no backup plan. Just me, Hank, Sarah, Patrick, the Dutch guy, our Chinese teaching staff, and about sixty misfit teenagers whose parents expected each of them to go to Harvard.

The expectations of the parents were not unusual; in China, rank is very important in the education system, and since Harvard was consistently ranked high in America and had branded itself internationally, everyone wanted to go to Harvard. If not Harvard, Yale. If not Yale, what the hell was the point of this expensive prep school, anyway? It was nearly impossible to explain to someone why Harvard might not be possible for their child—there was too much cultural baggage in the way to get to a clear line of communication.

All of us felt frustrated. We were pushing, constantly, against the hard, heavy wall of language. Hoping to budge it an inch backward. Setting grappling hooks of articles and nouns and pantomimed phrasal verbs. Our shoulders ached. We were in over our heads, and so were the students, many of whom cried on their breaks. As teachers, we struggled to know what to teach; we had no benchmarks other than that three years from now, our students were supposed to take an American GED exam in Hong Kong and be able to pass.

What made it worthwhile was the way the students stood politely and read silently next to their desks to prevent themselves from nodding off in class. Their broad smiles when they understood a joke; the physical humor and shared embarrassment of explaining a difficult concept. We could laugh with them, knowing that we were all floundering together.

When the dean left, I became the academic manager. I had never taught high school before. Aside from my teaching experience the year before, I had previously worked with an after-school program in Portland, Oregon, where I managed a few employees and helped corral thirty excited, exhausted second graders into group games. Supposedly, this qualified me to run a school.

I shared my responsibilities with Sarah, the teacher from Kansas. She specialized in student services and discipline, while I was supposed to design a high school curriculum. Although we both had experience working with kids, neither of us had ever worked in, let alone established, a prep school in China. Our students and their families now looked to us for answers, progress, results. We were supposed to get kids from "Teacher, what verb?" to Harvard in three years. How to do that was beyond me.

"What do you mean, we can't use the field?"

I was fuming. The elementary school's vice principal sat with a composed face, hands folded into her lap. It was December, shortly after the dean had left; I had been academic manager for about two weeks. The vice principal, speaking on behalf of the elementary school, had just informed me that our high schoolers constituted a danger to the younger students on the campus, and therefore we had lost our privilege of using the field, the track, the basketball and tennis courts. In effect, we had been restricted to our classrooms. Classes began at 7:30 a.m. and went until 8:00 p.m. As in many Asian schools, the students spent twelve hours a day sitting at desks. They were itching to run, shoot hoops, stretch their freedom. Now, they couldn't even use their breaks to play ball.

The woman nodded and said, "We are worried the students play too roughly."

"Well, they're fifteen. Of course they play rougher than a six-year-old." I was gripping my file tightly, trying not to fling it at her. "You can't restrict a bunch of teenagers to one classroom all day. They'll go nuts. They'll riot."

"You'll need to figure that out," she said sweetly. My first thought was: I'll take this to the top. We pay rent here; we get to access the sports facilities like everyone else.

"This is ridiculous," I told her. "I'll be speaking to the principal directly." But before I could do so, Amanda, my Chinese co-teacher, touched my hand. I glanced at her, and realized that something had been communicated that I didn't at all understand.

What I did know—what all of us knew—was that the student who attacked the dean turned out to be the son of the elementary school principal. Because we rented space from them, the principal's son was a VIP student. The young man had had discipline difficulties at other institutions, and after the baseball bat incident he had promptly been expelled. At the time, his father, the principal, had nodded gravely and said he understood. The Chinese teachers had tried to warn us about what that really meant, but we hadn't listened. We were used to people saying what they meant, that raw Western bluntness in which x equaled x. However, we were in China, and x did not equal x. The fact that we assumed everyone would learn our formulas, and follow our math, was part of the problem.

After my conversation with the vice principal, Amanda took me aside at her desk: a cubicle in a gray room that smelled of printer toner and green tea. She spoke with the reserved, precise tone that comes only from studying English as a second language: "They are punishing us," she said. "We have made the principal lose face, and we must suffer for that."

"His kid attacked a teacher with a bat! What does he expect?" I asked. "We were supposed to let him stay?"

"Of course not," said Amanda. She was probably my closest Chinese friend, and she had the rare ability to speak frankly to Americans, something many locals seemed unwilling to do. Her quiet voice conveyed patience with my thickheadedness. "But everything in China is built on face."

In other words, by expelling his son from his own school, we had shamed the principal publicly.

"He should have told us," I said. "Punish me, punish the teachers, but the students didn't do anything wrong."

With a small smile, Amanda chuckled. "That's not the way we do it."

I insisted on setting up a meeting with the principal's office. It was extremely cordial and everyone agreed that teenagers needed space to run and play, and that the facilities were in theory big enough for all of us. No one mentioned the principal's son, who we heard had been sent to military school. They served tea, smiled and listened, and nothing got better. With my American bluntness, my drive to solve the problem with open communication and brute force, I was missing the heart of the narrative. I didn't have some skill essential to negotiating here, a subtlety, a way to talk around instead of at the problem. Meanwhile, we hired a school bus twice a week to take the students from our empty, available playing fields to a gym a few miles away.

Kunming was an expat's dream city. With seven million people, in the foothills of the Himalayas, it had clear, crisp weather and blue skies—a rarity in polluted China. Dry, with a haze of red dirt that constantly dusted windshields and windows, Kunming had miles of mountain biking track that wove through small subsistence farms in the hills; a thriving city center with cafés and bars and a couple of sleazy clubs; a cadre of long-term, close-knit foreign residents whose main hobbies, as far as I could tell, were drinking imported whiskey at the local bar and complaining a lot.

Though I had come to China more for the adventure of it than any real interest in the country itself, in Kunming I felt at home. In November, Hank and I got a place with Sarah and Patrick on Longxiang Jie—Flying Dragon Street—to escape the teachers' dormitories on weekends. During the week, we lived at the school dorms; on Fridays we trekked into the city, an hour by public bus, to see urban China. Our downtown apartment was on the eighth floor and had no elevator. The windows had bars over them, as most buildings did—to stop suicides, we were told. Saturdays, Sarah cooked up Kansas barbecue in the kitchen, and Hank would go on long bike rides and bring back bunches of wild marijuana, scavenged from the side of the road, which we spread to dry on our kitchen table and smoked later, watching rip-off DVDs of American movies.

As the first semester drew to a close in January, Hank, Patrick, and I gathered in the apartment to write individual student reports. With finals exams stacked and graded, a bottle uncorked on the table, and laptops open, we tried to assess what progress we had made. The students were starting to distinguish themselves—some with a sharp curiosity emerging from beneath the burden of language; others struggling with the simple tasks of following instructions, doing homework, staying focused. We saw in some of them the beginnings of a transformation, the itching to change. In others, we saw nothing but resistance.

We told ourselves we were only in China for the "experience," which made the whole thing seem like a fun experiment. But we found ourselves worrying over a troubled kid or a bright one, drinking imported whiskey to forget that the futures of these children were inexplicably in our hands.

———

In revenge for the expulsion, the elementary school did little things to annoy us. Starting in the fall, they played calisthenics music during our first period; for fifteen minutes, we had to sit there, with the speakers outside blasting, unable to teach, shouting instructions across the room. The first day this happened, startled by the volume, I peered over the railing at the rows of kids in red-and-white track suits waving their arms in sync, like an army of marching candy canes. After a few weeks, it became an inside joke with my students: *not this song again*...I rolled my eyes, they giggled, and we all ignored our reading for a few minutes until it stopped.

When a hip-hop dance club caught on with our students, the elementary school restricted our hours of access to the dance studio, then accused our students of breaking lockers and roughhousing. Granted, they were probably roughhousing. We were banned from the studio. In the new year, when we finally developed a science curriculum, they wouldn't let us use the microscopes in the lab. They forced us to walk down two flights of stairs to use the bathrooms on the first floor rather than the third-floor bathrooms around the corner. Meanwhile, the middle schoolers got to bounce around our classrooms, banging on doors and running away, drawing rude graffiti on our bathroom stalls.

But if our relationship with the host school got worse, our relationship with our own students got better. There was a sense of living under siege, of surviving a thousand little cuts together. We huddled into English like it was our salvation—and for some of our students, it was.

"Who can tell me what the five senses are?" I asked my class. They sat in rows, prep school blazers draped over the backs of their chairs, staring up at the chalkboard. One girl with long pigtails, her eyes artificially widened by contact lenses, raised her hand.

"Smell, see, touch, taste." She paused, glanced uncertainly at a kid to her side. "Um, listening?"

"Hearing," I said. "Sounds." We were reading an excerpt from Annie Dillard's *Pilgrim at Tinker Creek* in which a large water bug sucks the insides from a frog. It's a horrifying scene, and great for teaching descriptive writing. I hoped it was gross enough to catch the attention of high schoolers.

"Let's make a list of all the words that have to do with the senses," I said, scratching a rough chart on the chalkboard. "We're looking for words that show us a picture of what's happening. Work with a partner and write down as many as you can." They huddled into pairs, awkwardly sticking long limbs into the aisles, too big for the desks. A taut breeze stirred the papers in the room. I circled the class, reminding two students not to speak Chinese, explaining what a "deflating football" was, asking one, "Is terrifying a sense or a feeling?" The hum of voices, the murmur of consent and disagreement, the flip of pages. A few months ago, we had been staring at each other across a divide of language and culture, asking, "Teacher, what verb?"

Spring was coming, and we were starting to inch forward. We could read—roughly, sort of—brief texts by real authors. We could talk about types of verbs: strong action verbs against stative ones. We could pick synonyms that made our sentences stronger. For that matter, we could write full sentences.

At the end of class, I asked the students to draw pictures of the scene based on what they had read. They held up disgusting pictures of a monster bug sucking the life from a frog, a curious woman bent over the water, her hair dangling over her shoulder. In the pictures, Annie Dillard was Chinese—narrow eyes and long, straight black hair. Of course she was—the "I" in the story came back to each of us, infecting our understanding of the story. The students grinned and laughed, pointing at the bugs on each other's pages. I don't know if it was Harvard, but it was a classroom of students in China, laughing about Annie Dillard. That was something.

We begin with the given of distance. To the teacher, a new class is a flock of unfamiliar faces. They speak a different language. They like weird foods. They don't know how to write a thesis statement or examine a primary source document. They begin as far away from us as possible.

Presented with the unfamiliar, we seek to transform it into something recognizable. As teachers, we draw out certain qualities in our students, suppress others. Sometimes it's more blatant: we mold a child into the image of ourselves. In an immersion language school, the teacher does not move. The students move. They begin to use our slang. They read *The Lion, the Witch and the Wardrobe*. They can name the US presidents and the houses of Congress. They learn the English names for the elements of the periodic table, for the parts of a cell. They learn the punishment for plagiarism. They are stripped of their own language and given a replacement language. They are forbidden from talking in their native tongue, or using modes of study practiced in their own country. They grow away from their own culture, becoming more like us: foreigners in a foreign land.

Suddenly, standing at the front of the classroom, the teacher no longer faces a room of foreign faces: she faces her compatriots, those with whom she shares cultural knowledge. She has given her students a vocabulary that will help them survive in another place.

I was very proud of them, but I am not sure I could do it again, in good conscience.

We gave our students open lunch; they usually left campus on their motorcycles, and came back in an hour. Then, in spring, the elementary school required them to eat in the cafeteria. We received a letter, notifying us of the changes. Students and staff alike were required to pay a daily fee to eat the cheap, crappy cafeteria food and share tables with six-year-olds. I tried it a few times, found a rock in my rice, got a bout of food poisoning, and never went back. Our students ignored the order and zipped away on their motorcycles anyway. The principal watched them go and said nothing to enforce the rule. This was how the game was played, I was learning: rules were made, and rules were ignored. You got by.

———

In our American GED social studies textbooks, a brief mention of the 1989 student protests and subsequent massacre in Beijing meant that the texts were seditious, treasonous, and dangerous. Our Chinese teachers were given the task of excising any reference to this bit of Chinese non-history.

"They're going to learn about it anyway," Sarah said as she watched Lee draw a thick black Sharpie line over the index reference, then cleanly tear away a page from the book. He did the same thing with the next book, and the next. "When they go to college someone is going to ask them about it. They might as well know."

"Maybe their parents will be upset," Lee said absently, ripping out another page. What he meant was *We don't have room to move on this.* What he meant was *You in your American privilege believe you can just say no.*

Of course, if you present a classroom of curious fifteen-year-olds, who are being trained to think critically and question authority, a book with pages torn out, they will ask questions. We avoided saying anything that could get our visas revoked while not denying that there was more to the story. The Chinese Internet refused to cough up search results, so they asked, and asked again, until I secretly told a few bright, persistent students about Internet workarounds. "Teacher Kate," one girl told me seriously the next day, "there are many informations to read."

In April, they staged their first rebellion—refusing to work in study hall. Too much time studying, too much English, too many restrictions on their freedoms. We talked them down and explained that sacrificing their studies wasn't the way to go. One student, a round boy with a loud, bossy voice, mentioned the Civil Rights Movement, and I recalled the first day of school, trying to get them to join me in their seats, modeling *sit down*. Now they were leading a sit-in. They began a letter-writing campaign to the elementary school president to get their playground privileges reinstalled. About a month later, they were.

———

At the end of the year, the staff held a banquet. It was at a local restaurant, made up to look fancy with marble counters and big chandeliers, but like many things in China it had one face and another reality: the bathrooms were dirty concrete slabs, and if you slipped your fingers behind the marble counters, you could feel shoddy grout that would likely give way in a few years.

We had reason to celebrate. After our first year of study, about ten of our students had taken an IELTS test of English proficiency and scored well enough for community college in the United States. They no longer talked about Harvard, but about places like UCLA, Berkeley, Wisconsin, University of Washington, NYU, Iowa. We had messed up a lot, but we hadn't completely failed.

Staff from the elementary school joined us at the banquet. I had written a short speech in which I hoped to address our power struggles over the last year and my hope for improved relations in the future. However, my boss was already several shots deep in *baijiu*—a strong Chinese liquor—with the principal by the time we arrived. They were laughing, arms draped around each other like old friends. I saw no acknowledgment of the snubs we had endured or the humiliations leveled on both sides. They did not give me time to read my speech. We sat together chatting about stupid things, and no one mentioned the blaring music, or the graffiti, or the school lunches, or the many other insults we had endured.

All was forgiven, at least on the surface, as we raised our glasses to the end of a successful first year. "To our partnership!" the principal said. "May it continue."

Slightly drunk on wine, I lifted my glass high into the air. Let bygones by bygones, I thought; we had done our fair share of damage here as well. We had given a bunch of kids a chance at life in the United States, but we might have also permanently damaged their sense of cultural identity. I wanted forgiveness, and I wanted to forgive.

"Put your glass down," hissed Amanda, who was standing next to me. I grinned at her.

"What? I'm happy for us. We did good this year," I replied. My glass clinked, high above the others, waving happily. We drank deeply.

She leaned into me, whispered in my ear: "When you raise your glass above the others', you insult them. You are proclaiming your superior position."

I frowned. "What?"

"You just told the principal and everyone that you were above them. They are your inferiors and must show deference." She smiled, took a long sip of her wine. "You're terrible at this."

I buried my head in my hands. So much of this job was fighting just to communicate basic, everyday things: *I understand you. I believe you. I have faith in your abilities.* Amanda rubbed my back and smiled. "Sit down," she said in Chinese. "You'll learn."

On My Own

Karen Kelley Perkins

"Just sit in my classroom during your conference period and then do what I do in all of your classes." Those were the words of Diane, a veteran high school biology teacher and dark-haired, Demi Moore look-alike, maybe fifteen years my junior. Sitting at her desk, she must have noticed the tension lines on my forehead, or perhaps my dilated pupils, as I gazed at the posters and taxidermy stuffed animals in glass cases on the walls of her classroom. It was the night before my first day teaching high school.

I had been hired during the summer by a charter school administrator who'd had no authority to issue an employment contract; the campus of multiple classroom buildings was barren—no teachers, no staff. Newly divorced, I needed a job. So I'd waited anxiously until Diane, whom I knew slightly, and the other staff members returned from their summer vacations, surprised when they showed up just a few days before school started. And now, half of my brain was on Brendan and Shannon, my eight- and nine-year-old children, who at that moment were running wild through the mid-century modern science building because I didn't want to pay for a sitter.

I scribbled notes on a lined yellow pad as Diane went point by point over her first-day lesson plan. Then she walked me next door to a storage room where spare silk prom dresses for teacher chaperones hung on wire hangers from full-length cupboard doors. Behind them were human bones (*were they real?*), displays of quartz and geodes, and archaic microscopes haphazardly placed on their sides. Diane yanked open a rusty file cabinet and pointed to manila folders of lessons, classroom activities, and lab protocols. "We have plenty of stuff to do with the students," she said. Brendan bolted into the room carrying an octopus specimen that was swishing around in a screw-cap jar of formaldehyde, but Diane remained unfazed. She handed me her one-page syllabus. "Here," she said. And so my high school teaching career was launched.

The next morning, as I was going out the door, Edith's minivan pulled up in front of my house. A plump, Hispanic mother of four, Edith would make my kids' breakfast and get them ready for school, drop them off, and then go to her full-time job as a housekeeper. I had been fortunate to meet her through a friend, just the week before. It wasn't easy trying to figure out life on your own in Los Angeles with two kids traumatized by divorce. As I drove down my street on the first day of school, I prayed that Edith would have no trouble getting them up and dressed.

Our street was lined with humble 1950s bungalows overlooking a chaparral and the Pacific Ocean, a neighborhood too expensive for me as a single parent. I had made a risky move and put a small down payment on a house near my children's schools, thinking it was a means to a normal home life. I felt lucky but nervous.

Teaching high school had seemed like such a simple decision, carried out for practical reasons, but in the weeks leading up to the first day, I had begun to understand the magnitude of the task. Just to begin, I had taken three state science exams, a test on the US Constitution, enrolled in a program to earn the preliminary teaching credential, and applied for an emergency teaching credential. There were little things, too—the TB test, the fingerprinting—all before I ever walked into a classroom.

The classroom was a hollow, echoing, cinder block space with twenty metal and laminated wood tables that creaked when you leaned on them. The chairs were worse, tilted. Bare screws protruded from the metal legs, some of which were different lengths. One chair had only half its wood seat. The other half was on the floor. That first morning, perched on my wooden desktop, I read and reread my notes from Diane, conscious of the rising thunder outside my door as the school's 2,800 students arrived from more than one hundred Los Angeles zip codes. When the first bell rang, it sounded like a fire alarm, and Diane poked her head in. "You need to open your door."

As I did so, forty teens of various shapes and sizes and shades screamed into my room, shooting me just a passing glance. I stood off to the side as the room filled past capacity. Then the second bell rang, and they glared at me.

"Hey, are you new?" a boy shouted from the sea of heads.

To say "I've never taught high school" would have invited trouble. I told them I had taught college, but was cut off by the morning announcements. The speaker shouted the name of our school with the charisma of Robin Williams in *Good Morning, Vietnam*. The kids laughed.

When the announcements ended, I formally took attendance. In the new-teacher orientation, I had been told that this was my primary responsibility, as it enabled our charter school to get its funds from the state. I clung to the imposed structure. What gave me anxiety was the upcoming getting-to-know-you game: too free-form. Yet I followed Diane's directions, and the kids scurried from their desks to find someone who liked chocolate, or who had read a book during summer break, or who had had their tonsils removed. I observed them in their comfort zone, but I didn't play along. I was relieved when each student had matched his or her identifier with a different student. Now we could get on to the biology syllabus, which was focused mainly on policies, such as no gum, no do-rags, no side conversations—on anything other than science.

I was midsentence, my mouth hanging open, my hand clutching my yellow lined pad of notes, when the closing bell sounded. The students got up and walked out—as if I had never existed.

Diane poked her head in. "How did it go?"

"Okay. What happens now?"

"You just do the same thing in four more classes." Diane seemed electrically charged, yet with a breezy confidence.

I was spent. My throat was dry, as if laryngitis were coming on. I hadn't slept much the night before.

Diane glanced at the clock. "At nutrition, we've got to go pee, otherwise you won't be able to go till noon." State law said you were not allowed to leave minors unattended, I reminded myself. It was only 8:49. "Nutrition," or snack time, would span a twenty-minute window, from 10:34 to 10:54. My life would now be measured by timers, the way I had long ago measured experiments. Before becoming a mother I had been a research scientist.

After the last bell of the day, at 3:08, I slouched in my desk chair under unforgiving fluorescent lights. My bones rubbed uncomfortably against the hardwood seat. As tension begged to drain from my joints, I pondered the evening chores that lay ahead. I would pick up my children, shuttle them to karate, thaw something out for dinner, coax them through homework and lengthy bedtime routines. Then my own homework would be due for my online teacher credential program. I took a deep breath and stared at the millions of holes in the white acoustic ceiling tiles. I thought of Dave, a man I had fallen in love with. Single and never married, he had gasped in dread when I told him I might teach high school to earn a living, might set the alarm for 5:30 a.m. every day. I had recently called him to break up. I couldn't fail by letting a man get in the way of what I needed to do, I told myself. I'd played that card of life, left a job for a relationship. Now my kids were at stake. Teaching and raising them was the only option. I added up the time till my youngest graduated: ten years. It seemed like a prison sentence.

Yet Diane seemed content. She mentioned she had recently married. The physics, chemistry, and marine biology teachers cavorted through the science building cracking jokes, borrowing each other's equipment, setting up the next day's activities. I wasn't like them, though I wanted to be. Staring up at the tiled dimpled ceiling, I made a vow. I would tell people I loved my job whether I did or not.

———

My resolve was tested on the third day of school when I was called to the principal's office in the administration building. She sat behind a mahogany desk in a corporate Ann Taylor suit and handed me my much-awaited employment contract. I saw my salary and gulped. I had perused the faculty salary scale and thought I had some idea of where I would fall on it. I had predicted double. The principal quickly informed me that teachers on emergency credentials were not eligible to be anywhere on the salary scale but at the beginning.

I complained profusely, bringing up my single parenthood, but she would hear none of my sad tale of woe. "If you don't accept the contract," she said, "you need to be out by this afternoon."

I signed. I walked out of her office with my head low. My eyes fixed on gum stains on the cracked cement path that led toward the science building.

"Hey, Dr. Perkins," someone yelled.

I looked up.

A blond girl from one of my classes waved to me from the outdoor cafeteria. Her biology textbook lay open on the table in front of her.

"Hi," I called. I could not recall her name, but I picked up my step.

I found Diane in her classroom with my daughter, Shannon, who had taken the city bus from her middle school. "All the kids take the bus, Mom," she'd said. So, fretfully, I'd told her to try it—one less thing for me to do. Diane asked me about my day, and I kept to my resolution. I told her it was fantastic.

Late that night while my children were in bed, I sat at the dining room table, the heat of a tensor lamp bearing down on the paper in front of me, the faculty salary scale. A teacher's earnings were based on two things: graduate units and years of teaching experience. The latter could include college teaching and up to five years of employment in the field in which you were teaching. I had done research for five years and taught college for four. Since my horrendous meeting with the principal, I now understood that none of this mattered. Fortunately I had chosen the fastest credentialing program in the city of Los Angeles. I would take out a bank loan to get me through the year.

I didn't head off to bed though. I developed a routine. I sat at the dining room table in front of my computer till one or two each morning until the credential was complete.

For the next few months, I did exactly what Diane told me to do. I didn't have much time for lesson planning on my own. When her classes dissected sheep eyes, my classes dissected sheep eyes. If her students baked cakes and decorated them with Twizzlers and M&M's to look like plant and animal cells, so did mine.

During my free conference period I sat at her desk, took notes, and watched her class. Students entered the room and deposited their homework into a "homework box," then headed for their assigned seats. When the bell rang, Diane put a black metal clip on the forty papers, to be graded after school. The day's agenda was posted on the board as well as a "warm-up" activity to engage the students. Diane would lecture briefly and launch into a lab. A student might come up to her and ask her something she had gone over three times, and I would be thinking, *you should have listened*. Diane made eye contact. Her voice was steady and soft as she repeated the instruction for the fourth or fifth time.

Diane's kind of patience was hard for me. I was all about getting the job done. My classroom, an extension of my life, was like an assembly line. I continued to tell everyone I loved my job, though I was really just getting through it. At bedtime my kids cried out for stories, their nightly routine while I was married to their dad. Now I pulled away from them, headed for my homework. Stacks of books, papers, drinking glasses, and plates with crumbs cluttered the dining room, which had become my office. I don't know what I would have done without Edith, who took to tidying up a bit while the children were getting dressed.

After about nine adrenaline-filled and highly caffeinated months, my credential completion letter arrived in my mailbox. The administrator in charge of "rating in," or determining one's salary on the scale, sat behind her desk. She was not the Ann Taylor principal, but an older administrator with black and gray curly hair who smiled even when she said something serious. Her office was a jumble of yellow envelopes, unfinished paperwork, and decades of high school yearbooks.

I handed her my graduate transcript and a letter of employment verification from UC Berkeley, where I had been a research scientist. She lowered her head. Her manicured nails paged through the documents.

"I was a researcher in the field of biology," I explained. "I have a PhD and 177 graduate units." The salary scale went to ninety-eight.

"But research…" Her bespectacled eyes met mine. "That's like, what, two hours a day?"

"It's a full-time job," I said.

"I'll need some proof." She handed me back the letter, smiling. "This doesn't say you were a research scientist."

I left her office dejected, mumbling rhetorical questions. *How could she not know that scientific research was full time? How did she think scientists had traveled to the moon or sequenced the human genome?* Later that evening, I sent my ex-boss an email and he replied with a glowing letter.

I hurried back to the administrator. Her eyelids fluttered rapidly as she skimmed the words of praise my ex-boss had written. I hoped she would see me in a new light. But, as though she were making a concession, she said, "I guess we can accept this."

That night I took my kids out to dinner. "Get what you want on the menu," I said. We ended up sharing two entrees anyway, but we splurged on dessert. Within a couple of months, the teachers' union won an 8 percent pay raise. I was making more than I had ever earned.

I've heard people say about teachers, "They do God's work." But I never felt I was doing God's work. Rather, I always felt I was not good enough, and that teaching as a profession was not good enough. I had been embarrassed to contact my former boss for a reference letter, embarrassed to be teaching high school. I kept repeating to myself, "Nobody listens to teachers," a line from my imperious older sister, a financial analyst. I had screamed at her when she said it. Mine was a family with rivalries of biblical proportions, and after my falling out with my older sister, my mother and my other sister stopped speaking to me as well. It would be years before I heard from any of them again.

But there were the other reminders of my low-ranking profession: the salary, though secure, was sufficient to get by, but not to save for the future. The pension, though helpful, would one day not be enough. The daily system of signing in and out on time cards felt belittling; the minimal lunch break left barely enough time to chew. I continued to fume over the principal's initial mandate that if I didn't sign the employment contract I needed to take my stuff and get out. I had secretly begun to think of my classroom as the dungeon, a place where I was locked up and not allowed to leave except to pee at nutrition and eat during the thirty-minute lunch break. But my anger motivated me.

Just before my second year at the high school, the physiology teacher resigned. None of the senior teachers wanted her position, which would comprise a full course load and a move to the physiology classroom. I took it. I outlined a new physiology course for honors students. I went to a school board meeting and asked them to fund it. After a ten-minute discussion they voted to award me more than my first year's salary for supplies and books. I applied to the University of California, and my course was accepted to their list of courses that would qualify a student for admission.

I was still probationary, however. I could be fired with the flick of a dry-erase marker. In California, a teacher is probationary for two years. By March 15 of the second year, the school is required to notify a teacher if he or she will not be "reelected" for the following school year. I received no doomsday letter.

I took four university courses to become an administrator—then I learned of the national test. Laughably, there was even a mail-order study-guide kit, which I purchased. The test was a breeze, giving me another credential.

When my children were barely old enough to stay home alone, I volunteered. I would drop them off and return to school. While I chaired committees, they would eat a meal I'd left on the stove. While I led meetings with families and teachers to help at-risk students, my own children struggled alone on homework, and sometimes my son just simply gave up and played computer games.

I was proud of my PhD, but it bothered me when one teacher said, "Just because you know your subject doesn't mean you can teach it." Again, I felt I had to prove myself. There was a pecking order among teachers. The most veteran teachers taught advanced placement (AP) courses, but my subject, physiology, had no national AP program.

A few of the science teachers had become National Board certified in teaching "Adolescent and Young Adult Science." This certification was more respected on campus than my four-year doctorate and published research. It was a rite of passage that would also raise my salary 15 percent, so I spent a year completing it. On the morning when test results would be emailed, I turned on the computer at six o'clock. Noticing my letter of congratulations, I burst into tears.

Shannon came out of her bedroom in flannel pajamas. Her brown curly hair went halfway down her back.

"I passed the test," I sobbed. "I can't believe I passed."

Shannon was now in tenth grade at my school. By the time we left the house that morning, she would be wearing ripped black stockings and black eyeliner. "Of course you passed," she said. "You're the hardest-working teacher over there." Likely fed up with my career insecurities dominating our lives, she stormed back into her room, and I ran after her for a hug.

At school, I relished the respect I had earned among my colleagues, but it did not fill the void inside me. During my fifth year teaching, I chaired our charter school board. At night I continued to spend hours at my desk. I hunted online for paths up the education ladder.

Finally, after five years of teaching, I landed a job as a high school principal at a different school that was not a charter but a science-based school, part of Los Angeles Unified, the second-largest school district in the nation. I hoped to make a difference.

There were three schools on my new campus, each with its own principal, and a total of 1,700 students. Located in an impoverished neighborhood, the campus was rife with gangs of different ethnicities. I was stunned to learn that as a principal, I would spend most of my day carrying a walkie-talkie, that the district did not budget for adequate security, and that the few school police were stretched among multiple schools. The principals patrolled the wide white halls and restrooms and the cement sidewalks where a student had been shot the year before. In the afternoons and evenings we supervised athletic events.

One warm spring afternoon, the teachers at my school held a meeting to plan curriculum. A former scientist, I considered science curriculum my forte, but my job as principal required me to supervise a soccer game. Grudgingly, I stood at the edge of the field, the sun in my face. Then I got hold of myself and took a deep breath. I had just convinced myself to relax and enjoy the game when a drunken student vomited at my feet. The Cokes the kids were guzzling had been laced with alcohol. The student's two friends picked her up and dragged her off toward the gym. I followed close behind. I was the only person on duty. The nurse had gone home too.

In the gym restroom I leaned against one of three sinks and stared at the shoes under the stall door. I plugged my nose to avoid inhaling the acid throw-up stench. I felt as if I were in an underground tomb, restrained by my walkie-talkie and cut off from doing any good to education, let alone myself, with the sour vomit suffocating us all, a live burial.

Convincing Los Angeles Unified of the absurdity of using principals as security guards seemed hopeless. I returned to my classroom at the charter school the next fall. In my smaller arena, albeit a dungeon, I thought I might find satisfaction by engaging academically with individual students in spite of yet another bureaucratic misstep, the

No Child Left Behind Act, which put a microscope on test scores as the only evidence of student learning.

Like many teachers I was astounded by the *Los Angeles Times*'s decision in 2010 to publish a database of teachers along with their students' performance on state tests over a six-year period. For some it was tantamount to a public stoning. One listed teacher, Rigoberto Ruelas, committed suicide three weeks later. A. J. Duffy, then president of the teachers' union, told the paper Ruelas had been depressed about his score.

I began to notice a change in students too. Responding to society's dissatisfaction with educators, they challenged every little thing I said, my lectures, my class policies, my science. A student seemed more intent to raise his hand to point out an irrelevant typo on a test than to actually study and pass the test.

Administrators at my school put teachers in groups to find out who was the best at teaching a lesson, as evidenced by the scores. I did as I was told. While I had never taught science with an eye toward test scores, I made it my job to call on every student every day, to grill them constantly on physiology. I spent less time playing getting-to-know-you games, during which even I had dared to participate. The school gave me an award when my students scored highly on the state biology test, which spurred me on.

Then, quite abruptly, as the political tide turned, the war ended. The new principal held a meeting. There were more than one hundred teachers at my school. We sat in foldable metal chairs in the large auditorium. The meeting was on the Common Core, the new approach to teaching. We would need to make changes in our teaching to pass the redesigned state tests. I shook my head.

One afternoon, I pushed my dining room table and chairs against a wall. I dragged in an armchair from the living room, and I placed it in the picture window. Sitting in the chair with a coffee, I stared at the chaparral. Ten years had passed since I had bought the house with this view. My daughter had gone off to college, and my son was at army basic training. Technically, my prison sentence was over.

My house had doubled in value. If I sold it, I could retire. I had made amends with my family. Dave, the man I once let go, had married someone else. I would have to accept that. But I had succeeded in my mission, raised good kids, provided stability. Had I been too selfish? Directed too much attention toward my work? Let my own insecurities about not being good enough take over? Keeping the inevitable mother's guilt in check, I told myself I had simply done my best.

I thought of a parent I had phoned the week before. Sandra's son Demont was struggling academically. She was raising him alone. He had never met his father. She had not "introduced them," was how she put it. "I made all the mistakes," she confided. I thought of a few of my own: leaving my children home at night and going back to work. "As single parents, we do the best we can," I told her.

We talked at length about Demont's behavior. He was jittery, the type to challenge any statement, to be easily distracted by his classmates. I did not really know how to help Demont, except to be someone he could grow to trust. He was a senior and I hoped he would graduate. As we were getting off the phone, Sandra said, "I'm so glad you called, I think I'm gonna cry."

The following Valentine's Day the school's leadership class delivered a rose with a card: *Thank you for being a great teacher—Anonymous.* I stuck the rose in an Erlenmeyer flask on the counter. I opened the desk drawer where I had tossed cards received from students, parents, and administrators over the years. A few of them caught my eye. They read: *Thank you for talking to me; Thank you for a great year;* and *You rock.* I placed the Valentine's card among them. Although I hadn't loved my years on the job, the job had clearly loved me. The years I raised my kids alone had been, perhaps, a time when I had needed love the most. Now that my prison sentence was over, I knew what I would do with my life. I would keep on teaching.

An Honor and a Privilege

Mary Ann Hutcheson

On a warm spring day in 1972, I headed across the university campus to my political history class. I was one year away from earning my coveted elementary education degree, and this was a required course. It filled me with dread.

The course itself was a fine one. It cultivated insight, encouraged problem solving, and expanded worldviews, vital skills for any teacher. It was the instructor, an exceptionally bright and somewhat brusque woman, who unnerved me. She favored the political science majors who comprised the bulk of the class, and revealed an air of disdain for us elementary education majors—a common prejudice I later witnessed both in and out of the teaching field. Many believed that it didn't take a genius to teach an elementary school curriculum. As students of the profession, we hadn't yet learned to ignore the slight and take pride in the significance of our calling. For me that actuality would arrive some twenty years later.

As I entered the classroom, I noticed that the coveted back row of desks had been, as usual, the first taken. I was one of the hapless few left to occupy a desk in the undesirable front row, so I sank down in my seat and did my best to maintain a low profile.

That day, gesturing with the black-framed eyeglasses attached by a long chain around her neck, the instructor advanced in a gradual but determined march toward my desk. I lowered my eyes to the ground and prayed to all saints Catholic to remain inconspicuous.

She asked, "What do you elementary education majors expect to teach when you have your own classroom?"

I was sure this was a trap; her questions were seldom this straight-forward. Math? Science? PE? How was I supposed to know? My specialty was yet to be determined at the time.

She reached my desk and stared at the top of my head. I squirmed, my invisible shield irrevocably breached, and my thoughts a jumbled mess.

With a flushed face and a sense of doom, I stepped boldly into her web. "Math and science," I replied, my voice a strangled imitation of a cartoon character's. A sly smile crossed her thin lips as she tilted her head toward her beloved political science majors and retorted, "You will *not* be teaching math and science; you will be teaching children!"

Like the Cowardly Lion trembling before the wizard, I considered a most clever retort: "But professor, you asked 'what,' not 'who,' you know." In my fevered state, I imagined a green disembodied head behind thick smoke, and booming columns of fire. I retreated into my shell and decided it best to hold my tongue. I needed that grade, and I had no intention of washing out of the course that semester. Better I wait a few decades and find another way to share my opinion of her teaching strategies.

If the woman had laid her unwarranted bias aside for a single moment, she'd have realized that she was preaching to the choir. I was twenty-one at the time, but I already knew *who* I was teaching. I had known for most of my life that my heart was that of a teacher. I did learn something important from that professor, which stayed with me for the rest of my career: I would not emulate her teaching methodology.

I write this story forty-three years later, three years into retirement from a successful career devoted to loving and teaching children. I would have a good deal more to learn in the years between my under-grad political science class and now. But even in 1972, I'd sensed I had the ingredients to do well.

I attended Catholic schools from kindergarten through twelfth grade, and I watched what worked and knew what didn't. I knew children well. In many ways, I was still one of them at heart. I under-stood their needs, their fears, their hopes, and their issues. I had lived every moment of my own childhood with an open heart and inquisitive mind, and I knew I could never forget how life worked for kids.

Like countless other emergent teachers, I spent my free time as a child "playing school." With a blackboard I'd requested for Christmas securely hung in our attic as my backdrop, I created a classroom for my favorite stuffed animals, eventually replaced by neighborhood children. I loved teaching them to read and telling them stories, enjoyed making them laugh and watching them improve their math skills. Love, dedication, and an innate understanding of the learning process were my strengths.

Sadly, I came to learn that such significant strengths would too often be overshadowed by the ever-expanding and unrealistic expectations in the teaching field.

Upon entering the profession, I intuited that teaching required more than assimilating the latest philosophies, methodologies, directives, and classroom management procedures to help children meet standardized test requirements every year. Moreover, those things changed yearly—sometimes, it seemed, monthly. Teaching was intuitive for me; that was not subject to change.

I was not enamored of methodologies that beamed, "Use a sense of humor in your classroom." I already *had* a sense of humor. Directing someone to "use it" is like telling her to use her mouth when she eats. Or, "Let children know you care, and then they'll care what you know." As a student of human behavior, I didn't understand how someone could engage the average child in the learning process without first earning his trust. Many of those methodologies seemed a waste of time to me. A prescriptive check-off script for teachers in the classroom was just another cumbersome piece of baggage I had to lug back and forth each day.

My fellow teachers and I leapt from one "best way to teach" stepping-stone to the next over the course of our careers. The trail twisted in all directions and invariably returned to its source.

We shifted from individualized learning to group learning. Then we annihilated phonics and praised brand-new programs like Accelerated

Reader. It wasn't long before the decision makers scoffed at programs like Accelerated Reader, and the East Coast joined California in its newfound solution for poor readers and spellers, christened "literature-based reading instruction." No Child Left Behind joined the parade and packed more file folders, paperwork, and accountability on teachers' backs as they struggled to keep track of their ever-changing curriculum requirements.

Technology entered the picture, and officialdom rattled its scepter and directed us to focus on problem-based learning, the creative and interactive use of SMART Boards, laptops, Classroom Response Systems, and the creation and use of instructional videos: *Get those kids' hands on things; they learn better that way.*

Didn't common sense already tell teachers that? Who didn't know that? During the 1973 school year, while studying Egypt, our sixth-grade students were building miniature pyramids in the classroom—before we were told it was good for students to get their hands dirty. They were writing and performing newscasts wearing proper Egyptian garb that they had designed themselves. Intuitive teaching is an art, and many of us were natural artists.

Soon Common Core and prescriptive instruction entered the classroom. SMART Boards were no longer so smart. Since there was no further need for the creative lessons made specifically for students to get their hands-on learning, the boards remained in classrooms as projection screens. Phonics was rediscovered and hailed once again as an excellent tool for teaching children to read.

Becoming a teacher now means navigating a complex network of hurdles and tunnels. In truth, I believe the act of becoming a real teacher involves little of that.

I did not consider myself a teacher in the full context of the word until the 1991–92 school year, nearly twenty years into my career. I worked at a pleasant neighborhood elementary school in South Carolina, where I taught fifth grade in a self-contained classroom, meaning I taught all the core subjects to my own class. We were family, sequestered together in one room the majority of the day, for the duration of the school year. Twenty-seven ten-year-olds arrived at my door that August, and they live in my heart today as one of the most amazing groups of children I had the privilege to know and teach during my career.

Among them was Ryan, whose mother, I was told, was terminally ill with cancer. Ryan was devoted to his mother, and I was asked to keep a special watch over him, an easy job for me. Ryan was an exceptionally kind and sensitive young man, bright and older than his ten years presented him.

Siobahn, a sweet, tiny girl, her paper-thin skin tinged an unhealthy yellow, was on dialysis; the family was waiting for a kidney donor. "Keep an eye on her, too, please," I was reminded. "Don't allow her to play too hard during recess."

Anekqua was a gentle and generous angel with warm brown eyes and a smile that illuminates the memory as I rekindle it today. Her family struggled to get by within their meager financial means. Her clothing and bearing were simple, but always neat and clean. Her Christmas gift to me that year was a one-eyed pink teddy bear, her "hug-companion" from infancy. My heart swelled with the offer of something so dear to her, and I insisted that I keep her bear by my side only for the length of that school year, after which I would return him to her. She accepted the deal.

Lisa came to us with serious physical issues; she suffered grand mal seizures. As an infant, Lisa had been tossed headfirst against a kitchen cabinet by her father, who had long since deserted the family, and the injury had caused the severe brain trauma that impacted the rest of her life. "Please keep an eye on Lisa," I was reminded. There was a procedure to follow in the event of an "incident" during class.

I assigned Ryan the desk behind Lisa. He learned the procedure in case Lisa suffered a seizure, and I knew he would perform his duties with great care. To prevent her from lurching forward, Ryan was to reach around and secure Lisa at her desk until our school nurse arrived. I hoped the responsibility might replace his own sense of powerlessness in the face of the impending loss of his mother with a task he could control.

There was Matt, the gifted and blind-from-birth student, whose volumes of Braille textbooks arrived in bulk the week before school started. "What are these books for?" I inquired. I had no idea how to teach a blind student, especially when I was so inclined to teach visually. I hadn't been trained for this kind of challenge. "Oh, he'll show you," the administrators told me. And he did, beyond anything my imagination anticipated.

Kim was our beloved "class mother." Her immutable smile, framed by dimpled cheeks and warm eyes, hid a deep secret in her life, one that would unfold in due time. In the meantime, it was Kim who created get-well cards for the class to sign when a classmate—or the teacher—was sick with the flu. Kim gave the best hugs in the class, and I was sometimes the lucky recipient at the end of a difficult day. Her heartfelt kindness was a constant presence in our classroom.

And then there was Jamal. Jamal was repeating fifth grade as a twelve-year-old. I was told he was a handful, and that his home life was harsh and unyielding. His threatening demeanor, made more threatening by his now-older, stronger body and unpredictable mood changes, added yet another challenge to our classroom environment. His legs were his weapons of choice, his kicks aimed to harm, and he stole from his classmates at every turn. How would I protect my students, especially little Siobahn, from the serious risks Jamal's anger might unleash upon them?

My job description dictated that I teach these children the full fifth-grade curriculum in all subjects and make sure they passed the standardized test at the end of the year. With flying colors, if possible. The task of preparing students to perform well on standardized tests, while juggling complex classroom behavioral issues, plays out in every school, every day, around the world. It is the area of teaching for which none of us are prepared or trained. It challenged my dedication, determination, resiliency, and patience. It forced me to unveil creative problem-solving skills I didn't realize I had.

Yet I can say, with deep conviction, that this was the year I understood, in its finest interpretation, what being a teacher means.

Our problem with Jamal had reached desperate proportions by midyear. One January afternoon, during his absence, my students shared that they had had enough of Jamal's manipulative and aggressive behavior and they needed help.

Sending a student like Jamal to the office was not an option. It did nothing to change his behavior, despite the wonderful support programs and personnel available at our school. Acting out was an excuse to avoid work on his part. Sending him home meant more physical abuse and less time to learn in the classroom. Jamal wanted to stay in our classroom, but I believed he had no idea how to fit in. I thought I had tried everything. I hadn't.

I asked the students if they could proffer a list of transgressions they experienced at his hands. It was a huge list.

"He kicks me, Mrs. Hutcheson, for *no* reason!"

"He stole a box of Kim's World's Finest Chocolates, Mrs. Hutcheson, and she never told you. She paid for it herself out of her allowance!"

"He stole money from my cubby!"

"Yeah, he stole one of my pens and some paper from my Trapper Keeper."

"He makes it hard for us to pay attention because you always have to stop him from doing something when you're teaching us!"

Out it spilled, until we had compiled a large list of complaints on the board.

The room was eerily quiet, the students spent. I had no idea Jamal's misconduct had escalated to that level. So much of what Jamal did was on the sly, and the students had been afraid to tell me.

For the most part, I had experienced positive results from my disciplinary methods in the past. Once my students trusted me and knew I respected them, a bond developed between us. Strange as it may seem, the idea of a broken trust, or the perceived loss of my respect for them—coupled with a stern, disappointed look and a private talk—almost always settled the problem. It sounds simplistic, but it worked.

It bothered me deeply that this young man had unleashed such chaos and damage to his classmates, in spite of my best efforts. This was his family. How many talks had I had with this group about our classroom being a safe place? No bullies allowed. I made sure of that.

I wasn't doing such a great job.

My students deserved a plan. There was always a "plan." Where my plan might originate this time, I had no clue.

Several days passed before an idea occurred. In a stroke of luck, Jamal was absent from class for several days, so I had another chance to address the issue with the class. If they agreed with my idea, it was a go; if not, we'd try another approach. But, I assured them, we would fix this problem one way or another.

Ever the optimists and always eager for something fun they might do *with* their teacher, the students were my ultimate motivators. Their reaction was quick and enthusiastic. "What, Mrs. Hutcheson? What are you thinking about doing?"

Smiles and curiosity flooded the room from every direction, and they hadn't even heard my plan yet. This was a desperate bunch of kids.

"Okay, here's my plan. What if I put a large bag under my desk, where Jamal will never see it? Then every day for a month, before he arrives," (Jamal could be counted on to bring up the rear just after the bell rang each morning) "we donate anything from the list we posted on the board—items he has stolen or articles he needs—and place them in the bag? Simple things we don't have to buy, items we no longer use but are still in good shape. At the end of the month, we will hold a special class meeting and present our friend, Jamal, with his bag of surprises. That way, he'll know we hold no hard feelings toward him and we can assure him we want him to feel safe with us."

Silence. A long silence. I expected an immediate rebuff for this crazy plan. Things like: "Why in the world would we give more things to a person who has done nothing but take from us?" "Won't he just laugh at us for being so weak?" "Why should we reward his bad behavior?" "What if we insult him with our plan? He might think we're making fun of him and think he is poor or something."

Oh, but those are the things adults think about—or *should* think about. I was one of those adults, and I knew we were treading a very treacherous path with this plan. The students knew simply that it was a secret surprise plan, a fun plan, something none of us had ever tried before in our lives. We could do it together, and for them at least, that made it worthwhile.

"*Yes!*" they responded. "Let's *do* it." A buzz of excitement permeated our little classroom.

"I have an old Walkman. It still works great, but I don't use it anymore," volunteered one of Jamal's victims. "I'll bet he could use one of those, right, Mrs. Hutcheson?"

From another child, "I keep spare change in a jar in my room. I don't mind pulling some of that out and contributing it."

"I have a lot of loose-leaf paper in my binder that I never use," said Matt.

And from Erin, "Jamal never has anything to use; he's always borrowing stuff."

Children. Their greatest good exists just below the surface, and this particular group of children, struggling in their young lives with so many serious issues of their own, were the best of the best.

So each day, without Jamal's knowledge, the children snuck behind my desk to tuck treasured gifts into the large paper bag I had hidden below. I added to the pile. Jamal was never the wiser.

During that month, students behaved less like victims around Jamal, perhaps because they felt they had taken control of their situation. Sensing the shift in climate, Jamal seemed less prone to display his usual aggression. Or maybe that was my own starry-eyed faith in simple goodness.

The prearranged day arrived. Students made their usual exuberant entrance from recess, their excitement tinged with anticipation. I asked the students to settle themselves so we could start class. Jamal scanned the room, searching for someone to tease, or perhaps for a classmate to engage in a little lesson distraction with him.

On cue, little Siobahn, we called her Bonnie, pulled a single chair into the center of the room and asked Jamal if he would be so kind as to have a seat. His dark brown eyes found her slight frame and he offered a confused grin. Bonnie was nothing if not persistent, and she requested his presence once again so we might put this ball into play.

At this point, let me now confess, I knew we were on the precipice of either the best experience in group dynamics, or the worst disaster in the history of gut intuition.

Like a wary cat, Jamal rose from behind his desk, his hesitant curiosity driving him toward the chair in the middle of the room. Bonnie moved to my desk, retrieved the brown paper bag, now bulging with items from her classmates, and placed it on the floor before him. She delivered her unrehearsed speech with great conviction and love, blond curls framing her diminutive features and bright blue eyes.

"Jamal, we wanted to give you some things that we thought you might like to have," she began. "We think sometimes you might feel like you need to borrow things from us, so we've been putting those things aside for this day so we can give them to you. We hope you'll accept them with love from all of us." She moved back to her desk.

Ryan and Lisa, Matt and Anekqua, Tiffany, Kim, Erin, Blakely—everyone leaned forward to take in the feel of that moment.

Jamal turned back to me, and I agreed with a smile that his classmates wanted him to have these things, that it was a sign of love from them.

The fleeting moments that last forever in our memories come few and far between. This was one of them. Cautiously Jamal reached down into the bag—and pulled out a jacket. A jacket? I hadn't surveyed the contents of the bag in recent weeks, and it surprised even me.

Out came a Trapper Keeper, then the Walkman, and notebook paper, and a set of pens and pencils, and loose change in all sizes. A rare smile bloomed, and then blossomed at the discovery of each new gift. Then, quite unexpectedly, tears appeared along the furrows his smile had created, dampening his cheeks and dropping from his chin, slowly at first, then irrepressibly. The students were watchful, the mood reverential. No one spoke.

The students and I witnessed something that day I doubt any of us will ever forget. We felt the intensity of active loving, loving someone who probably deserved it more than most, and received it from the very children he had victimized.

I warm to that moment now, almost twenty-three years later. I was so proud of this extraordinary group of loving children, so relieved and moved to see Jamal receive the gifts with gratitude and emotion. So glad it worked!

The next day, Jamal arrived on time to our classroom for the first time that year. As I began class, he reached into his book bag and extracted his new Trapper Keeper. The pens and pencils came next, thoughtfully and evenly lined up beside it. He opened to a blank page and peeked at me with a wide grin, to let me know he was ready for class. The students were watching, and spontaneous laughter and smiles erupted in the little classroom.

There were no further incidents of kicking, fighting, or stealing that year from Jamal. Our class melded into the family I wished it to be.

There is a coda to Jamal's story. Have I mentioned that this class was an exceptional group of children? Kim, our miniature "class mother," the student Jamal had cost a box of World's Finest Chocolate, was shot and killed by her father, in a drunken rage, as she watched television in her home during the first week of summer vacation. He murdered her mother along with her, and then took an axe to their home. Kim had concealed her sad secret with great aplomb that school year. Her warmth and smiles fooled us all.

I read the story in the Charleston newspaper on that warm June morning with shock, disbelief, and an incalculable sense of loss. In an attempt to equalize the amount of publicity given to the atrocious act, and to the man who committed it, I wrote a letter to the newspaper, telling the story of who really mattered, the beautiful child who lost her life in such a senseless act.

After publication, I received numerous letters about Kim. One was written in pencil, tucked into a simple envelope, and delivered to my mailbox at our elementary school. Jamal had enclosed two dollars and a short, touching note. *Dear Mrs. Hutcheson,* he had written, *I am so sorry about what happened to Kim. Please use this money to buy a rose for her funeral. Thank you, Jamal.*

And I did.

I don't know if this was his way of returning what he had taken from her, but I do believe it was an act of love and understanding for the acceptance and forgiveness she had shown him that year. It is what I hoped for Jamal, and it conveyed an earnest testimony for the little girl who helped teach him love.

My students performed well on their standardized tests that year. They learned and behaved because they knew it mattered to me and it mattered to our cohesion as a group. Neither they nor I were perfect. We were human and we made mistakes. Hopefully, I taught them more than just producing for a test. I'll never know for sure, as I have not seen any of them since the year they moved on to the middle school. Soon afterward, my husband's job moved us to another part of the state, and I began a new journey in another school.

I would love to know where my fifth graders are now, what they are doing with their lives. I heard that Ryan's mother passed away at the end of that school year. I'll never know if Siobahn received her transplant, but I once found Anekqua online and learned that she had become quite a talented hairstylist. Fear suppresses my curiosity about Jamal's path in life after that year. I don't know if one year is enough to change a life predestined to trip and slide into old habits. I'd like to believe our time together made a difference.

I think back on that day in my political science class forty-three years ago, and the professor who poked fun at those of us standing at the threshold of our careers. The instructor didn't know who she was challenging that day, and I believe she underestimated our worth in the profession.

Hopefully, every teacher begins a career with the conviction that she will help children define their strengths, face the tough decisions, and stand up for themselves and others when they are called to do so. The teachers who make a difference will give their children the love and dedication of one special person who cares for them every single day for an entire year. For some children, it may count for the rest of their lives. Our profession has become more and more demanding and I worry that teachers no longer have the time to focus on this most important aspect of it.

Each year I created a love letter to my class and tucked it within their final report card. The letter I wrote my children that amazing year ended like this:

You are one of the most loving groups of children I know, and it has been a privilege to be your teacher. You make me proud, and your parents are lucky to have you as their children. I want to see you grow up and be kind to one another and treat others fairly with love and respect. I see you learning that already and doing very well at it. That makes me happy. I like that you will be the adults running our world when your parents and I are rocking in our porch chairs years from now. I love you. —Mrs. Hutcheson

You Can't Wrestle Windmills

Chris Girman

I peel an orange in long spirals with the side of my thumb and spark my lighter under the table. I draw stick figures on a napkin. I downsize my wallet. I finger my eyebrows. I write down—in red, green, and yellow highlighter—how much money I shelled out for this six-week emergency teacher certification course. I sigh into limp fists, exhausted from my first week of teaching. Around me sit five young first-year teachers and an older woman named Juanita, whose story I can't quite figure out. I flick the lighter through my pants pocket.

It's our third night together, the last session of the week. We meet in a small second-floor conference room in south Texas, about twenty minutes from the Mexican border. The others started teaching three weeks ago, at the beginning of the semester, while my position opened up just last week. I notice a Ramirez & Associates sign outside the window. Abandoned. Another first-floor law firm succumbing to the Rio Grande Valley's late August heat. I tap my fingers on the table and make eye contact with Juanita, the only Mexican American in the class. A blond girl to my right presses down on her pen and draws a large checkmark at the top of a handwritten student paper, the first in a high stack. She circles the title with a quick motion of her wrist: "Idealism in *Don Quixote*." I notice the book to her right. On the cover, the old Spanish knight clutches a long sword; he's perched atop a skinny horse.

Watching her reminds me that I still haven't turned in my first-week lesson plan to our seventh-grade curriculum specialist, nor do I know what part of Texas history I'll teach my students next week. I coax up phlegm, dramatically, from the back of my throat and look around the room to see if anyone notices. I adjust my seat for my theatrical departure. A guy across the table rolls his eyes at me and whispers something to the blond girl grading papers. They're on to me. I twist sideways and crack my back. I swallow mucus.

My classmates are articulate and well informed, sipping soy lattes and looping red pens like licorice over student essays. *High school* student essays. I'm not even sure my seventh graders know how to read. Several of my fellow teachers work on slender Macintosh iBook computers and share a bag of organic potato chips. Today I forgot my World Wrestling Entertainment notebook, the one a student of mine left behind after fifth period. I write on a nearby napkin instead. Before class, downstairs, I heard several of them discussing new educational theories. They exchanged lesson plans and dished the latest gossip from their respective schools. I smoked a cigarette.

I finish peeling my orange and wrap a long piece of rind around my wrist. My creativity impresses me. I hold my fruit-wrapped wrist a small distance from my face and notice one of my classmates reading a Teach for America pamphlet.

"Oh," she says, when she notices me watching her. "I almost volunteered for Teach for America."

She closes the pamphlet and slides it over the table to me. I look at the smiling young woman on the cover. She looks like the blond girl across from me, the one grading papers. The actual, three-dimensional girl speaks in some monotone Anglo accent. Probably from the Midwest. I look more closely and notice her hair is more brown than blond. Freckles dab her face. She looks like a *Samantha*—something about her upturned nose. Maybe *Karen*. A strand of hair hangs in her wide, ceramic mug. She looks like my sister. I remind myself to talk to her later. And I should call my sister, too.

I glance back down at the pamphlet and open it. On the inside cover, the sad eyes of a black youth stare at me. Under him are the following words:

Of the 13 million children growing up in poverty,

About half will graduate from high school.
Those who do graduate will perform
On average at an eighth-grade level

You can change this

I laugh, unexpectedly, much louder than I had intended. The boy across the table gives me that look again. This time he doesn't roll his eyes: they bug out instead. Perhaps he's right: maybe I'm not teacher material. I place my hand in my pocket and finger one of the business cards I've emptied from my wallet: *Dennis St. James and Associates.* My friend's dad back in Austin said he'd help me if I ever needed a job. I imagine the once-bustling law firm below us, visualize Barrister Ramirez thumbing through her preliminary draft motions. She removes her glasses. *I can almost imagine.* But then the blond/brown-haired girl whispers something to the bug-eyed boy and points her long fingers toward a passage in *Don Quixote.* Together they laugh.

I have nothing against Don Quixote. It's only that his idealism is a long way off from my present predicament. I remember vaguely the tired old knight, protecting the Spanish Golden Age of justice, respect, and reverence. I've nothing against idealism either, nor would I begrudge Quixote his fanciful descent into madness. *Quixotic*—the word's an enigma: on the one hand, it means "visionary, though often impractical." The other definition is more like me: "impulsive, unpredictable." How else could I explain how I ended up here?

I studied politics at an expensive East Coast university and spent my summers interning at various high-powered think tanks, including the Institute for Foreign Policy Analysis, where I swallowed my conscience and spent the semester analyzing the international weapons contracts that killed thousands of innocent civilians each year. I moonlighted for a variety of lobbyists, including several foreign governments that thought nothing of bribing United States senators. I completed my mandatory study-abroad semester in Lima, Peru, where I acquired a love for colonial history and chilled pisco. I finished my final year of college and, because I had no idea what to do next, applied to law school.

Unfortunately, I soon discovered that I had no passion, or use, for the law. I felt like an Eskimo clutching a can of mosquito repellent. While those around me furiously traded multilayered outlines in elaborate study groups, I bartended at a downtown hotel. Thankfully, I graduated. However, while other students had parlayed their summer internships into lucrative associate positions, I continued bartending. After a year I decided to take that *other* bar exam. With the help of an expensive bar review course, I learned more about the law in the next two months than I had the previous three years. I passed the bar exam with an astonishingly high score (astonishing, at least, to the instructor of the course, who'd asked repeatedly if I'd actually graduated from an accredited law school), donned a pale gray suit, and conveniently forgot that I'd rather chew glass than file a deposition. My job as an immigration lawyer lasted only a few months.

I'd given as much thought to becoming a teacher as I had to walking on the moon. Yet when a friend told me that school boards down in the Rio Grande Valley, an area comprising some of the nation's poorest school districts, had offered to pay back student debt in return for teaching service, I looked at my meager bank account and decided it was worth a shot. Besides, I'd kept very few clients from deportation as an immigration lawyer, and wondered if I might have better luck getting through to twelve-year-olds.

So here I am, two months after quitting that job—impulsive, unpredictable. Quixotic: that's me. I return my attention to where I left off in the Teach for America pamphlet:

It is this—the clear potential of students—that makes the disparities in educational outcomes so unconscionable and fuels our sense of urgency and responsibility to do everything we can to ensure educational opportunity for all.

I feel like I've entered an Al Gore documentary. Desperate for an emotional response, I pinch my forearm under the table. I think of dead kittens floating in a bathtub. Nothing. Maybe if I keep reading...

> *We accomplish [our mission] by building a diverse, highly selective national corps of outstanding recent college graduates—of all academic majors and career interests—who commit two years to teach in urban and rural public schools in our nation's lowest-income communities and become lifelong leaders for expanding educational opportunity.*

The Marine Corps battle hymn comes to mind:

> *From the halls of Montezuma*
> *To the shores of Tripoli...*
> *You will find us always on the job—*
> *The United States Marines.*

I breathe slowly and maintain my composure. Why can't I feel emotion for the thirteen million children growing up in poverty? I am overcome, instead, with a wave of skepticism. I look around me. Why have I so quickly come to despise this roomful of optimistic first-year teachers? The girl grading papers looks up and smiles. Her hair still dangles in her coffee cup; I hope she falls in.

I've had a bad first month here at B. L. Garza Middle School. Unlike Don Quixote, I stay in my idealistic phase only as long as it takes me to realize—about four weeks in—that someone in my seventh-period class has thrown gum in my hair. "Truly I was born to be an example of misfortune," lamented Don Quixote to his loyal servant, Sancho, "and a target at which the arrows of adversary are aimed." Faced with a world of fraud and deceit, malice and greed, the fictional Spanish knight succumbed to fantasy as a way of preserving his idealized image of *how the world should be*. I understand Don Quixote's despair. I explain to Rafael in the front row, as Don Quixote explained to several goat herders, that before the fall of men, Mother Nature had provided all that man needed. "That means," I say to Rafael, gripping his little hands until he drops the whiteboard eraser, "that stealing was unnecessary."

"Who's Don Quixote?" he asks.

"This guy," I say, holding up a copy of *Don Quixote* I borrowed last week from the girl in my certification class. Her name, Bev Friedmont, is written in permanent marker on the inside cover of the book. "An old guy," I continue. I return the eraser to the board. "He was romantic, believed the world needed his immediate presence."

"Why?" Rafael asks. He's a small boy with dark skin like caramel who started asking questions the first day we met and hasn't stopped since.

"He just thought that some people in this world need to be protected," I say. "To be looked after." I return to my podium. "Don Quixote would never steal."

"He sounds dumb," Rafael says. "And I didn't steal the eraser. Roxy *gave* it to me."

"Did not!" Roxy shouts, and stands up, her large loop earrings dangling like lanterns.

I remind myself that these are twelve-year-olds. On top of that, they're from Edinburg, one of the poorest school districts in Texas, a mostly rural region of dry ranches and agricultural land struggling to keep up with the demands of surging immigration. Roxy and Rafael are two of thirty-five students in my seventh-period class. The least I can do is be more understanding.

But then they surge toward each other, and I'm interrupted from my daydream. "SIT DOWN!" I scream: a clear violation of teacher certification rules. Rafael and Roxy sulk back to their seats. "Does everyone have the page number?"

"I don't have a book!" Isabela shouts from the back. "Manny took mine."

"Enough!" I yell.

"Okay," Rafael says, lowering his head. "You don't have to yell."

"The order of knight-errantry," I read from *Don Quixote*, "was instituted to defend maidens, to protect widows, and to rescue orphans and distressed persons." A girl in the back rolls her eyes. I suddenly realize that I've got it backward: I am here to protect myself. I *am* the distressed person.

"Okay, then," I say, closing the book. "Now back to Texas history. Do I have any volunteers to read?"

"What page?"

"Nine. Okay now, do—"

"What page?"

"Nine. How many times do I have to say it?" I see a raised arm in the back of the class. "Yes, Jimmy?"

"Sir, my page nine doesn't have a picture." The boy holds up his book next to the book of a girl sitting beside him. "See, her book has a big picture."

"That's the wrong book," interrupts another, much smaller boy. He reaches over, closes Jimmy's book, and compares it to his own. "You have the wrong book, Jimmy."

"Thank you, Javier," I say.

"You've got an American history book," Javier continues, looking at Jimmy. "We've got *Texas* history." He picks up Jimmy's book and holds it next to Jimmy's dark face. It's my fault, I realize. I have given Jimmy the wrong book. "Your cover is blue, not brown," adds Javier. He slams his brown book on Jimmy's desk. "Don't be such a dumbass."

I channel the spirit of Don Quixote and answer in a chivalrous manner. "Please get another book off the cart, Jimmy."

Jimmy walks toward the front of the class, looks back at me, and stops at the wobbly silver cart. "Are you sure it can take it?" he asks.

Several students snicker, sharing Jimmy's concern. Because I was hired two weeks after the semester began to meet the growing number of newly registered students, I wasn't assigned a classroom. Thus, I wheel around my daily necessities—thirty-eight textbooks, campus plan, pencils, Kleenex, hand sanitizer, all the essentials—to the far corners of our poorly designed middle school. Jimmy looks at the battered cart as if it were a tousled old street dog napping after an alley brawl.

Don Quixote's horse, Rozinante, is described as follows: "Ill-shaped, long-haired, short-maned, big-hoofed, knock-kneed, sway-backed, broad-eared, watery-eyed, slow-paced, awkward." The same description fits my cart, Betsy. "But in the eyes of his master, Don Quixote, he was the handsomest and the wisest steed that had ever lived." Together Betsy and I ride bravely out into the world, lance in hand, notebook paper flying aimlessly through the air, prepared to fight injustice, heal the sick, and teach dumb children how to read. Betsy serves me as faithfully as her bony metal construction allows, wobbling through the treacherous hallway as bravely as Rozinante struggled up Castilian hillsides. I pull on her reins and charge down the hallway. Woe to thee who dare cross our path!

And then she collapses. The moment Jimmy lets go of his blue American history book, Betsy heaves and sighs, struggles mightily to keep her weak joints in place, and buckles in a ghastly heap of corrugated metal legs and tiny plastic screws. I bow my head in reverence, interrupted moments later by Javier. "Way to go!" he yells at Jimmy from the other side of the room. "You big dumbass."

In the certification class later that day, I explain my situation to our instructor, Mrs. Randolph. "Sounds like you're not having such a good time of it," she says. She's a kind middle-aged woman in a long denim skirt. She tilts her head to the side and looks at me softly as if she were my grandmother. "Okay, class," she says, "since this is our last week together, I think I want to try something new." She asks us to write down three reasons why we selected a career in education. Agile fingertips lightly tap keyboards across the table. Juanita writes in her marbled composition book.

"Is this yours?" asks Mrs. Randolph. She holds up my WWE notebook. "You left it yesterday." She hands me the spiral notebook, her stare lingering on several stickers of half-naked men and buxom female wrestlers posed in battle. On the back cover, one of my seventh-period students wrote *Eat me* and drew huge hooters over a female wrestler's metallic bikini. Probably Javier. I pretend not to notice.

"Five more minutes," Mrs. Randolph announces. I turn another page and massage my temple. I desperately try to answer the question.

<u>*Why I Became a Teacher*</u>
1. To make a consistent income
2. To go to bed at a decent hour
3. Summer vacation
4. I have no f***ing idea

Mrs. Randolph notices my open notebook and asks me to share my responses with the class. I do as she asks. I skip number four. Several students stare into open computer screens. Bev, the blond girl I mistook for a Samantha, breaks the silence.

"I think I have more of what you're looking for," she says. Mrs. Randolph, a former theater teacher, maintains a neutral expression.

"Okay," she says. "Why don't you share for us, Beverly."

"Bev," corrects Bev, who's still correcting Mrs. Randolph this last week of class. "I like to be called *Bev*."

"All right, Bev, then have at it. Why did you become a teacher?"

"First," Bev begins, "I became an educator to improve the sorry state of our educational system." Several people bob their heads in agreement; someone crunches a potato chip. "Second, I want to share my unique knowledge of the world." Mrs. Randolph smiles. "And third," Bev says, nearly rising out of her chair, "I love children so much and want to be an *advocate* in their lives." She stresses the word *advocate* as if opening a jar of pickles tightened by the stiff hands of those who were *not* advocates. She looks at me as she says the word. I don't blame her. "I think of myself as Don Quixote," she says. "Pure idealism."

I make a note to retrieve the Dennis St. James and Associates business card from my dresser drawer.

By the end of October I feel like things are getting better. I no longer dread each day. Then I find a drawing taped to the wall. The drawing depicts a man in a green shirt, his hands resting in his conservative

khaki pants pockets. He looks annoyed. I look carefully at the picture—I recognize myself immediately. A name is drawn across the top
of the man's shirt: D-Generation X. Smaller lettering in the middle
of the shirt displays an odd message—"We've got two words for ya:
suck it." At the bottom of the page is my name, Mr. Girman, and a
small arrow pointing toward the man in the picture.

I feel sad. How have they come to despise me in two short months?
I turn over the drawing and slam it on a small student desk next to
me. I slide my legs inside the desk and sit. I turn the picture over.
The man in the picture looks angry, as if he carries his hands in his
pockets so he doesn't strike someone. Is that what they think of me?

In mid-December I see Bev in front of me in the checkout line
at the grocery store. She wears a charcoal-gray business suit over a
wide-collared white blouse, accented by a turquoise scarf over her
left shoulder. Her hair rests in a loose bun, a shiny silver pen poised
behind her ear. She looks good. I unload my basket of school supplies
and lean forward.

"Beverly," I say, purposely using the longer version of her name and extending my hand. "How have you been?"

She turns around and looks at me like she can't quite place my face, but a few moments later something clicks and she smiles. "I'm great," she says, staring at the mound of plastic scissors I dump onto the checkout counter. "I see you're still teaching."

"Uh, yeah." I pull the last of several notebooks from my shopping cart. "How's it going for you?"

"Better," she says. "*Now*." She unloads several bags of cookies from her cart and continues, "How can you stand it? I quit a few weeks ago."

I am stunned. "Oh, yes. I…I know what you mean. It's not for everyone."

"It's not that," she says. "No one should be expected to put themselves through such hell. Those rotten little kids."

I nod uncomfortably. "Sometimes it's—"

"They didn't want to learn. None of them." One of my plastic scissors falls to the floor; Bev doesn't notice. "I can only do so much," she says. "I am not a savior." She raises her arms in the air and looks defiantly toward me.

"So, um, what are you doing now?"

"I'm a legal secretary," she says. "I'm starting at Stanford in the fall."

"You've applied and been accepted at Stanford?" I ask incredulously.

"I've applied, yes."

"Like, Stanford *Law*?"

"My parents met there."

I hardly know what to say.

"I'll never have to go home again coated in glue and colored markers like you." She looks at my stained khaki pants, then looks up at my face with a satisfied smile.

I turn toward the cashier. "Well, okay then, *Beverly*. I wish you the best of luck."

"I won't need it," she says. "My parents are—"

"Uh-huh," I interrupt. "Yes, right, parents are lawyers."

"You should really think about law school." She drops a large tub of ice cream on the counter, nearly smashing a pair of my scissors. "Don't waste your time teaching."

The next day in class I wonder how Beverly turned from a wide-eyed optimist to bitter cynic in only two months. Was it really that bad? Was this *really* just a stop on her way to becoming a lawyer? What happened to the smiling girl with big dreams for our most needy children? Was she fooling herself all along?

"Look at their white arms reaching out towards us," Don Quixote warns his trusted squire, Sancho. "Daring us to combat."

"Pardon me, sir," replies Sancho, "but those are windmills."

I close the book.

"For real?" asks Gloria, a little girl with her curly hair usually buried in one of her *Twilight* books. Her soft brown face looks earnestly at me from the back of the room. This is serious business. "He thought a windmill was a person?"

"Well, not exactly," I say, returning my gaze to the book. Then I think about Beverly—maybe she was fighting windmills all along. Undeterred idealism can skew one's vision. I make eye contact with Javier just before he reaches back to launch a pencil across the room. I squint my eyes and mouth the word *no*; I run a finger across my neck in a slow slashing motion. He likes it when I do that, says he'd like to do the same to his stepfather. I hope he's joking but I'm not entirely sure. I hear rumors that Roxy's mother makes a living by bringing recent immigrant men into her home. It's not easy being a kid. Maybe my cynicism protects my own sanity. Javier smiles and puts down the pencil. I smile, too. Perhaps I'm no cynic after all.

The more I get to know my students, the more comfortable we become in class. Javier has stopped cussing, and Rafael no longer takes erasers but instead helps me clean the board. I know now that there are reasons for the things they do. That's not to say, however, that I don't still have my challenges. How does Don Quixote turn the intrepid innkeeper's daughter into his fantastical princess Lady Dulcinea? I can't even get Roxy to spit out her gum.

Another week passes and I am sitting in the cafeteria listening to the science department's rousing performance of "Noche de Paz." I organize a large green binder, silently mouthing the English version of "Silent Night." A teacher named Ms. Perez laughs, then leans over the table and pulls the drawing of D-Generation X out of my binder.

"How cute," she says. "Who did this?"

"Who knows. I found it a while ago."

"They got it perfectly," she says, looking closely at the drawing. "Even your expression."

"My expression?" I ask. I wish I'd thrown the picture away. "What's wrong with my expression?"

Her eyes retreat into their sockets. "Nothing," she says. "It's just how you get when you're mad." She tenses her face and balls her hands into fists.

"Suck it." I point at the picture. "That's a bit harsh."

"Hey, that's what they say."

"Huh? *Who*?"

"They're not telling *you* to suck it. Don't you know who D-Generation X is?"

"But it says here, 'we.' Doesn't that refer to the students?"

She takes the picture from me. "You're the *we*. It's plural because D-Generation X is two people, like a tag team." I remain silent. "You're telling *them* to suck it," she continues. "The kids." I look at her blankly. "They're saying you're like the wrestlers, like don't mess with me."

I learn that D-Generation X is the name of a popular World Wrestling Entertainment tag-team duo. They are infamous rebels—even in the wrestling world—and are known for their outrageous antics. Their signature slogan, *Suck it*, has become a rallying cry against authority figures of all types. They are most famous for something called a "crotch chop," in which they place their arms on the sides of their crotch, fingers pointing toward their explicit region. I return my attention to the drawing and notice eraser marks in my crotch area; the artist had originally drawn me in the "crotch chop" pose, but ultimately decided to place my hands in my pockets instead.

"See," says Ms. Perez. "I told you they like you." I realize the drawing is intended as a form of flattery.

"And if you ever saw it," I croon, rising from my plastic chair and clapping to the principal's stiff gestures onstage, "you would even say it glows." *One more day till Christmas break!*

The next morning I surprise Javier from behind and place him in a faux sleeper hold. He's growing taller every day. He reaches behind him, struggles playfully against my weight, and pretends to fall asleep. Jimmy wraps his arms around me, lifts me up surprisingly high, and gently returns me to the ground. Rafael pretends to punch me in the stomach. He and Javier slap hands and hold up their arms in victory. On my way back to my desk, I flick Rafael in the head with a pencil. "Where's your make-up work?" I ask.

"Crap," he says. "Can I bring it tomorrow?" We both know tomorrow is the first day of winter vacation.

I make him wait a few seconds. "Sure," I say, "just make sure it's right." He taps my chest with his pencil.

The bell rings and everyone sits down. Ms. Perez peeks in from across the hall. "Maybe they'll buy you a new cart for Christmas," she says, staring at tired old Betsy in front of the room.

"Maybe."

"I can't believe the custodian managed to piece that old thing back together."

"Yeah." I lower my lip in Betsy's direction. Several boys laugh. Roxy sighs sullenly.

"Betsy doesn't look so good," says Jimmy.

"Yeah," Javier says, lifting his small body off his seat. "I think we can help."

The class spends the next fifty minutes fixing up Betsy. Javier reconnects Betsy's joints with several metal hangers he took from the locker room; Rafael reinforces the middle shelf with layers of electrical tape; Gloria glues fringe from her purse along the top of the electrical tape. They remind me of a NASCAR pit crew. Roxy adds a braided tail. Their enthusiasm is compelling. Watching them, I consider the love Don Quixote felt for his horse, Rozinante. I feel something, too. Javier glues on a few more glass beads he stole from someone's science fair project. Roxy tilts more Christmas glitter on wet glue. She turns toward me and smiles: "Looks good, huh, sir?"

I place my hands in my pockets and tilt my head in agreement.

"Now you can fight those windmills," says Javier. He offers me a soft sucker punch in the kidneys. I throw up my arm and lower my elbow, stopping inches above Javier's head. I look out at the scurrying mass of students before me. These children are not victimized charity cases, as the Teach for America literature would have me believe, nor are they long-armed enemies. You can't wrestle windmills. Instead these are real children with real problems—ranging from abusive parents and unidentified learning disabilities to the simple self-doubt and acne that plague children the whole world over. They are, simply, kids.

"Finished," Javier says after a few more minutes. He wheels Betsy toward the podium. I look at Javier and then at my horse. He beams with pride. The class surrounds him, inspecting their good work.

"Venerable sage, wise enchanter, whatever be thy name; thou whom fate has ordained to be the compiler of my history," I read aloud. "Forget not, I beseech thee, my trusty Rozinante, the eternal companion of all my adventures!" The class claps on cue, all except Roxy, who—a thousand times more beautiful than Lady Dulcinea—takes the gum out of her mouth and reinforces Betsy's tail.

Sealed Forever: On Becoming a Teacher

Cynthia Miller Coffel

"You taking a shit, babe?" Jasmine asked the baby on her hip. I ran my hand along the cold half-opened lid of an ebony casket with gold swing-bar handles, studied the white pleating of the bed's fabric, fingered the quilted velvet of the lid's inside panel, and wondered, *is that any way to talk to your child?*

Twenty-five years old, I was a first-year teacher in May 1980 in the gritty mountain city of Ogden, Utah. I wandered, with the students in my Death in Literature class, around the showroom of the local mortuary. Poor girls, my students—eight teenage mothers working toward their high school degrees—could only dream of someday sleeping in coffins like these, like the empire casket with blue crepe interior, the stainless steel rose casket with copper-plated handles. Did the cheery funeral director, our tour guide, tell us that the bronze casket up on a dais in the middle of the room was "our Rolls-Royce"? I believe he did. I remember the sense of him watching us kindly, hands behind his back: watching pregnant little LaDeane looking up at the wedding-cake chandelier; watching Dainty racing her child's beat-up stroller along the shiny floor; watching me in my maroon now-I'm-a-grown-up teacher dress. I remember agreeing with Majesty, who held her two-year-old daughter Star's hand, that after this, neither of us could ever be buried in any cheap old thing made of fake wood. I remember my irritation at the exuberance of Rosie—usually my favorite—as she leaned into an oak casket open under a spotlight and said, "I have dibs on this one!" She called across the room to me, "Which one's yours, Cindy?"

The Young Mothers Alternative School, a program for married, pregnant, and mothering teens, was located on the second floor of the old
brick Washington Junior High School building downtown. Students
came to Young Mothers from all over the city because of the special
services the program offered: one of the school's five rooms held a
daycare, with white cribs shoved against the walls, where students left
their toddlers and babies to nap and play with a preschool teacher;
in another room a business teacher, a Mormon mother of six, taught
prenatal care, parenting, and budgeting classes; in a third, Sally, the
program's unofficial director, taught a service-learning course combin-
ing English and history. I was expected to teach child development,
foods, economics, one traditional English class, and a set of short
English classes I could design myself; the students earned credit by
taking any of my English courses they chose.

Sally made the program homey. Though the school had no cafeteria
or lunchroom, no science lab, no gym, and few textbooks, it did have
wall-to-wall carpeting, so babies' knees wouldn't scrape when they
crawled across classroom floors; it did have, in Sally's room, a piano and
pillows and plants whose vines climbed up the windows; it did have,
on wintry days, cocoa that Sally served to girls who came in on time.

The Washington Junior High School building housed other alternative schools, too: down the hall from Young Mothers, kids just out of
jail studied for the GED; on the first floor, older people from Vietnam
and Cambodia learned how to pronounce English vowels. Next door
to those elderly refugees, Sally's husband, a former lawyer, ran a school
for gifted students—many of them kids whose ideas about life didn't fit
well with the prevailing Mormon culture. The gifted students named
their program the NEW School: the letters stood for Nonconformists
Entitled to Wisdom.

Everything seemed great in those other programs, but in my classes
the students were obstreperous, and the amount of information I was
supposed to learn and teach was daunting.

"She is the sorriest teacher!" I heard big, giggly September Jones mutter in my English class one day early in the school year, and back then, in October 1979, I knew it was true: at that point I'd failed at every classroom activity I'd tried. In foods class, the girls laughed when I burnt the stew. In English, when I read Grace Paley's short story "Gloomy Tune" out loud, they claimed to be shocked at Paley's profanity. In child development, in a lesson on self-esteem, I demonstrated how it feels when someone treats you badly. Holding an apple up I said, "Every day people take bites out of you, like this," and bit into the apple—*crunch.* I'd found the idea in a book on teaching, but the girls didn't seem to get the point. For days afterward they slid into my classroom with the baby-bottle warmer and their children's pink-and-purple finger paintings taped to the windows and asked, "You going to eat a peach for us today?"

Was it good, that they asked that question? Was it bad? Some of them asked if I'd ever smoked pot, or if, single as I was, I knew anything about sex. *What should I say?* And none of them turned their homework in.

Back home in Indiana, where I'd started toward the master's degree in alternative education that this year of teaching would complete, I'd imagined my classes running like clockwork, every girl excited, every hand raised, every student remembering me, and praising me, for the rest of her life. When Sally and her husband—graduates of Indiana University, like me—had interviewed me, explaining what Ogden and the school for Young Mothers were like, I'd thought I was ready for a town of cowboys and teenage brides, snowy Wasatch Mountains and Latter-day Saints. I'd thought I was ready, as a critic of traditional high schools, to teach in an unconventional school for girls ages twelve to twenty-three, excommunicated or still-believing Mormons, young women who were black or Latino, white or Navajo or Shoshone. An intellectual and a feminist, I wanted to teach my students not just Jack London and Harper Lee—standards of the high school curriculum—but Milton and Woolf and Morrison; I wanted not just to educate my students, but to make their lives all better, too.

Instead, I struggled. Over and over, those first months, I made tactical errors: I wanted all twenty-five in my English class to read Shelagh Delaney's play *A Taste of Honey*, whose main character becomes pregnant out of wedlock. But while making illegal copies of the play at night, I broke the school's mimeo machine, so I sheepishly asked my students to share. I set up independent study sessions with fourteen-year-old Sunday, who wanted help disciplining her two-year-old, Amos, but as we read *Children: The Challenge* together, I wondered out loud whether it was healthy for Amos to be snuggled in bed every night between his mother and his aunt; offended, Sunday stopped coming to class. Proud of my powers of persuasion, I convinced the principal of Ben Lomond, one of the city's two traditional high schools, to send over his outdated textbooks so we'd have reading material I didn't have to mimeograph, but, leafing through the battered books, the girls rebelled. "Hawthorne?" they asked. "What kinda shit is this? You just don't be using your head. We're pregnant, we got things to think about. We can't be doing this homework."

Still, when I was assaulted—in late November, on the day before my twenty-fifth birthday—walking home from teaching an evening class to the refugees at Washington Junior High, the girls seemed sympathetic. Sally rushed over when I called, calmly, from my first-floor apartment with the Murphy bed, the five close-to-the-ground windows, and the plate-glass door, my apartment in what Sally optimistically called a transitional neighborhood.

"I'm okay, really," I said when she answered the phone. "But I was molested a minute ago, and I thought it'd be good for me to talk to someone."

"What?" Sally asked. "You were what?"

"Molested? I don't know what to call it. Attacked? That seems too strong. This guy out on the street—but I'm okay, you don't need to come over, I'm not hurt, he didn't rape me or anything. It's just kind of late at night, and I thought it'd be good for me to talk to somebody before I went to bed."

"Call the police," Sally said. "I'm coming over."

By the time I got to school the next day Sally had told all of the girls at the school my story. How a man had come up behind me and said, "Chilly, isn't it?" then grabbed me and shoved his hands between my legs; how I'd screamed as I'd run back to my apartment. How, at the Arctic Circle restaurant across the street, a stranger had heard me yelling and chased the molester, tackling him in Lester Park. How the stranger had told the molester he was a cop who'd blow his brains out if he didn't identify himself; how he'd come away with the molester's driver's license. How the stranger had run to my apartment, shouting, "I didn't do it. But I know who did." How I'd looked through my glass door and seen the stranger, mistook him for the man who'd grabbed me, and yelled at him to go away, then, dragging the phone in with me so I could call the police, locked myself in the bathroom, pounding on my walls so my neighbors might come and help. All Sally had heard, when she walked up to my dark apartment, was me yelling, and all she could imagine, she told me later, was that the molester was still out there, ready to attack her. She'd pounded on my door so hard she broke it down, glass flying all over my living room rug. The girls had heard about how, at ten at night, the characters in the story traipsed through my broken door: Sally with her frizzy hair and dark coat, crying; the stranger, my savior, whose name I never learned; my neighbors—an explosives expert and a seventeen-year-old single mom; and the policeman who'd come in his black-and-white patrol car when I'd called. The students had heard about the way the policeman, taking down names, jerked his elbow at Sally and asked, "Who's Wonder Woman over there?" They'd heard that the stranger said, "I nearly busted that guy's balls off," and, to me, "You sure can scream, sweet-heart. That's your best quality. You major in screaming?"

My students were suddenly kind to me that day. Some of the girls stood silent and respectful beside me when the policeman in a snazzy blue suit spread photos on my desk so I could identify the pervert. ("The cop's cute," one girl said, "maybe you can snag a date.") They nodded solemnly when I said that if the police found the bastard I'd be happy to testify against him. "Bert O. Peel," the girls said. "We'll remember that jackass's name."

Even though my teaching life improved after that day—I no longer cried on my walk home, no longer dreaded going back—I realize now, thirty-five years later, that my students' kindness didn't help me understand their lives. A daughter of privilege, I didn't know how exciting pregnancy and motherhood can look to a poor girl when there's trouble at home and no work to look forward to after high school. A Midwesterner, in the city just for the year it would take to complete my service and get my degree, I didn't know much about the Mormon culture in which many of my students had grown up, a culture that expressed the American can-do spirit, tied up in a colorful package complete with angels and the lost tribes of Israel; a culture that promoted belief in the perfectibility of man, even after death (I'd seen the paintings of men floating up into the clouds, holding their briefcases); a culture that encouraged girls to marry young and have children rather than living independent lives, and in which large families were—to my mind, anyway—overvalued.

Most especially, back then, I didn't know anything about being a mother. I know more about that now—my son just turned twenty-four—and I can imagine what the girls must have felt when they sat bored in my classes that year. I know now what the texture of time feels like when you're caring for an infant—ragged, coffee-edged, pale, night bleeding into day bleeding into night; I know now how the very color of the light changes when it's your own child you're holding in your arms.

The day after I was assaulted, I think my students began to see me differently. I think they began to see that despite the gaps between us I was like them in some ways: out in the dangerous world on my own and too young for the work I'd taken on; both sentimental about life and angry at it; a little confused, often depressed, sometimes mistreated by men and—even though I was older, wealthier, and more worldly than they were—vulnerable.

Slowly, then, with the help of my colleagues, I began to learn how to teach. Sally told me to invite speakers in or to take students out: to let the community educate. She gave me ideas about how to work around the lack of books. She asked questions: What was most important for these young women to learn and what was the best way to help them learn it? She told me not to require the students to do anything in class they could do on their own; she said that if the teacher wasn't learning, nobody was. She showed me how to organize a semester's work into nine-week chunks. I put together classes on subjects that interested me—on the interpretation of dreams, on the literature of love and literature the students might read to their children. A small group of students liked my style and the topics I presented: they began to take every English course I offered. Toward the end of the year, with my serious pushing, this group agreed to a nine-week course on death.

This topic—all the rage in the late seventies—was perfect for the very young woman I was then. Theologically minded, hungry for gloom, I'd studied the connection between confession and autobiography in college, and had read Carlos Castaneda's *Journey to Ixtlan*. I recalled how the fierce Yaqui wizard don Juan reminded the anthropologist Castaneda of a time he hunted a white falcon, and first shivered with the sense that his own death was sitting to his left, at an arm's length, watching him. "In a world where death is the hunter, my friend, there is no time for regrets or doubts," don Juan tells Castaneda. "There is only time for decisions." Knowledge of our own death, the wizard says, is "the only wise adviser that we have."

Remembering don Juan, I had the students in my death class read the chapter from *Tom Sawyer* called "Pirates at Their Own Funeral," and act out the scene from *Our Town* in which Emily watches her twelfth birthday from the grave. My students wrote their own obituaries ("Brenda Williams was a very sweat girl"), listed objects they chose to be buried with (*The Book of Mormon*, a baby's first pair of shoes, all of their Pink Floyd albums), and planned their own funerals ("Just have a party, drink your asses off, but remember how pissed I am that I can't be there"). They learned the words *maudlin* and *lamentation* and *sepulcher*, and recited Emily Dickinson's "I heard a

Fly buzz—when I died." In my black-and-white-speckled notebook I reflected on students' reactions to the course ("the girls don't seem to take death seriously"), and described my intention to ask a lawyer to explain how to have a will drawn up, because one student worried that her son's father, a gang member, might have rights to her child if she died. Around the room I put quotations: from Rabelais on his deathbed, "I go off to seek a Great Perhaps," and from Hesse, "Look, soon *death will get us too*, and we'll rot in the field and the *moles will play dice* with *our bones*."

Can it be that I was ever the person who designed such a class? As I read my letters from that period I seem so strong, out there all alone among the Mormons. I look at mementos I've kept from the trip my students and I took to the mortuary at the end of the class: a pamphlet in which a woman says, "But I never made funeral arrangements before!"; the Lord's Prayer on a bookmark; a glossary of terms: *cremorial, companion lawn crypt, entombment.* Among the mementos there's a letter I wrote my sister as I was preparing to teach the class, saying I was nervous because "Death, as a topic—it's heavy."

In *Getting Schooled: The Reeducation of an American Teacher*, teacher and minister Garret Keizer writes that he trusts people who have taught school over those who haven't not only because public school teachers have "encountered humanity in all its rawness and variety," but because, as they try to shape that humanity, teachers are forced to experience themselves "as naked as a human being can get." When I remember my first year of teaching, I feel chagrined and a little sorry for my students: I feel naked all over again.

That first year is all about learning who you are up in front of a class, trying on different styles of management and pedagogy until you find the one that feels right. On the trip back to school from the mortuary I thought, for the first time, that I'd figured it out. For much of the year I'd felt like an imposter—a feeling typical among beginning teachers. More focused on content than on the students I taught, loving organizing my curriculum but not comfortable delivering it, I hadn't yet determined what kind of authority to wear or how to perform myself in front of the students: I sometimes disciplined too harshly and other times watched passively as girls spoke cruelly to each other. Most tellingly, perhaps, I didn't hold the students' babies, afraid of those squirming, unpredictable masses of wet; didn't play with the two- and three-year-olds who sometimes toddled over from the school daycare center. There had been moments of connection: students had told me personal stories, asked my advice, invited me to baby showers. But it was only at the very end of the year that I started leading with some skill, and started seeing myself as having something worthwhile to give.

You could say the trip to the mortuary was a disaster; you could say that during the tour I showed very bad judgment.

Nervous about entering a funeral home, I couldn't stop thinking, as I walked into the building, *there are dead people here, there are dead people here.* My students showed no anxiety, though; excited to be out of the classroom under a blue-silk Utah sky, they bounced up the mortuary steps, pointing out the phlox and rhododendron bursting on the mortuary's manicured front lawn, marveling at the heavy, tasseled curtains in the rotunda, propping up their diaper bags against marble pillars while I told the receptionist who we were.

As we waited, Jasmine—blond today but a redhead yesterday—sat on a green silk chair, opened her blouse, and nursed her baby. Was that appropriate behavior in a funeral home? Who knew? I ignored Jasmine and watched Rosie, standing next to a potted fern in sweatpants and mascara, arguing with her daughter, little two-year-old Nina. Eighteen years old and pregnant again, Rosie worried me every time she opened her mouth, a mouth so sharp an attorney who volunteered with our students said he wished she had the money to go to law school. Rosie treated me as if we were equals, loudly complaining that she hadn't had sex in five months; noticing, and commenting on, my awkwardness with the children. In particular, she saw my confusion about her relationship to her daughter, whom she sometimes pushed roughly in the swing that sat in my classroom, whom she called "my little bad girl," to her face. "Cindy, do you think I'm a mean mother?" she'd asked once, and I'd struggled to answer both honestly and kindly: I thought Rosie didn't act toward her daughter the way a caring mother should.

But there wasn't time just then to think about Rosie; when the funeral director appeared, he seemed delighted to squire eight teenage mothers in T-shirts that said "Precious Cargo" and "The Devil Made Me Do It" around his place of work. The girls quickly befriended him, asking, as he showed us the embalming room, what kind of makeup he used on a dead person's face ("I'm thinking of becoming a cosmetologist," Carmen explained); pestering him to describe why faces turn green after death; wondering, when he took us to look at the shiny metal box he called the crematorium, if he ever got people's ashes mixed up. My students cheerfully understood when he told them he'd become a mortician after flunking out of dental school. "We know about flunking!" they said. I followed behind, holding onto baby blankets, picking up dropped pacifiers, asking questions designed to keep the girls in line, and designed to teach.

When, after we'd wandered through the casket-filled showroom, the funeral director quietly asked if I thought the girls would mind looking at the infant coffins, I assumed that my charges would continue on, cheerful and tough. I called out, "You guys, want to see the baby caskets?" and led them, unhesitatingly, toward Baby Land.

We shoved into the alcove made to look like somebody's idea of heaven, a place with a white carpet, satin walls, and a plaster angel blowing a trumpet. Picking up a teddy bear ready to be placed into a coffin, tracing the embroidered words *my little angel* on a heart-shaped pillow, looking over the little blue caskets and the little pink caskets, touching the velvet lining of a white one made especially for newborns, I forgot about the girls, and about the funeral director hovering at my shoulder—until thirteen-year-old, pregnant LaDeane started talking in a rush:

"You know about dreams, don't you, Cindy? You taught that course? Sometimes I have this dream that my baby dies and I'm not sad, I'm happy. Does that mean I'm a bad mother? And then I dream that my husband Ricky dies, too, and I go out to see *Superman II* with my old boyfriend—what does that mean? My husband and I were married in the temple, we're sealed forever…"

"You guys, I'm outta here," Rosie said. She picked up her diaper bag, slung Nina over her shoulder, and marched out of the building.

"What's with her?" Jasmine asked, but I barely heard her. I think I told Jasmine to make sure the girls got back to school; I think I gave LaDeane a quick hug. I know I rushed over the plush gold carpet and under the chandelier, through the wide double doors, down the long flat steps, past the manicured lawn, down Washington Boulevard, and after Rosie.

I found her kneeling on the sidewalk, straightening Nina's pink dress. Rosie's face was wet; her mascara smudged.

"I couldn't stay there one more minute," she said.

I crouched next to her, picking up the diaper bag lying on the cement. I put my hand on her back for a moment.

"I was glad to get out, too," I said. She fussed with Nina's dress, then hoisted her onto her back. We started walking, slowly—what else could we do?—down the few blocks back to school.

"You don't have to give us a test over this day," Rosie said. "I don't think I'll ever forget it."

We walked past El Toro Market and the hamburger place. We walked in rhythm together, silently, Rosie's hands cupped around Nina's ankles, Nina's arms around Rosie's neck. I worried about the girls I'd left unsupervised at the mortuary. Somebody would reprimand me. When we got back to school, I told myself, I'd call and thank the funeral director.

Rosie swung Nina back onto her own two feet. I put my hand on Nina's curly, tough-silky hair.

"I just kept seeing her in one of those little boxes," Rosie said. She turned to me. "I know you think I'm a mean mother, I've seen the way you look at me. But…do you remember that girl that was in our English class last semester, that girl who moved, Heidi?"

"She wanted to be a psychologist," I said, remembering blond Heidi and her ladylike little daughter.

"Do you remember she told us after her baby was born she shoved her hands through the window in the hospital and scraped her wrists back and forth across the glass? Showed us the scars? I was just like her, before I had Nina, I wanted to kill myself, I didn't want to live. But I didn't shove my hands through a window like Heidi did, and I didn't get drunk every night, either. Instead I went out and fucked every guy I could find. I was balling all the guys from my neighborhood, and that's how I found my boyfriend, and that's how I had Nina, and I had her on purpose, Cindy. I've never told anybody, but I wanted to get pregnant. Now that I have her, I have a reason to get up in the morning."

Rosie looked down at her stomach and said, "But this one was a mistake."

"I thought you didn't like Nina," I said, surprising myself with my honesty. Maybe a mother's behavior toward her child didn't always express the way she felt toward that child; maybe I was learning something. "I've seen you be really mean to her."

"She's my little bad girl. She got into the terrible twos and I don't think she'll ever get out. Wait till you have a kid, you'll see! But that's why I'm planning on getting my tubes tied after I have this baby. I did everything right, I got on the pill and took it every day but then here about February I found I was pregnant again."

"You got pregnant even though you were on the pill?"

"I kept bleeding all the time," Rosie said. She told me she'd bled for two weeks straight. She'd thought that you couldn't get pregnant when you were menstruating, so, she said, she thought she was "all right." She stopped walking, squeezed Nina's hand, and faced me, exasperated.

"I don't understand it!" she said. "I don't want any more kids right now, I want to finish high school, I want to be somebody." She started walking again, frowning, looking down at the cement. "So I think I'd better get my tubes tied, I think I'd just better get myself sterilized."

Since my conversation with Rosie I've spent many years teaching. I've taught English as a second language to the daughters of the

Venezuelan oligarchy and test preparation to boys on welfare in upstate New York; I've taught college students, too. More recently I became an educational researcher. All these long years later, I still carry the girls I knew at Young Mothers in my heart: one of my research projects has been to study the literacy lives of teenage mothers.

In my research, I've heard many teen mothers explain why they had their children. I've talked to white girls who had sex with black boys simply because they thought "mixed" babies were cute; I've talked to girls whose pregnancy earned them celebrity among their peers; and I've heard teen moms defend their moral selves by saying, "I'm not one of those that'd leave my baby in a trash can." I've also known girls for whom having a baby has been salvation. If it weren't for their children, some of the girls I've known might be alcoholics or addicted to drugs or dead. I've known girls whose lives have been changed by having a baby, forever, and for the better.

At that time, though, during my first year of teaching, when I was twenty-five, in Ogden, Utah, in May 1980, I hadn't had many conversations with my students like the one I've just described with Rosie. I hadn't yet told my students that I wasn't a virgin, but on that walk back from the mortuary I told Rosie.

"I know that sometimes, when you're on the pill, if you're bleeding, it means there's not enough estrogen, it means the pill's not working," I said. "I think after you have this baby you should go back to Planned Parenthood and get a stronger pill. I don't think you should get sterilized, Rosie, you're only eighteen. What if you meet a great guy and want to have another kid? I don't think you should cut off your options just because of one mistake."

It seemed to me Rosie was telling me about having her tubes tied because she didn't want to do it; it seemed to me that she was scared and angry. I almost offered to go to Planned Parenthood with her, but she shook her head and said, "I think I need to stick to my decision."

"No," I said, surprised at the fierceness in my voice. "You need to take the long view on this." I wanted to tell her how important it is to keep knowledge of your own death to your left, at an arm's length, when you're making big decisions; I wanted to remind her of how many mistakes I'd made myself that year. I decided then, and I believe it now, that as a teacher you don't always push your students or lead your students, but rather you sit beside them, keeping watch as you both move through time, as you learn from mistakes you made yesterday and anticipate mistakes you'll both make tomorrow. I looked back in the direction of the mortuary and saw my students coming toward us: Dainty and Carmen pushing strollers; Jasmine lugging her baby on her hip; Majesty strutting along next to her little Star; September, Brenda, and LaDeane waddling behind. I took Nina's hand.

The Substitute

Marcia DeSanctis

The call came in the morning between cups of coffee as I stood in the kitchen searching the room blankly for a map to follow in my now-familiar quest for a meaningful day. The September air outside the window was clear blue and sparkling, and although it was chilly, the grinning early weatherman had promised me ninety degrees of summer heat by midday. I knew the time would present itself in an instant of clarity regarding when I could shed my heavy sweater. It was the only plan I had for the day, one that would unfold like many in the two years since I had left New York and my job as a network news producer, and moved with my family to rural Connecticut.

My husband had lobbied for years to relocate from our six-hundred-square-foot apartment in the city to our weekend crash pad, an unfinished wooden house perched on the side of a lush, tree-strewn, and very remote valley. He is a sculptor, a carver of massive stones, so it stood to reason that he would seek permanence and happiness in the place where he actually could do his work. Also, our children were already strapping schoolkids, and had fast outgrown our space on the fifteenth floor. The decision to pull up stakes and leave work and the city I loved was more complicated for me. I stood on the precipice of middle age and I was terrified of isolation, geographical and otherwise. But even as I grieved for the urban life we had abandoned, my excitement grew to dive into the work I believed I was destined to do, but had never had the time or the courage to pursue. Finally I had the space—mental and otherwise—to write.

In April 2004, I had written the last sentence of a novel that had gripped me and consumed me with purpose—and helped me ignore how much the exteriors of my life had changed. But by August, too scared to face literary failure that seemed inevitable, I walked away from it. That moment of reckoning had come swiftly one morning on a family trip to Hawaii, which we took courtesy of my parents, as was most of our travel when the kids were small. Ripples of heat rose from the ground at high noon as I turned my back on my children who swam in the hotel pool while I fretted and my husband went mountain biking. I snuck into my room, towel tucked around my waist, to check for an email from an agent who had been promising for five months to read my book. There was nothing in my inbox. It was the last disappointment I could face, and when I picked my face up from the faux mahogany desk, I decided I would pack up my unfinished manuscript and shove it out to sea on a homemade raft made of reeds. I'd add a stack of unpublished essays to the pile, maybe light a match to the whole damned thing.

So on that September morning, as I tried to think of anything but writing, the phone rang and shattered my aimless reverie. It was my new good friend, the wife of a faculty member at a nearby prep school. We had met through my son and her daughter, who were second-grade classmates.

"You speak French, don't you?" she asked.

"Sure," I said, figuring that she, an adventurous cook, needed help with a recipe.

"Well enough to teach?" she asked.

"Well, I speak French well enough to speak fluent French," I answered, genuinely unsure how to answer her question. I had learned French at school, and mastered it breezily and well. I visited France often, and in my twenties, there were a couple of Frenchmen from whom I learned the saltier bits of language. There was even an upstanding Soviet citizen in Moscow who preferred intimacy in Voltaire's native tongue, rather than Stalin's. Later, when I began to work for ABC News, I sallied forth to the Paris bureau whenever I could finagle a stopover there from Moscow or Berlin, an obvious ploy to butter up my colleagues in the hopes of getting hired to work at the gilded bureau on Avenue d'Eylau. When I was twenty-nine, I moved to Paris anyway and on my own steam after the European Union—then known as the European Economic Commission—gave me a press fellowship. Once I was dug into Paris, I stayed for four years. I went back to ABC, then moved to CBS and had a spell at a French network, where a fog of cigarette smoke created a permanent haze inside the office and fumes hung in the air from wine drunk during endless lunches. I bought a sixth-floor walkup, got married to the sculptor who is still my husband. Living there, I learned the cadence, the slang, the quirks, and broke all the rules I had studied so diligently in high school. So, yes, I spoke French—clean and dirty. But I had not thought about grammar in decades and I knew my spoken language could be lazy and riddled with little errors, now habit.

The school, my friend reported, was on a frenzied hunt for a French teacher to fill in for a woman on urgent medical leave, and she was certain I was up to the task of stepping into the semester that had only just gotten underway. Mostly, she knew I needed something to take me away from ruminating about failure and from my self-imposed social quarantine that seemed to be slowly doing me in. I could use a project to divert me from this self-pity jag, something to fill my day and temporarily give my life a point, and a paycheck. Either way, I saw this job prospect as easy deliverance.

"How hard can it be?" I asked.

"I think you can do it," she said.

"Is there really nobody else?"

"French teachers aren't growing on trees in northwest Connecticut," she said. "You'll be great. I promise."

My interview was a formality. They were desperate; so was I, and still I overstated my qualifications, if not my enthusiasm. The school hired me to teach twenty classes—five levels—each week. Their leap of faith had me a little incredulous. The parents who could afford it paid about $45,000 for their kids to attend this rolling idyll, and those kids who had scholarships were there for the prime opportunity a school like that could offer. My appointment felt vaguely like a bait-and-switch. But I would prove to them that this substitute was no flunky. I was a former television producer who had lived a huge life in France.

The language head delivered two towers of textbooks and teacher's companions, which I stared at for a week. As the day approached, I decided to jettison all that. Screw the deadening, mundane curriculum. I would teach them real-life French. I would be the teacher they'd all remember in future awards show acceptance speeches. I would be the teacher who changed them.

Instead of discussing grammar, we would screen *Les Enfants du Paradis* and *The Passion of Joan of Arc*. I wanted them to know the devastatingly gorgeous sixties pop singer Françoise Hardy, and to understand why "Non, *Je Ne Regrette Rien*" was not just Edith Piaf's song but an anthem for all of us. I wanted to inspire them to make off for Paris as Audrey Hepburn did in the film *Sabrina*—as every sensible person should—and know the singular thrill of driving a car through the Place de la Concorde at midnight. I would urge them to close the books first and then their eyes and speak the language, imagining the thrill of mastering another tongue. To really feel it: pucker the lips, shrug the shoulders, add dramatic inflection to every other syllable, to act like a French person and fly. I would tell them about an American news bureau chief I had once known in Paris who did not speak a word of French, and how embarrassed I was for him, and of him. My teaching gig would be, of course, *du gateau* and what was more, I had a new focus and it was not my writing career that was dead in the sand.

The following Monday, my anxiety rose like steam off a lake as I walked across the green toward my first day at work. My boots thudded past sugar maples and teenagers with backpacks, faces rife with curiosity and secrets. *Were they my students? Could I teach them? Would they like me?* My confidence vanished. When I crossed under the two-hundred-year-old arch into the school and realized the enormity of what I was called upon to do, it was too late to run home.

I had a strong sense that I had jumped, all too readily, into rapidly churning waters that were, by the way, far too deep. The stone hallways gave me a dark premonition, as if to telegraph to me the reality that all teachers know: soon I would meld into the corridors, become part of the building, and barely leave the place. This would be my new home, locked as I now was into pure, low-paying devotion. What was I thinking? I was no teacher.

What was worse and even more irreversible, I had belabored my outfit for an hour in the darkness that morning. I felt too flashy and a bit ridiculous; my skirt was too tight and my designer boot heels were too high. I was dressed as I had been for years as a television producer. But for a French teacher in a bucolic boarding school, I was all wrong.

I had fifteen minutes to introduce myself to other faculty members before my first class. But my nerves had emerged, chafed and raw, so I spent twelve of those fifteen minutes fighting nausea in the restroom and finally vomiting out of sheer, helpless terror. When at last I took my place at the head of the classroom, in front of twenty pairs of staring eyes, and realized I had to put on a show, I understood the gastric upset: it was stage fright. Now, I had to entertain them, the kids in Honors French 2, my first class of the day.

"*Bonjour classe,*" I said, my cracking voice revealing, I was certain, my insecurities and pathetic qualifications. "*Je m'appelle Marcia DeSanctis,*" and I turned around to write it on the board, realizing with horror that those same eyes were now on my too-tight skirt and forty-three-year-old backside. "But I guess you call me Mme DeSanctis, here at school." I desperately wanted to add, "And I am not a French teacher, just a French-speaking former journalist who was lucky enough to be handed this job just when I needed one. And I have no fucking idea what I'm doing here."

My knees wobbled as we went around the class, as each earnest student gave me his or her shortened biography. When Tanya, a perky blond, asked if I was collecting the homework, and Donald, a serious brown-eyed boy, asked if the chapter exam would still be the following day, my deep shame was illuminated. I had taken every teacher I'd ever had, and every teacher my children had ever had, for granted. This was going to be work, tons of it, and all my posturing about real-life French went out the window. These were serious students, some of them brilliant, and they needed to learn, get good grades and into college.

"Madame, will the extra vocab be on the exam?" asked one girl.

"Madame, will the test cover just chapter five or everything since the beginning of the year?" asked another.

I had not prepared any test. Neither had the regular teacher, Mme Mazarine, who had been incapacitated by a medical emergency. I had barely opened the textbook. I assured them that there would be no break in their program, not to worry a bit. "I am going to postpone the test until Friday," I said.

"We don't have class on Friday," said a student. "Hi, I'm Hannah. How about a week from today?"

After class, a boy named Grayson came to see me in my office. "I need some help on the imperfect," he said.

You and me both, buddy.

"Sure thing," I said. "Let's see. Can I borrow some paper?" I wrote down a verb: *manger,* to eat. "The imperfect is easy. I'll show you." After fifteen minutes with him, a swelling sense of resolve rose up to greet me. He was my student now and I wanted, almost needed, him to do well.

"Is this any clearer?" I asked, a blatant cry for validation.

I had four classes left to teach that day. I needed a drink.

Those first days, I moved as if buoyed by water, propelled by the relentless and satisfying drift of the school day. I taught five lessons, tried to learn the students' names, and already, I was ashamed to say, had formed opinions about them. I could already see who was serious and who hated French class and who hoped their substitute teacher would give them a free ride. I sensed who was sucking up, and who made excuses for missing homework, and I tried my best to nod compassionately and believe them. It surprised me how quickly— sometimes just by an intensity in their gaze—I could spot a student with a ferocious drive to excel, and they popped up regularly.

I did not realize that despite how democratic was the process in theory, a teacher was just a human being and that being fair was sometimes a necessary contrivance. I was supposed to like them all equally, and the best I could do was to pretend that I did. Similarly, I had to possess an equal trust in their abilities and efforts, and not penalize them for lack of enthusiasm in a subject they despised. Even if I knew that Billy, for example, found French class to be a torture chamber, I could not hold that against him. I was partial to two kids, both stars of the school drama program who had a way with accents. Neither of them could complete a homework assignment or hand it in on time, but their incorrect spoken French was gorgeous. It would propel them, I hoped, around the streets and cafés of Paris or Aix-en-Provence and serve them well. They were better suited to dream their way across the world as I had once, more than the robots who scored perfectly on grammar but could not speak a decipherable word.

I tried to look the other way when a student fell asleep in class. It happened all the time, and who could blame them, considering. Grammar is a deadly hell. High school students have enormous demands on their time and to be truthful, for those not born with a gift for languages it can be a struggle to stay alert, not to mention awake. Still, I was mortally wounded when a student dozed off; I took it as a personal betrayal, but I wailed only on the inside. When students checked their watches or craned their necks to see the wall clock, I was similarly stung. They were right: I was boring. I took to throwing candy at my first-year students in a shameless effort to buy their love and attention in the long, starved hour before lunch break. I kept bowls of Halloween-sized Snickers and Twix bars on hand, and once even gave a kid money to go buy snacks for everyone at the vending machine. I wanted them to like me, and gifting them with a few bags of chips seemed a good way to ensure that.

I am certain my students did not know the hours I put into making up tests, correcting homework, planning the next day's lessons. How could they? I had no idea myself until I stood, by accident, in front of a classroom for the first time that fall morning. My own family life went on hold while I negotiated the learning cliff of a first-time teacher, and my husband patiently took over. And when I was rewriting a student's stilted homework paragraph at midnight—eighteen hours into my workday—I did it with the same passion and facility I remembered from writing my own stories.

Like an actor who gets her big break, I got used to, and even motivated by, the performance anxiety, the brief wooziness from adrenaline, and finally the utter clarity that was required of me as I stood in front of the students. I enjoyed walking in as the figure in charge and, usually, my nerves quickly settled into the classroom's groove. I was working harder than I ever had, and though much of it was grueling, I looked forward to my lessons and the responsibility that came with them.

The students, for their part, may or may not have sensed that I was growing fond of them, or protective, and of the teaching rhythm that had become the engine of my life. I anticipated some of their essays with curiosity, and I felt a new intimacy. You can learn a lot about a person by a small homework question—that he did not make the varsity hockey team, or that she hates the violin her mother forces her to play, or that his greatest wish is for his parents to reconcile, or that she dreads the upcoming holiday vacation with her stepfather, who drinks too much and *n'est pas sympathique*.

By the time finals and the semester had ended, it was December vacation and my job was over. There was no party for me, of course. Everyone was exhausted from correcting exams that last bleary week. There was snow on the path when I crossed the green the last time toward my car. With the stone building behind me, and the arches at my back, I wept with near grief. I cried for the students who had affected me so deeply, but who I feared had forgotten me already in their exuberant exodus for the holidays. I had gotten myself out of the house and in so doing had rejoined the family of man, which teemed with purpose and devotion and commitment. I would miss those kids and was grateful for one thing they could not know: they had emboldened me. All teachers know that the reward is mutual—you give, you get—and now that sweet secret was mine to hold as well. But I missed the breakfast and dinner routine with my own children whose Christmas lists sat folded up and neglected in my wallet. And my writing—I was scared to face it but now it stood before me, all consuming but less urgent than three months earlier. I had hurled myself before my students and in so doing, I had seen what mattered and it wasn't me.

I sat a spell in the parking lot. The life before me seemed vacant, the one just behind me was full. I looked up to see a smiling Hannah at my car window.

"We will miss you, Madame," she said. "Are you coming back?"

"I'm sorry to be leaving, too, Hannah. I'll miss you so much," I said. "I loved teaching your class. Every minute, really."

"Then stay," she said.

"Mme Mazarine will be back in January," I said. "She's a great teacher and much more qualified than I am."

"That's too bad," she said. "So what do you do normally?"

"You know," I said, "I'm a journalist. A writer actually. I have lots of ideas to tackle. Or tame, I'm not sure which."

"That's cool," she said, "but why don't you teach French instead?"

Why, indeed.

They deserved more than I could offer. And in truth, I had my own work to continue, and it would demand doggedness, diligence, and all my attention.

A week before my teaching job started, I had sent my manuscript to another agent, a friend of a friend, a smart woman whose judgment I was told to trust. I had pushed it, almost entirely, from my mind. The first thing I did when I got home from my last day as a French teacher was email her. I was too tired to care what she said about it, but the time was right to search for answers and write my fingers raw.

Merry Christmas, she said in her response. *I like your book, so far. Keep working on it. Don't give up. But maybe*, she suggested, *you should put this one away for now, and start another one.*

And so I did. This is the place where I belong: alone, in the liberating confines of my writing room, spending several hours a day face-to-face only with myself. Fear is as invigorating in my writing life as it was in my teaching life, but it is still fear and needs to be confronted every day. One project gives way to another. Like life, my work changes, amends itself, and throws me a few surprises. It took five years for an editor to show faith and publish the essay that ushered in my career, and almost ten until my first book came out. My writer's life is full of riches, even if frequent recognition and the satisfaction it brings are not among them.

About two years later, after one long day embroiled in rewrite, my phone rang. It was Alison, the head of Modern Languages at the school where I had taught. There was a new crisis in the French department: a beloved teacher had fallen ill and it was just the start of the winter semester. Would I consider coming back?

"Hmmm," I said. "Depends how long."

"It could be indefinitely," said Alison. "At least till the end of the term."

I said nothing but the possibilities tossed around my brain. I could commit to a few months. I missed the students, the adrenaline, the human race. Hell, I missed speaking French.

"What do you think?" she repeated.

"Sure," I said. "I'd love to come back for a while."

It Took an Island: Why I Became a Teacher and Stayed

Deborah Meltvedt

Medical Science, Health Professions High School, 2015

In anatomy classrooms throughout the world, we teach about the heart. We have our own language: ventricles and atrium, septum and superior vena cava, cardiac reserve. The purpose of the cardiovascular system is to deliver oxygen, and the purpose of teaching, in my eyes, is to help kids not only learn science and math and how to write a thesis statement, but also to discover the wildness and bravery of their own original thoughts.

I wasn't the kid who always dreamed of being a teacher—who picked up abandoned chalk and made her little brother or sister *sit still* as she bit her lip and pretended to diagram a sentence on an imaginary chalkboard. But I learned later, after volunteering as a health educator in adolescent clinics and getting a degree in health science, that I was good at breaking down complex physiology into terms my friends could understand. And I fell in love—with language, world news, scientific theory, the anatomical words for my own biology. But it was more than that. Science, sociology, and women's studies classes all taught me, after years of self-hatred and a brief flirtation with anorexia, to make peace with my own body and to realize the empowering quality of knowledge. I stayed in teaching because I wanted to give back power, especially for children at risk for self-loathing and risky behavior. Moreover, I found that, in giving kids tools for self-respect and healthy behaviors, I also taught myself to reclaim a small slice of self-love that I had lost so many years ago.

And then there are scenes like this: a warm Friday afternoon in May. It is almost four thirty and I'm packing up for the weekend's work: papers to grade, new health science standards to catch up on, medical journals to try and decipher. Four students linger in the classroom, waiting for rides, hanging out. Their voices jump from homework groans to gossip giggles and eventually settle on an array of philosophical talk: religious views, immigration laws, terrorist threats, teen pregnancy. Their conversation is a microcosm of California society. I ask, "What does the other side say?" "Why do you think you believe that?" They argue, laugh, they intersperse the serious talk with a fashion question, a joke, a line from *Criminal Minds* or *American Idol.*

And then they give me more. With pulses rising and blood zipping through veins, they tell me what it feels like not to have enough money for breakfast; they let slip the shame of being undocumented or the anger of never having had a teacher of the same race. And deeper still, they may share the color of blood from a friend's gunshot wound or the sound of sorrow when the very best grandfather passes away.

Pulmonary: lungs. *Pericardium*: the heart enclosure. *Apex:* point of the heart toward the left hip, where the ventricles meet. *Chordae tendinae*: heart strings.

I became a teacher because in what other job in the world do you get to witness the heart ripped open and, instead of using a surgeon's knife, teach a child how to use their own medicine to stitch up heartache and to stand up against any further blows?

Rachel, Valley High School, Late Nineties

I am teaching skin anatomy when Rachel summons me over and whispers, "I'm a witch." She is sitting dutifully in a front seat of my classroom, only sixteen years old, but like a seasoned college student, copying notes in a frenzied, neat style. She is dressed in green and yellow, except for her sneakers, which are purple and red. A pink bandana hugs her bony skull. It has been just three months since her diagnosis. Three months since her family was told *she might not make it to graduation.*

"But don't witches wear black?" I ask.

"Ms. Meltvedt, I am here to tell you a secret: real witches, like me, *love* color, its energy. The colors you see are the ones reflected in your soul." She stretches out the word *love* the way a Southerner would. Or a true believer. And Rachel smiles the rare smack of young people in love, not with a first boyfriend or childhood crush, but with something else, something deep down—something that, less than ten years into my teaching career, I am still looking for in myself. But in Rachel's disclosure of identity, as my students label their epidermises and sebaceous glands and the warmth of a September sun comes sneaking through the window, I see bravery up close. Rachel, who has been through rounds of chemo and radiation and has come back to school, not only ready to ace a test or write a good composition, but wearing the brightest colors from head to toe, as if to tell the world *as long as I'm here, you will notice me, you will want me*; Rachel, who has curiosity dripping off of her like sweat and a brain that inhales the world, will dart inside my heart and stay.

There are other forms of toxicity, not just the cancer cells that soared through Rachel's lymph nodes. There is the quieter invader that I think most people experience from time to time when we try to find meaning in our lives. For me, it was trying to find purpose in public education—where everything from bureaucracy to union fights to political agendas to teaching five preps with little pay to make ends meet made me question whether I chose the right career. It was also hearing each day how we were all *failing our kids.* And it was watching some kids give up and not being able to find the right ingredient, *the magic wand,* to make their low expectations or their family dysfunction go away.

But it was Rachel, and so many others, who got up each day and got to school—*despite everything*—who made me get up, who reminded me why I stayed.

The Beginning, 1965

In kindergarten, Miss Weismann gave us chunks of wood and placed slices of metal between our awkward stubs of fingers and watched us saw new life. We became five-year-old mothers and fathers birthing donkey heads and rabbit ears—and, miraculously, the only cuts to us were small ones into fleshy palms. But we became ready for battle. Our teachers made us ready by saying *it's not that bad* and thrusting our tiny hands under the faucet where we watched the water turn red. Later, we licked our tears and, wearing big white shirts for smocks, painted the donkey's head gray and the rabbit's ears pale pink. The shirts smelled of bleach and our fathers' aftershave, and we breathed in again their stories of war and what it was like to shed more than blood so we could be free to go to school and cut imaginary shapes into wood.

Miss Weismann taught me how to lick my wounds when I fell down and how to be a Big Girl. The teachers who followed taught me to read the words of our forefathers, the honesty of Anne Frank, and the causes of World War II. But I didn't learn to speak up. I didn't learn to reach down so deep into secrets that went beneath a surface cut and pull out emancipation. I didn't learn to show and tell heartache. Awakening would come later, and not with scientific theory, but with the release of private knowledge that had been ziplocked in our own mouths—because we believed that shame and secrets and family battles had no place in the classroom.

Don't tell. Without a word said at home, I *knew* that telling would be shame. In the 1950s and '60s, it was the unwritten code of suburban families. The generation of past war heroes and nuclear families that smiled prosperity and happiness on the outside. But inside our homes lived the fallout of a horrific war. So when my world at home began to crumble—when my father's one drink became five or six, when the shouting was so severe that I slept in the closet, when I began to hate the ones I should have loved—I didn't tell a soul. Especially my teachers. Telling would be far worse than sleeping in closets. I knew instinctively that nobody could know about my parents' verbal fights, which were so loud that I learned how to hide just as well as my father had years before, in a Belgium field, escaping German enemies. Only my shame was without bravery. My guilt was in the *wanting desperately to tell*, but cowardice held court, and I remained a good girl in class, often hating the thought of ever going home.

The Defense

Teaching is a battered, beloved profession. The dichotomy of wanting so much to give away a piece of yourself that will settle into the hearts and minds of the next generation, and the daily defense against accusations that you are failing the hearts and minds of the next generation. And in all the debates on what is wrong with education today, the simple word *teacher* leaves both a mouthful of admiration and a bitter aftertaste of blame.

Picture yourself in front of a school board, at a doctor's office, a cocktail party. Picture yourself defending the belief that every kid deserves the best education. And insisting that most teachers don't leave for home when the last school bell rings. Picture yourself explaining that every kid isn't a politician's version of the right answer on a multiple choice test.

Almost Losing Rachel, Late Nineties

The day before Thanksgiving break, I learn that Rachel is getting worse. *No wait!* I scream inside, *I just got her.* The other teachers tell me, like an afterthought. One minute they are discussing standards and grade checks and then suddenly: *Oh yeah, the tumor returned. It's in her eyes now, and the back of her spine. Doesn't look good.* One of them makes a slitting sign across his throat.

In the classroom that day, Rachel is quiet. We've moved on to the skeletal system, and posters of irregular bones decorate the classroom. Rachel squints one-eyed into her paper, lip bit, her hand like an arthritic old woman's. She grips her pencil so hard it dents her thinning skin.

At lunch, she tells me, "You know, Ms. M, no one wants to hear this. Not really." Her voice is raspy now; there is the deep gulp of breath before each sentence. "But I do want it all, college, marriage, kids, a house. I still think it's gonna happen."

"I know," I say. "Everybody does."

"It doesn't even hurt much," Rachel insists. And we sit there for a moment, eating ordinary tuna fish sandwiches, Rachel's bracelets clanking loudly every time she takes a bite.

The Defense Goes On

At the school board meeting, everyone is shouting. In a two-minute rebuttal, you can't tell them how confused you are. You want to shout: *We're doing what you asked! You told us don't teach to the test—but the test scores will judge you. You said put up a flag, don't put up a flag; talk about character but not religion; prevent teen pregnancy, but don't hand out condoms. And—despite poverty, homelessness, apathy, child abuse, drug addiction, violence, budget woes—dear God, teach them to stop bullying, to take AP classes, to shut up and listen.*

At the cocktail party, somebody asks, *Which schools are best?* You want to answer, *Mine, mine!* But even you, the teacher, know that despite all talk of education equality, if they're rich enough, they'll put them in private school. You wish deep inside that private schools were outlawed; maybe then, maybe then, everybody would care.

It Took an Island, 1989

Because I could not save my family from fighting or myself from self-hatred, I decided instead to save the world. For years, I harbored the fantasy of being brave *somewhere*. If I couldn't stop my parents from hurtling insults, it was my duty to pluck courage from my heart and do good *somewhere*. Like a civil rights protester or a nurse on the Western Front, I needed a risk. If I couldn't save my father from the ghosts of German pilots he had blown out of the air, I would free drowning kittens from burlap bags thrown in rivers and travel to Asia to feed the starving babies in Bangladesh.

I have always wanted to be brave. But I was too sensitive—the girl with tangled hair flying, eyes averted, feet running away. I gauged my cowardice by how often I ran from boys who seemed to sniff my fear like the neighbor's Doberman pinscher. I rode my bike carefully and snowplowed my way out of ski accelerations. Sometimes I would whisper to myself, *Just do it*—get to the higher branch, talk to the new boy, raise your hand in class. But I knew well the safety of staying seated and never raising my hand, my voice, or any threat at all.

Invisibility is a strange thing. I've learned since that children raised in alcoholic or verbally violent homes suffer, like veterans of war, from PTSD: my father's and my shared legacy. And even though my father has changed, made amends, those years of hiding when his voice was raised, when glasses were thrown and threats were made, led to such anxiety that my body rebelled. In crisis, there is fight, flight, or freeze. Without me knowing why, my body froze. Insomnia, stomach twists, tension headaches.

When my parents' voices rose and grew too loud for sleep or safety, my sister Betsy would confront. She would risk punishment, a possible slap. Betsy took chances in everything: boys, driving recklessly on the freeways, sneaking out in the middle of the night. I didn't confront, but cleaned up broken glass and mended the aftermath. I wanted to save the world, but I froze along the way. Got swallowed up in body rebellion and adolescence and stayed there until the scars of acne, the headaches, and the pain of rejection sat on my shoulders so heavily it was years before I could stand up straight and make myself visible to the world. Always haunted by the times my knuckles froze midair when I tried to raise my fist against my parents' bedroom door, and yell back at them: *Stop! Don't you know I'm here?*

I hid my weakness well. I avoided public bathrooms because my shame froze my bladder. Every imperfection of puberty—frizzy hair, acne, round thighs—was more ammunition for me to hate who I was, and I spent hours searching for ways to cover up flaws. Eventually, I found a way to control—with what I ate or didn't eat. A little starvation, what we know now as an eating disorder, was the final card thrown to seal my invisibility. It would be years later, in college, when fear started to thaw. Curiosity happened. Learning about injustice worldwide struck a chord. Women's studies taught me to love my body again. In sociology classes, I read about the "ideal" equity of a public school system, the ethic that all children, no matter how rich or poor, deserved a good education. The health sciences taught me that knowledge of our bodies could prevent a pregnancy, disease, even the taking of our own lives.

I decided to reclaim bravery. I would help stop homelessness and the spread of AIDS. I would go back in time and take the gun away from the girl who sat next to me in my family studies class and later blew her brains out on a lonely Saturday night. I wanted to keep babies from being born without limbs and girls from hating their bodies.

And so, at the age of twenty-eight, I joined the Peace Corps.

I saw myself sunburned and thin in a tiny grass hut teaching children to read or dropping malaria pills onto eager tongues. I saw myself sacrificing my skin and hair, blood and health, so others could see me doing something good. I joined up quickly and spent my twenty-ninth birthday en route to the South Pacific. I left behind my job, my ex-boyfriend, my aging dog, and friends with shiny diamond rings and newborn babies.

Four weeks later I was back on American soil, a Peace Corps dropout. There aren't any support groups for us. And when I arrived back home it was hard to explain that it wasn't poverty or bad water or nighttime raids; it is harder to explain when you are simply running from yourself.

Rachel on Her Way

On the day before Valentine's Day, the school holds a special graduation for Rachel. Our principal wears a low-necked formal and reads a speech written by Rachel's teachers. They are all so proud. *Look, look, you made it!* By now, Rachel is almost deaf and we need to bend low to speak to her. Her head cocks to one side, her legs stick out like those of a figure in a child's drawing. When I hug her, her arms feel doll-like: cold and plastic, barely bending. For a moment Rachel whispers in my ear, "Why?"

You Can't Hide on an Island

I can still taste the Solomons—mangoes and pawpaws, poached eggs clinging to slivers of thin, burnt toast, the lukewarm sweetness of coconut milk. Although there are many islands in the Solomons, we were stationed on Guadalcanal, a place I knew only from World War II movies before I'd left home. I found thick tropical forests, shell beaches that cut my feet, and heavy humidity that felt like the familiar cloaks of heaviness I was on the edge of naming.

My roommate was Sandra, Baltimore born and raised, a thirty-five-year-old divorcée. At night I watched her grease and roll her hair, her brown hands moving rapidly and expertly. She flossed her teeth for over an hour, and when she laughed, her smile took me in like firelight on a winter's night.

On day three on the islands, I was unabashedly and joyfully sick. The symptoms were real—dull headache, body aches, the slow rise of nausea in my gut as we walked through the middle of Honiara, the main island town. I had a fever, a burn deep down behind my eyelids, making me giddy and grateful. I had expected this. They had warned us of the certainty of food poisoning hidden in a single piece of unwashed fruit. Sandra brought me warm 7-Up and burnt toast. By nightfall, I rushed down the bathroom hall, throwing up, and laid my head against the room's cool tile. And, again, I thought, *Oh yes, this is what they told me.* Physical sickness would hide the growing power of depression, giving my body respite from a different type of pain.

Once again, courage began to unravel. Fear hovered on my lips after a chug of Foster's beer drunk in late afternoon talks with other volunteers. It hung in the moldy walls of our communal bathroom, as we examined ourselves, women without makeup, in the aching honesty of our hotel mirror. Fear came back and recognized my twelve-year-old self and found a familiar home. A fog began to linger somewhere between the thin cotton sheets and the heat that seeped in our paneless window. The uncertainty was overwhelming. I was like a small child lost in a crowd, my hand slipping from the grasp of my mother, the hems of foreign women whipping my face. The words *I may have made a huge mistake* stayed pierced inside my brain, and I was flooded with familiar shame.

And we waited. Solomon life was slow. But still I learned: Pidgin English, island customs (*kastams*), and taboos (*tabus*). How women died in childbirth, of rapes inside the "bush," the accepted ritual of wife beating, and the lack of female independence. After eight days of training in the hotel, we traveled to our assigned *vilaj*. My family host was Vetalina, who "storied" each night, revealing blackened teeth, decayed from betel nut, and large sunken breasts that swung side to side with the sighs of her tales. She told us of dead souls reincarnated into the bodies of sharks and reptiles, so that finally, by the second night, I dreamt of these spirits, calling from the sea. But their form wasn't fish-like, but of women, torn and broken, screaming for help, their voices drowning in the waves.

The island began to shrink for me. None of the women, foreign and islanders, were allowed to swim or canoe or go into town without a male escort. Close to the shore, I learned to stand distant, cutting my toes on shell beaches, and staring into the sea. The sharks were out there swimming, in masses, hiding beneath sunlit waves. Behind my back, the trees towered thick and impenetrable.

In the fit of one August morning, I lay awake in the Solomons and knew I would go home. My sense of connection to my own body had left me once again, before the birds awoke, when the island was dead tired. As in childhood days, when I dissociated for survival, I hovered, watching myself, void of feeling. I saw what it was like to feel utterly alone. Under a mosquito netting in the middle of the South Pacific, melancholia had finally won out, and I didn't make a difference at all.

I hitched a ride with Australian divers out of the *vilaj* and back to Honiara. After a conference, the Peace Corps granted me leave and I returned to the hotel. My director was kind and she told me a story. When she left for the Peace Corps, her father told her that no matter what, if she left early or stayed late, he would always be proud of her. Her words made me buckle. I couldn't imagine anyone ever being proud of me, especially now. I closed my eyes and tried to imagine what it must be like to win praise for simply taking a risk.

It took two days to fly home. At the Brisbane airport, I met a South African man, with dreadlocked hair and flashing smile, who wanted to know my "story." Everything spilled, even the fact that I missed my dog and feared he would die while I was gone. His eyes listened the most, and he leaned over and told me, gently, "This just wasn't the right time, give it time, you will know when to really give back, give it time." And he was gone. He will never know how long I carried his reassurance inside my head. How often I held his words in future times when I still couldn't forgive in my own voice.

Years later, I tried to answer all my questions. *Was I right to leave? Did I give it time? Will I ever make a difference?* My friends told me how proud my father really was to see me go, but I never heard those words myself.

Sandra, my roommate in the Solomons, made it three years in the Peace Corps. She wrote me in her second year, asking to visit me in California. She asked if I would help her get an abortion. She was too afraid to tell the staff, too afraid to come forth about how island *tabus* carried over into the domain of American women too. We met only once in Los Angeles, and she told me of others who'd dropped out, that I wasn't alone. Sandra had her abortion and one year later got engaged to a Solomon man, a lab technician who worked at the same hospital she did. They were married and she wrote of bringing up two island children, who I like to believe have bellies well fed and whose hands catch the saltwater waves full of shells and giving spirits.

For a while, I tried not to think much about being brave. I did travel again. Small trips to Africa and South America. I can merge into five o'clock California traffic with the best of them, and I've learned a thing or two about how to make eye contact in late-night bars and crowded airports. I was there when my dog died—when I let them put the thin, poisoned needle into his crippled collie body and held him as he released his final breath. And I like to think that was important. That somebody needed me.

Rachel

The last time I see Rachel is on a cold March day at lunch in the school yard. Rachel states she is no longer a witch but a Christian and that her funeral will be held at the United Methodist Church, and, of course, I am invited. Rachel tells me *she is ready now.*

The sky is white blue and hurts my eyes. Rachel sits in her wheel-chair, dwarfed; the wave of her hand as a friend passes by reminds me of sugar cane swaying in a field. Waving and dancing, waiting for the inevitable slice of a sickle, where her sweetness will be packaged and delivered to the open mouths of sugar-starved kids. I shiver and the ivory hands of Rachel come down, pox-scarred and thin, and grab mine. "They're so cold, Ms. Meltvedt, so cold." There is a rhythm to her touch: rub, rub, blow warm breath, rub rub. Rachel brings them back to life. For a moment, I feel a rush of heat and pleasure soaking into my bones. The air around me shimmers from the tiniest bit of energy Rachel still brings forth. Rub, rub, blow warm breath, rub. And in a flicker of late afternoon twilight, I can almost feel the ghost of Rachel, months down the road, zipping up a graduation gown in June, walking down a rose-petal aisle, even bandaging the skinned knees of children not yet born.

Another Kind of Peace Corps, 1991–2015

There are pupils of mine in the United States who make me think of fear. Third World students in America. These teens have replaced the images I once held of hungry Honiara children. Some parents have thrown them away—handed them over to grandparents, foster parents, even the streets. Others have loving parents, but something wild and threatening often lies beneath the child's surface as adolescence and the world's sadness collide. I've listened to Juanita's fear of being disowned by her parents because she loves both boys and girls, of Petra's third suicide attempt, of Cassie's trip to visit her father in jail. I've been there when they confessed—to not using birth control, to vomiting food because two ounces is two ounces too much, to wishing they could just slip away. And I've read about their deaths at the hands of an angry foster dad or underneath a mangled car. And yet. And yet. They aren't forgotten. Or invisible. Sometimes we just didn't listen hard enough to their screams.

I teach adolescents because it is hard and the classroom is where I choose, wrongly or not, to change the world. I teach adolescents because I have a crazy belief that we have to remember that kids matter. Even older children—the ones no longer so easy to keep still and make them *do what we tell them*. They matter. And because my students remind me more and more, not of fear, but of courage.

Because I teach, I get to see Cesar, shy in September, nail a thirty-minute presentation at the end of his senior year. I get to discuss racism with Seraiya and Natasha who trust me, a white woman, just enough to let me in on what it feels like to them to grow up black in America. I still hear from Priscilla, whose multiple sclerosis has kept her in a wheelchair for years, who fights for breath daily, who talks about her two majors and her college degree. I get to watch them all—give blood, recite poems, be the first in their family to apply to college. I get to hear from students who thought they could barely graduate, who write me from college classrooms or global travel about how, in their own way, they are changing the world. I am not their Miss Weismann in kindergarten giving them their first blade, but instead I hope I give them voice on the page or stage or in the community.

On the flight back from the Solomons, I sat with knees crunched up against my chest, unable to imagine a world that still needed me. I was a failure. I had tried trading one form of adrenaline for another, hoping I could finally tame the darkness that rode tandem with me since childhood. But we find a way. I did in teaching. Learned to starve out sadness. Learned to let go of an image of my fist that never pounded on a closed door and dropped that image thirty thousand feet into the sea, where I imagined it eaten by ancient sharks. In the end, we all have outstretched hands.

Because of Rachel

At Rachel's funeral, I walk into the middle of it all. Into the awkwardness of my colleagues' hugs, the echoes of the weeping teens—dramatic sobs, backs of hands splattered with mascara, a few boys choking back the bubble of thickness rising in their throats. Their mouths release the true pain of sorrow, the much-too-early reality of loss. They are all so beautiful in their grief.

At the podium, in front of Rachel's coffin, all of them step up. The English teacher reads one of Rachel's poems, the best friend of the family admits Rachel was the daughter he never had, and Amy and Elinor, good friends of Rachel's for years, all heavy-haired and shoulder-slumped, recall the glory days of childhood. When it is all said and done, when none of them have ever known a girl to be as kind, as brave, as funny as Rachel, when her passions—the color pink, the NBA—have been thrown out and reeled back in—the reverend gazes across his flock and smiles. He stares at Rachel's classmates, her oncologist, her uncontrollably weeping aunt and her can't-cry-anymore mom, at me where I sit squirming like a five-year-old. When he at last speaks, he says what everyone has been waiting to hear: that Rachel is better off. God has called his angel home and she is free. Free of needle jabs and nausea, free of a scalp that burns for days, free of diseased lungs and ravaged veins. All those years of suffering have been quenched and replaced with a spot next to Jesus. Pain free.

My first impulse is to slap the reverend's face. *Better off? Better off than graduating or going to college or experiencing the awkwardness of first sex? Better off dead?* But another part of me wraps tight the revelation. I want to believe in this analgesic ascension which replaces sick, skinny, bald-headed Rachel with the version of her I want to see: smiling, strong-armed, with thick, glossy hair, pink cheeks, and wings. No pain at all.

But what I really know is the slow truth of what Rachel gave me. Of what I get back as a teacher—the witness of bravery in an unjust world. The remarkable witness of a young girl's life and death. To be the one, just for a moment in her short life, who got to hear her say, one day, *It's not fair*, and who said back, *Yes, yes, it's not, but I'm proud of you for trying*. And on the toughest teaching days, I can still see her smile and feel her gift of warmth, as her hands hold mine and the rhythm of *rub, rub, blow breath, rub rub*, seeps into me. This is why I stay.

Contributors

Sara Ackerman is a writer and kindergarten teacher. She lives with her family in Ethiopia.

Anne P. Beatty is a National Board Certified Teacher who lives, writes, and teaches high school English in Greensboro, North Carolina. Her writing has appeared in *The American Scholar* and *North American Review.*

Jane Bernstein's most recent books include the memoirs *Bereft: A Sister's Story* and *Rachel in the World.* She is also an essayist, a lapsed screenwriter, and a member of the Creative Writing Program at Carnegie Mellon University. Visit www.janebernstein.net to read some of her shorter work.

Cynthia Miller Coffel is the author of *Thinking Themselves Free: Research on the Literacy of Teen Mothers* (Peter Lang, 2011). A literary essay, "Letters to David," won the *Missouri Review* Editors' Prize in 2007; other works have been listed among the notable essays of the year in *Best American Essays* 2005 and 2008. Her PhD is in literacy education.

Michael Copperman teaches low-income, first-generation college students of diverse backgrounds at the University of Oregon. His prose has appeared in the *Oxford American, The Sun, Creative Nonfiction, Salon, Gulf Coast, Guernica, Waxwing,* and *Copper Nickel,* among many others, and he has won awards and garnered fellowships from the Munster Literature Centre, Bread Loaf Writers' Conference, Oregon Literary Arts, and the Oregon Arts Commission. This piece is a part of his memoir, *Faces Bright, Voices Loud,* forthcoming from University Press of Mississippi in September 2016.

Lynn DeFilippo is currently a fifth-grade teacher in Barrow, Alaska. This is her thirteenth year teaching in Alaska.

Marcia DeSanctis is the author of a *New York Times* Travel Best-Seller, *100 Places in France Every Woman Should Go* (Travelers' Tales, 2014). Her work has appeared in numerous publications including *Vogue, Marie Claire, Town & Country, National Geographic Traveler, More, Tin House, The New York Times,* and *O, The Oprah Magazine.* Her travel essays have been widely anthologized, and she is the recipient of four Lowell Thomas Awards for excellence in travel journalism, as well as a Solas Award for best travel writing.

Caitlin Dwyer graduated with a master's in journalism from the University of Hong Kong in 2013. She taught English for three years in China and now lives in the Pacific Northwest, where she works as a freelance writer and English teacher. She has written for a range of publications, including *Creative Nonfiction,* the *Los Angeles Review of Books,* the *Asian Review of Books, Europe Up Close,* and *Buddhistdoor Global,* where she is a columnist.

Chris Girman is an attorney and PhD candidate at the University of Illinois at Chicago, where he teaches creative nonfiction. He is the author of two books: *Mucho Macho: Seduction, Desire, and the Homoerotic Lives of Latin Men* and *The Chili Papers.*

Leslie Hill taught English and library skills for twenty-five years at inner-city high schools in Toronto, Canada. She left teaching after the death of her husband, Paul. In 2012 she published a memoir, *Dressed for Dancing,* about grief and recovery. She is currently completing an MFA at the Northwest Institute of Literary Arts.

Mary Ann Hutcheson retired from teaching in 2012. She now freelances for magazines and is working on a memoir chronicling her family's history, beginning with the late nineteenth-century immigration of her Italian ancestors. Before she chose her career as a teacher, Mary Ann's passion was the theater, and during her college years, she trained at the Herbert Berghof Studio in New York City. One of her writing rewards was her friendship with Pat Conroy, which was cut short by his death.

Ann V. Klotz is a teacher/mother/writer; she is head of school at Laurel School in Shaker Heights, Ohio. Her work has appeared in the *Brevity* blog, *Mothers*

Always Write, Independent Ideas: The Independent School Magazine Blog, and *Community Works Journal;* she blogs semi-regularly for the *The Huffington Post.* Ann shares her life with three children, three rescue dogs, two cats, one patient husband, and a goldfish named Shark. She is a proud alum of Creative Nonfiction Foundation's online Boot Camp class taught by Joelle Fraser.

Shannon LeBlanc teaches middle school English. She holds an MFA in creative writing nonfiction from Boston's Emerson College. She has previously been published in *Redivider*, Emerson's graduate journal, and *Catch & Release*, Columbia University's new online journal. She lives in Louisville, Kentucky.

Kristin Leclaire teaches high school English. Her nonfiction has appeared in *Literary Mama* and *The Bohemyth*, and she recently won the Denver Stories on Stage flash fiction contest. One of her essays made *The Masters Review* 2015 shortlist and was selected as a finalist for the *Bellingham Review's* Annie Dillard Award for Creative Nonfiction. Her writing has also been featured at readings sponsored by the Lighthouse Writers Workshop and Making the Mountain. She lives in Littleton, Colorado, with her husband and two toddlers.

Deborah Meltvedt is a high school teacher and project coordinator who loves to combine health and medical topics with creative writing, both in her own writing and as prompts for her students. She has been published in the Sacramento Poetry Center's *Tule Review*, the *American River Review*, and the true story anthology *Under the Gum Tree*. Deborah lives in Sacramento with her husband, Rick.

Karen Kelley Perkins teaches physiology and biology at a charter school. She earned a master's degrees in botany and biochemistry, then completed a doctorate in molecular biology at the Albert Einstein College of Medicine in New York. She worked as a cancer research scientist at Memorial Sloan Kettering Cancer Center, Johns Hopkins University School of Medicine, and at UC Berkeley, where she was a Damon Runyon-Walter Winchell Cancer Research Fund fellow. Her essays and articles have appeared in a wide variety of publications, ranging from *Science* magazine to *The Hispanic Outlook in Higher Education Magazine*. She lives in Pacific Palisades, California.

Anne Raeff is proud to be a high school teacher and works primarily with recent immigrants at East Palo Alto Academy. Raeff is a 2015 recipient of the Flannery O'Connor Award for Short Fiction for her collection of short stories *The Jungle Around Us*, which will be published in October 2016. Her essays and stories have appeared in *New England Review*, *ZYZZYVA*, and *Guernica* among other places, and her first novel, *Clara Mondschein's Melancholia*, was published in 2002. She lives in San Francisco with her wife and two cats.

Lori D. Ungemah spent eleven years teaching English in secondary schools in Brooklyn, during which time she most likely learned a great deal more than she taught. After receiving her doctorate in education from Teachers College, Columbia University, she left teaching high school to be a founding faculty member at Stella and Charles Guttman Community College, where she continues to teach English.

Kate Ver Ploeg has lived and biked throughout the United States and abroad. She now lives where she grew up and studies in the University of New Hampshire MFA writing program. Her writing has been published by *Brevity*, *Calyx*, and *The Fourth River*, among others.

Sherri Wright spent her entire career in education, first as an elementary school teacher, and later focusing on educational programs for at-risk youth at the University of Minnesota and the US Department of Agriculture. Retired in Rehoboth Beach, Delaware, Wright runs, practices yoga, works out, and volunteers at a center for the homeless—all of which figure into her writing. Her work has been published in *Hill Rag*, *Letters From CAMP Rehoboth*, *Aspiring to Inspire*, *Words of Fire and Ice*, *The White Space*, and *Clementine Poetry Journal*.

Acknowledgments

Any book is the work of many people. *What I Didn't Know* was made possible by the almost 400 educators who submitted their stories for consideration for this project; Matt Spindler for managing our dedicated readers; Hattie Fletcher, Anne Horowitz, Josie Fisher, and Chad Vogler for their editorial efforts; Ellen Ayoob for managing the production process; and Victoria Blake for her ongoing partnership.